REGGIE WHITE IN THE TRENCHES

The Autobiography

with Jim Denney

A
JANET
THOMA
BOOK

THOMAS NELSON PUBLISHERS

Nashville • Atlanta • London • Vancouver

Published in Nashville, Tennessee, by Thomas Nelson, Inc., Publishers,
and distributed in Canada by Word Communications, Ltd., Richmond,
British Columbia.

The Bible version used in this publication is THE NEW KING JAMES
VERSION. Copyright © 1979, 1980, 1982, 1990 Thomas Nelson, Inc.,
Publishers.

Library of Congress Cataloging-in-Publication Data

White, Reggie.
    Reggie White in the trenches : the autobiography / Reggie White.
        p.   cm.
    ISBN 0-7852-7252-6 (hc)
            0-7852-7123-6 (pb)
    1. White, Reggie.   2. Football players—United States—Biography.
3. Football players—Religious life—United States.   I. Title.
GV939.W43A3   1996
796.332′092—dc20
[B]   96–41509
                                                            CIP

Printed in the United States of America.

9 10 11 12 — 02 01 00 99

DEDICATION

I dedicate this book to the most wonderful person that I have ever known, my wife of twelve years. I love you, Sara! To our two wonderful children, Jeremy and Jecolia. You two are so special to me. You have taught me a great deal on what love is about. To all of the hurting souls out there, many of whom have been called by God, who have been judged and ignored by man. Please forgive us for not loving you for who you are and for not representing God the way we should. Remember, sometimes we go out on our own, and we do not act accordingly; therefore, don't take our stupidity out on the One who created you and loves you . . . God. Sara, Jeremy, Jecolia, and I send our love out to you.

CONTENTS

ACKNOWLEDGMENTS

I would first like to thank my wife, Sara, for being such a patient and loving mate. You are truly a Proverbs 31:10–31 woman. I LOVE YOU! To Jeremy and Jecolia for being such honest, caring, and loving children. To my mother, Thelma—my love for you has never changed, you are the best mom. To my grandmother Mildred Dodds, whom we affectionately call "mother"—you mean so much to us. To Aunt Janette and Jackie and Uncle Ronnie—I love you guys. To my brother, Julius, and sister, Christie—you guys mean the world to me. To my father, Charles—no matter what, you are my dad. To my in-laws, Charles ("Pop") and Maria Copeland—thanks for loving and supporting me for who I am. To Steve Fate—you have taught me what a true loving servant of God is. To my sister-in-law Maria and her husband, Wayne Dozier—you guys are the best of the best. To the other sis-in-law Liz Taylor and her husband, John—use that name, girl! To my brother-in-law, Mark, and his wife, Liz—keep your faith and watch God work. To my pastor and best friend, Jerry Upton and his wife, Janice—I really do not know where Sara and I would be if God had not put you two in our lives. Thank you, Jerry, for battling in the trenches on our behalf and for talking to me in the late hours of the night.

To Bro. Billy and Betty McCool—thanks for being so loving to Sara and me. Mark and Jamie McCool—Mark, you are my man and a valued friend. Gino Magdos—stay away from my house when you have golf clubs. Love you, buddy. Lee Jenkins—thanks for being a friend. To Brett and Cynthia Fuller—Sara and I really love you guys. You will always be special to us. To Max Siegel, our lawyer, agent, and friend—thanks for helping us build God's kingdom and supporting the vision. To Henry Cisceneros and Nelsen Diaz—you have been true helpers and friends. To Marvie Wright—an angel sent you to me and Sara. Thanks for grasping our vision and dedicating yourself to it. To Jim Wade—thanks for your friendship. To Nelson Peltz—thank you for believing in me and for caring as much as you do. You have a wonderful family and a great partner in Peter May. I thank God for friends like you. Dick and Chris Monfort—Dick, it's been a short friendship, but I feel like it has been a lifetime. Thanks for believing in me and Sara. Thank you, Calvin and Devorah, for being so great, and to Walter Lewis for a friendship that lasts a lifetime. And, of course, to the Thomas Nelson family—thank you, Jim Denney, for all your help; Janet Thoma, for seeking me out; and Todd Ross, for making all my changes.

To Bishop Isaiah and Dr. Gloria Williams—we love you two very much. To Harold and Brenda Ray—thanks for your love. To Jimmy and Kyle—a pair who have represented me well. To Coach Robert Pulliam—you don't know how much you mean to me. You taught me toughness. I am blessed to have had you as a coach, friend, and mentor. To Coach Tyler—thanks for your caring and discipline during middle school. To R. V. and Frances Brown, keep up the great work with O.T.A.Y. ministries. We love ya. To Lurone and Candy Jennings—thanks for your ministry and friendship. To Herman Prater—remember, no matter what anyone says about me, never let it affect your heart and thoughts. Thanks for knowing my heart and being a good friend. To Rice and Greg—thanks for your ministry and helping me in time of need. To Rev. Samuel Spence Montgomery—thanks for being my first pastor and friend.

There are so many people who have been instrumental in my life and in Sara's. We have had great neighbors in New Jersey, Tennessee, and Green Bay. We thank you all for being part of our "normal life." Special thanks, but not limited, to the most "Leave-it-to-Beaver" family we know, the Klarners (you guys are wonderful); the Wehner family; Hood family (Val, Terrence, and Jecolia); John, Lisa, and Gina; Kouser family (keep up with the pigs); Odell family; Sanderson and the A-Team; the entire BDR family—you got it, Nancy! To John and Kelly and John and Cindy—thank all four of you for allowing us to be part of your wedding days. John, I want Sara at 10 percent body fat soon. The Schmit family—thanks, Debbie, for helping give Sara some sanity.

Thanks to my past and present teammates. You all know who you are and what kind of love, as well as headaches, you have given me the past ten seasons. Oh, I can't forget about Big Daddy Kent Johnston and the entire Holmgren staff that has helped me accomplish, hopefully, my dream of winning the Super Bowl; only time will tell. God has always put so many great athletes on my teams to make me look better in the trenches. Also we thank the team that our faithful friend and accountant, Mike Weisberg, has put together. They have helped us for the past twelve years to put our money up to preserve life, not only for our family but others too. Thanks, Mike, for helping us with all our finances; you are the best. Oh yeah, you can finish the last nine of thirty-six holes at Royal Oaks too; I am sure Jimmy Mac will be happy to test it out. Thanks to your staff, of course—Karen K., Karen W., Eddie, Jason, and you all know who you are. Peace out and thanks.

The final thanks is saved for the One who brought me out of the life that I could still be in—Jesus Himself. Your grace is truly sufficient for me and my family. Teach us daily how to love more and, most important, how to love others as we love ourselves. Let us not judge others by what we see or hear from outer appearances, but love by what we see and feel from our hearts. Give us compassion for others that they may come to know You personally and that they may see us as living servants for Your kingdom. THANK YOU!

PROMISE KEPT

Promise kept, Vince. We brought your trophy home.

I made that promise in the first edition of this book, which came out a few weeks before the start of our championship season. I predicted that 1996 would be our year, that the Green Bay Packers would go all the way to Super Bowl XXXI, that the Vince Lombardi Trophy would come back to Green Bay where it all began—and we did it.

Promise kept.

When Brett Favre came into training camp in July of '96, he had already gone through some incredibly tough battles, including a dependence on prescription painkillers and the death of a close friend—yet he was ready for war. "I'm going to beat this thing, and I'm going to win the Super Bowl. Don't believe me? Then bet against me. I'm telling you now: This year, it's Super Bowl or bust." Uh-huh!

Promise kept.

We played a tough schedule. We played under pressure. We suffered a heart-grabbing loss on the turf at the Metrodome and back-to-back losses at Arrowhead and Texas Stadium. We suffered injury after injury, lost starter after starter—Robert Brooks, Antonio Freeman, Mark Chmura, Kenny Ruettgers, Earl Dotson, John Michels, George Koonce, and more. But every time one man fell, another stepped up. Together, we battled back. We stayed focused, and we stayed together—and we finished the season 13–3.

The 'Niners came to Lambeau for the divisional playoffs. We put a hurt on 'em. The Panthers came to Lambeau for the NFC championship. We sent 'em packing. Then we packed our own bags for New Orleans and the Super Bowl. Last time Green Bay won a title, I was five years old—Brett Favre hadn't even been born yet! But we did it. We went to the Super Bowl—and we won it.

Promise kept.

In the biggest game of my career, I saw the most incredible things. I saw Brett Favre play one of the most flawless games of his career, including a Super Bowl record 81-yard touch-down pass to Antonio Freeman. I saw Desmond Howard return a kickoff 99 yards for a touchdown—another Super Bowl record. I saw Brett run to the corner of the field and plant the ball just an inch across the goal line, even as his body was airborne and sailing out of bounds—touchdown! And me? I hauled Patriots quarterback Drew Bledsoe onto the turf for another Super Bowl record—three sacks in a single game.

When it was over, the scoreboard read Green Bay 35, New England 21. With my heart in my throat and tears in my eyes, I grabbed the Lombardi Trophy and ran around the field, holding it high. I understand there were three Cheeseheads for every Patriots fan in the Louisiana Super-dome that day—and from the roar of joy that washed over me from the stands, I believe it! I wanted those fans and all the people back home to know: This trophy belongs to you as much as us! You, the fans, lifted us on your shoulders at the beginning of the season—and you carried us all the way to New Orleans. Together, the Packers and the community of Green Bay, Wisconsin, brought the title back to Titletown.

Promise kept.

After the first edition of *Reggie White: In the Trenches* appeared, I began getting letters from people all over the country. One letter stands out in my mind. It was from a man who said he was a racist before reading my book. He read it because he was a fan of football. But by the end of the book, he repented of his racist attitudes and asked God to forgive him. Now he's working to really understand people who are different from him. That letter alone made the book worth writing—yet I received not one, but scores of letters like that. Incredible!

I have seen and experienced many, many awesome things since the first edition of this book appeared. So I just had to come back and tell you the rest of the story in this expanded Super Bowl edition of *Reggie White: In the Trenches*. At the end of this book, you'll find a whole new chapter covering the Packers' championship year, including a turf-level look at Super Bowl XXXI.

Thinking back over my twelfth season in the NFL, I am totally in awe of all that God has done in my life since this book first appeared. You may have seen the games, you may have read the accounts in the newspapers or in *Sports Illustrated*. But you haven't heard the *whole* story, the *inside* story, until you've heard it from me.

So come back to the trenches with me. Let me tell you the Green Bay Packers story, the Reggie White story, that you won't see on TV or read about in the papers. Let me tell you about the promise we made . . .

The promise we *kept*.

Chapter 1

LIFE IN THE TRENCHES

I had been playing pro football for more than ten years, and I had never missed a game. I had injured my knees, elbows, ankles, ribs, and hamstrings before—but those injuries had never kept me from lining up the following week. I had played 166 straight games, and the only time I ever sat out was during the players' strike in 1987. But on December 3, 1995, as the Green Bay Packers were leading the Cincinnati Bengals, something scary happened.

With just 6:43 left in the game, the Bengals had possession of the ball, and were trailing 17–10. The ball was snapped. I beat the tackle off the ball, coming around the corner. I saw the tackle dive at me to hit me with a cut block, so I jumped high to avoid the hit. As I landed and planted my feet, I heard a loud *pop!* from somewhere down around my left knee. I felt pain—not excruciating pain, but more of a cramping-up sensation. I instantly felt weak and hobbled on that leg. I grabbed my left leg and hopped on my right, watching the action. The Bengals quarterback, Jeff Blake, was rolling out of the pocket and pulling back to throw a pass. When he fired the ball, it fell right into the hands of my teammate, LeRoy Butler, for an interception.

When I saw we had the ball, I hit the ground. I stayed down on the field for a minute while our head trainer, Pepper Burruss, and the team doctor, Patrick McKenzie, came out on the field and looked me over. LeRoy and Sean Jones had to help me off the field because I was hurting, and I couldn't put any pressure on that leg. I lay on the sidelines for over half an hour, and I knew the game was over for me. Worse, I was afraid the season might be over as well.

In the end, we won that game, 24–10—but there had been a price. I had ripped a hamstring, one of the tendons in the hollow behind the knee that anchors the rear muscles of the upper leg. The muscle had detached from the back of the knee and was bunched up in the upper back part of my thigh. Since the hamstring muscles provide most of an athlete's power for pushing off and running, I was effectively crippled as a football player.

I've seen guys whose careers were ended by a hamstring injury. At the least, I knew I might be out for the rest of the season—and the Packers were having their best season in years. We were headed for the playoffs. I couldn't imagine the Packers in the playoffs, playing for the NFC title, maybe even in the Super Bowl, without me.

I missed the next game against Tampa, breaking my 166-game streak. It was hard to miss that game. They narrowly beat us, 13–10, and I knew in my heart if I had been out there we would have won. I felt I could have made something happen for us just with my presence. It was pure torment, having to watch that game from the sidelines, feeling that the season was over for me. It had been an incredible season for the team. I was leading the National Football Conference (NFC) with 12½ sacks, and the Packers offense—led by league MVP quarterback Brett Favre—had been absolutely awesome. We were confident that the '95–'96 season was going to be our year, the year of the Packers. Suddenly, all of our championship dreams were in doubt.

On December 14, 1995, sports pages across the country carried the headline, "Injury Ends Season for Reggie White," and bemoaned Green Bay's future: "The Green Bay Packers suffered a devastating blow to their Super Bowl aspirations yesterday when they learned that their star defensive end, Reggie White, would be lost for the season."[1] But hold on! The next day—I mean, *the very next day!*—those same newspapers carried *this* headline: "'Miraculous' Recovery for White." Now, the newspapers put that word "miraculous" in quotes, because they don't believe it. But a miracle is exactly what it was. Later on in this book, we'll talk more about that and other miracles that have happened in my life, but for now it's enough to say that I was able to play in the very next game against New Orleans.

We won, by the way, 34–23. And that paved the road to the playoffs.

"WE DID IT! WE DID IT!"

We went into San Francisco's Candlestick Park—excuse me, I mean, 3Com Park—to face last year's Super Bowl champions, the 49ers, on their home turf. Despite having Brett Favre powering our offense, the oddsmakers had us down as 10-point underdogs. Let me tell you, that made us mad! Sure, we had lost two of our outstanding stars from previous seasons—wide receiver Sterling Sharpe (retired because of a neck injury) and defensive lineman Bryce Paup (gone to Buffalo as a free agent). Also, our biggest guard, Aaron Taylor, was out because of knee surgery. But hey, we had managed a record of 13 and 5 for the season versus San Francisco's 11 and 6! Even though the oddsmakers hadn't learned to respect us yet, the Pack had come to prove a point: For the first time since the Vince Lombardi era, Green Bay had reemerged as one of the elite teams of the National Football League (NFL).

For the past three years, the NFC championship had been a contest between just two teams—the 'Niners and the 'Boys from Irving, Texas. We aimed to put a stop to that. As our coach, Mike Holmgren, told the press before the game, "We're gonna win it all—why not?" We weren't just happy to be in the playoffs. We fully intended to take it all home—including the Super Bowl.

Was I nervous before this game? Me? Reggie White? You bet I was nervous! I always get pregame jitters before a big contest— and this was one of the biggest. I don't try to tamp down the emotions, I try to harness them. Being nervous before a game doesn't mean being fearful—it means being *pumped*. That emotional tension is an edge you use to power your performance, to get you off the ball faster, to get you into your man harder, to get you into the game with more drive and intensity. When emotions run high, man, you go with the flow. Of course, that nervous edge does have its downside. Like, it makes you have to go to the bathroom . . .

It was exciting to walk out onto the field and see literally thousands of Green Bay fans in the stands at San Francisco. You can spot a true Packer fan by the foam cheese wedge he wears on his head—which, of course, is why our fans are called Cheeseheads. Packer fans are the greatest, most devoted football fans in the world. As I walked out on that field and the announcer called my name, I heard a loud chant of "Reg-gie! Reg-gie!" When you hear a sound like that, your heart starts pounding a little harder, the adrenaline starts coursing through your veins, you feel a surge of pent-up energy quiver through your nervous system, and you are ready for anything. Most fans probably never realize how important they are to our game, and how much the men on the field need them, how much we appreciate the emotional charge they give us.

The tide was with Green Bay from the 49ers' first snap. 'Niners quarterback Steve Young hit fullback Adam Walker with a swing pass. Half an instant later, Green Bay outside linebacker Wayne Simmons barreled headfirst into Walker, his helmet popping the ball out of Walker's hands like a cork out of a bottle. The runaway ball was scooped up by our rookie cornerback, Craig Newsome, and he carried it all the way for his first-ever NFL touchdown. The quick score on turnover by the Packer defense set the tempo for the rest of the game. On San Francisco's next drive, we held them to one yard and a punt.

Our defensive coordinator, Fritz Shurmur, came up with a brilliant defensive scheme that enabled us to keep Young and the 49ers' superstar receiver, Jerry Rice, under control. Our defensive objective was to shut down the 49ers' running game first, force them to pass, then shut down the passing game. Using the nickel defense and three rushers, we pressured them, double- and triple-teaming Young, while hammering back their receivers at the line of scrimmage. I didn't get any sacks in the game, but the 'Niners were forced to concentrate a lot of offensive strength on me, which opened up the lanes for other Packer linemen to get through. Our defensive powerhouse in that game was wild-eyed Wayne Simmons, who produced twelve tackles and a sack.

Meanwhile, my man Brett Favre was awesome on offense. It took him less than two minutes to drive to a second touchdown with passes to Keith Jackson (35 yards), Robert Brooks (20 yards), and Jackson again (3 yards and TD). He clinched a third touchdown with a pass to Mark Chmura in the second quarter. By the end of the game he had thrown 21 of 28 for 299 yards. Brett's performance was so flawless that day that even when something went wrong, he turned it into perfection. On one snap, he slipped and fell, jumped back to his feet, and fired a beautiful pass to Keith Jackson.

And let me tell you about Keith Jackson! He and I used to be teammates with the Philadelphia Eagles. When I went to cold, frozen Green Bay in 1993, Keith went to warm, tropical Miami. Then, in '95, Keith was traded to the Packers—and he didn't want to go! He said he'd rather retire than play on the frozen tundra at Green Bay's Lambeau Field. He stayed out the first few weeks of the '95 season, then reluctantly joined the Pack—and am I ever glad he did! In the playoff game against the 'Niners, Keith caught four passes for 101 yards and a touchdown.

For a while in the second half, it looked like San Francisco might be coming alive. The 49ers turned the second-half kickoff into an 80-yard drive, giving Steve Young his one and only trip into the end zone. But he paid for it—big-time. I could see by the way his face twisted and the way he kept massaging his throwing arm that he was hurting from his own exertion and from the pounding we were giving him. Meanwhile, Young's main receiver, Jerry Rice, was taking an awful pounding of his own. Though he somehow managed to snag 11 passes for 117 yards, we held him to zero yards after catches. Sure, Rice could catch the ball, but we refused to let him run with it.

The 49ers' frustration was underscored when their center, Bart Oates, reached out and snatched the helmet off the head of our defensive tackle, Darius Holland. Oates sent that helmet flying way downfield—lucky thing Darius's head wasn't still in it. That move cost Oates and his fellow 'Niners 15 yards.

When the final gun sounded, we had beaten the previous year's Super Bowl champions, knocked them out of contention—and we had moved to within one game of a Super Bowl of our own. It's hard to convey in words how it feels to beat the defending champs in

their own backyard. There is a surge of total exhilaration, a powerful wave of emotional energy that simply has to be expressed in a
physical way. I was jumping up and down, grabbing my teammates, and running around the field yelling, "We did it! We did
it! Man, we did it!" I looked up in the stands and I saw hundreds
of Cheeseheads jumping up and down and yelling too. So I dashed
out to the stands and ran all the way around the stadium, high-
fiving every Packer fan I could reach.

We stayed on the field for a while, talking to the fans and the
TV commentators, then headed into the locker room. The place
was jammed with trainers, coaches, teammates, and guys from
the Packers board and management. Everybody was hugging each
other, slapping each other, yelling and laughing and clapping each
other on the back. The players headed for the showers, and some
were so excited they still had soap dripping off of them when they
came out to pray. We said the Lord's Prayer together; then Mike
Holmgren stood up on a bench and gave a little closing speech. It
was along the lines of, "Hey, you guys did great out there, but
don't forget you've got an even bigger game coming up next week."

We all knew Mike was right. We had to look beyond the euphoria
of the moment if we were going to get to Phoenix and Super
Bowl XXX. There was one more team to beat—either the Philadelphia Eagles or the Dallas Cowboys, depending on which team
won its playoff game. I sure knew which team I'd *rather* face on
the way to the Super Bowl. The Packers had never beaten the
Cowboys in the three years I'd been wearing Packer green and
gold. So in the locker room after the game, when the reporters
asked me if I had anything to say, I gave them two words: "Go
Eagles!"

My paycheck for that game was $13,000—but I only kept a little
bit of it. The rest of it went to my teammates. For a couple years,
the Packers players had been running an incentive program. We
all contributed to a fund for the players who made big plays. When
the fund ran out of money near the end of the season, Sean Jones
and I kicked in some extra cash to keep the program going. The
newspapers called it "smash-for-cash" and claimed we were paying a bounty on bone-crushing hits. That wasn't it at all. We were
rewarding big *plays*, not big hits—a practice that the NFL has
okayed and that is no different from a quarterback buying gifts for

the offensive linemen who do a good job of keeping him alive in the pocket. Did the money motivate us to play harder? I don't know. All I *do* know is that the only money I made on the 49ers game was the $500 I earned for a takedown I made on Steve Young.

In all my years in the NFL—eight seasons with the Eagles and three with the Packers—I had never been as close to the Super Bowl as I was at that moment. In fact, in all my years playing football—from high school, to the University of Tennessee, to the Memphis Showboats in the United States Football League (USFL), to the NFL—I had never had a single championship season, not one. Yes, I had logged more quarterback sacks than any other player in the history of the game. Yes, I was assured of a place in the Hall of Fame. And yes, I had received ten straight appointments to the Pro Bowl in Hawaii. But I would have traded all those Pro Bowls for just one Super Bowl—in a heartbeat. I thought, *Maybe, just maybe, this is gonna be my championship season!*

GOING HOME

The trip back to Green Bay after a big road win always seems short—but this was one of the shortest ever! Everybody on the plane was noisy and excited, knowing they'd be greeted by about eight or ten thousand cheering fans at the airport. We just couldn't wait to get home. I was really looking forward to a great, intense week of preparation for the next game.

Even though God had healed me in a miraculous way the previous month, I didn't have quite the same quickness and mobility I had enjoyed before the injury. I knew Coach Mike Holmgren was concerned about playing me too much—he wanted me in good shape for the '96 season, and he didn't want me to reinjure that hamstring and maybe get knocked out of the game for good. But I promised I would be honest with him if the leg was really bothering me, and he gave me playing time in both the New Orleans and San Francisco games. I was really grateful for the chance he had given me to play in one of the most important games of my career. So, on the flight home, I went up and sat beside Mike Holmgren and told him how I felt.

"I just really want to thank you, man," I said, putting my arm on his shoulders.

"For what, Reggie?" he asked, giving me a puzzled look.

"For putting me in the game," I said. "For letting me play for a championship. Coach, I've never been this close to a Super Bowl before. It feels great."

He seemed really touched that I would thank him like that, and we both just sat there, basking in the moment. Then he looked at me again and said, "Reggie, you're not getting my Bud Light."

At least that's what Mike Holmgren told reporters he said to me. Fact is, everything I just told you is exactly the way I remember it—except the punchline about his Bud Light. Now, I don't want to say that Coach exaggerates, but I will say that he's a great story-teller—and the way he remembers our conversation is a lot funnier than the way I remember it!

The thrill of a big win sticks with you for a few days. You sleep well. You dream good dreams. You feel pumped up and energized the moment you pile out of bed. You get dressed quicker. You're ready to go. That's how I felt when I started my day on the Monday morning following Saturday's win in San Francisco.

Nothing could have prepared me for what that day would bring.

A FIERY BEACON

I strolled into the training facility at Lambeau Field to get ready to practice. There, I picked up the phone and called my answering service to get my messages. One of the messages was from Skip Lackey, a reporter I knew with the *Knoxville News-Sentinel*. The message said that my church, the Inner City Church in Knoxville, had been firebombed early that morning, and the sanctuary had burned to the ground. Skip wanted to get my reaction for the next edition.

For a few minutes I just sat there, not knowing how to react. I had to let that sink in. Together with Pastor Jerry Upton and Pastor David Upton, I had helped found the Inner City Church in 1993. I tried to picture that building, always so alive with music and praise, now reduced to blackened rubble. For several seconds, I simply couldn't believe it. But then I thought, *Man, I need to believe it, because too much good has been happening. Now the devil has reached out and he's trying to shut us down. We must be doing something right for the devil to come against us like that.*

I didn't immediately return Skip's call. Instead, my first call was to my pastor and friend, Jerry Upton. "Jerry," I said, "what happened?"

Jerry's voice shook with anger and pain as he told me. Sometime in the dark early-morning hours of Monday, January 8, 1996, someone broke into the church. They painted racial slurs in white paint on the brick walls of the church—"Die, niggers, die," "White is right," and "Nigger lovers." In the sanctuary, offices, and classrooms of the church, several gallons of gasoline and kerosene were sloshed all around. When the walls, carpets, and furniture were saturated with fuel, Molotov cocktails were lit and tossed into the building. The sanctuary was engulfed in flames.

My immediate response was, "Jerry, the devil hasn't beaten us. God is getting ready to do something even more tremendous than the things we've already seen. You know what's been happening through the Inner City Church—not just in Knoxville but around the country. Every week, I call you with news about the things God is doing through our church, even way up here in Wisconsin. You just wait, Jerry. Even greater things are going to happen in the days to come."

And throughout that week, I began to see some of the great things God could do through a tragedy like the burning of a church. I got calls from attorneys, businesspeople, and Packers fans who wanted to help raise money to rebuild the church. One man, a Wisconsin lawyer named John Hugel, held a press conference the day after the fire, announcing the formation of a rebuilding fund for the Inner City Church. We got letters from architectural firms in Wisconsin offering to prepare plans for a new church free of charge. Several nurseries donated almost $10,000 worth of greenery for the landscaping. Lumberyards offered free construction materials, delivered to Knoxville without charge. Church youth groups volunteered to go to Knoxville to supply labor. A local radio talk show in Milwaukee devoted three hours to the subject, and dozens of callers phoned in their support, from little kids offering their pennies, to business owners and retirees opening their checkbooks. Most of these offers came from Green Bay and around the state of Wisconsin, but other offers came from all around the country. My wife, Sara, and I were so moved by the outpouring of love that we both wiped away tears many times during those days.

On one occasion that week, I was walking to my car in a parking lot when three young men approached me. They started to talk to me, but I was in a hurry, so I said, "I'm sorry, but I've got to go." I got in my car and started the engine. As I was backing out of the parking space, I felt God speaking to me: *Reggie, you'd better go talk to those guys.* So I pulled my car around and rolled the window down. "I'm sorry I didn't stop a moment ago," I said. "You guys want an autograph?"

"No," said one of them. "We want to give something to help rebuild the church." And each of them handed me a $20 bill.

I had that same experience again and again—people stopping us on the street or in a restaurant, writing us a check, saying they were praying for us. One child sent a card with 92 pennies attached to it—the same number of pennies as the number on my jersey. A couple from the South sent us a check for $1,000. One woman stopped us in a restaurant and asked us to pray for her because she had breast cancer, so Sara and I prayed for her in the restaurant—and she gave us a check for the church.

When I called Jerry and told him all the things that were happening in Wisconsin, he said, "Reggie, we are getting letters and phone calls from Wisconsin all day, every day. I just can't believe that people in another state are sending thousands of dollars here to Knoxville to rebuild our church!"

But that was just the beginning of what God was doing.

After our church burned down, I learned that ours was not the first black or interracial church to be burned in the South. Fact is, in the previous three years, nearly twenty churches had been torched—and I hadn't heard of even one of these until our own church was firebombed. The pattern of burnings extended across the South, in state after state, from Virginia down through Louisiana. Yet despite evidence of a possible conspiracy against black churches, the news had been buried in the back pages of the nation's newspapers, if it was covered at all. Only when an NFL star's church was burned to the ground did it finally make headlines.

When I learned about this pattern of racist terrorism, I was shocked. I was disgusted. I was hurt because of what Jerry and David and the members of our church and so many other churches were going through. Yet I was also excited—excited because the darkness had finally been pierced. The silence had been shattered. The world could no longer ignore this crime. When the Inner City Church burned, it became a fiery beacon in the night, shining a light on the suffering of so many other churches in the South.

I believe it was the devil himself who inspired those sneaking, night-crawling people to torch our sanctuary and scrawl Satan's slogans on our walls. But the devil has made a major tactical error. A church is made of people, not bricks and stone. The building has burned down, but the people are still standing. The devil has come against us. He has wounded us. He has destroyed much of what we have built. But the war is not over. The devil has not won.

And the devil will not win.

CLASH OF THE TITANS

Meanwhile, I had another battle to think about. The Dallas Cowboys beat the Philadelphia Eagles in the playoffs, so we were headed for Texas Stadium for the NFC title game on January 14, 1996. As game day approached, the press had a lot of questions for me: How would I block the burning of the church from my mind on Sunday? Was the attack directed at me or at the church? Would there be any extra security measures taken to protect me during the game?

"Look," I replied, "I don't know and I don't care if this was an attack against me or against the church. All I know is that the people who did this thing are demonic, and the devil himself is behind it. It's not going to be a distraction from my game. It's gonna be a rallying point. I've committed my life to kicking down the doors of the devil's kingdom and pulling people together. I'm just gonna keep doing that, because the only way to beat an enemy is to rally all your people together. They're not gonna hurt Reggie White, and we're not going to let people walk up to us and slap us around. I'm not gonna be afraid of nothing, and neither is my family or my church."

Not surprisingly, the Pack went in as nine-point underdogs. We had lost five straight games in Dallas over the past three years by an average of almost 16 points per game. The last time Green Bay had seen the inside of a Super Bowl stadium was exactly twenty-eight years earlier, on January 14, 1968. The Cowboys, on the other hand, had won three NFL titles in their past four seasons. The Dallas roster boasted an incredible fifty-two Super Bowl rings—and man, that's a lot of jewelry.

Our whole team looked forward to that game with a deep sense of Packer tradition. The Super Bowl trophy is named after Vince Lombardi, who coached the Packers to five NFL championships from '61 to '67. We wanted nothing more than to restore the glories of the house of Bart Starr, Jerry Kramer, Paul Hornung, Ray Nitschke, and, of course, Vince Lombardi himself—and we believed in our hearts we could do it.

The media loves to play up the drama of any sporting event. One of the dramas they began spotlighting in the days before the game was the contest between me and the Cowboys' big offensive tackle, Erik Williams—"clash of the titans," they called it, or "the best D and the best O in the NFL go head-to-head." The Fox network, which broadcast the game, made the White-Williams matchup the focus of its coverage. Sure, there was a lot of hype involved—but it wasn't *all* hype. Because to get to the Super Bowl, I had to get to Cowboys quarterback Troy Aikman. And to get to Aikman, I had to go through Erik.

Wearing Eagles green, I had lined up against Erik in the NFC title game in Texas Stadium, January 1993—and my Super Bowl hopes were dashed, 34–10. The next year, wearing Packers green and gold, I lined up against him again for the NFC title, again in Texas Stadium—and again my team went down, 27–17. By January of '96, I was tired of seeing my chance for a Super Bowl ring get stomped into the turf at Texas Stadium by 6-foot-6, 325-pound Erik Williams. I was determined to get through Erik—and I was determined to ruin Troy Aikman's afternoon.

Let me tell you a little bit about Erik Williams: People say Erik plays dirty. Well, *dirty* is a subjective term. Erik is a high blocker, and sometimes his hands get in your face as he's coming at you. But I don't think Erik's the kind of guy who's out to do serious damage or bust someone's career. One time in a previous game against Dallas, he hit me in the face; then after the play he came over to me and said, "Hey, man, that was me. I'm sorry I hit you." And I knew he meant it. Sure, Erik will watch to see if the officials are calling the game loose or tight, and he'll get away with whatever he can. But I wouldn't call him a dirty player.

People say I've got a grudge against Erik or that I'm mad at him because of the way he plays. No way! I like and respect Erik Williams. As a player, he's tough to intimidate. He plays furiously, challenges you hard, and keeps coming at you—and that's what the game of football is all about.

Erik grew up in South Philly, and he tells people he was both an Eagles fan and a Reggie White fan before joining the Cowboys as a third-round pick in the '91 draft. At age twenty-three, he quickly gained a rep as one of the few offensive linemen in the game who could make trouble for Reggie White. In October of '94, Erik was involved in a car crash that destroyed much of his right knee. He was lucky to be pulled out of the wreckage alive. When they wheeled him into Parkland Memorial Hospital in Dallas, it looked like his playing days were over. He had torn two major ligaments and a lot of muscle in that knee—an injury that made his broken ribs, broken thumb, and face cuts seem trivial by comparison.

On Halloween day, 1994, Erik underwent massive reconstructive surgery that left him with an ugly eight-inch scar on his knee—and a fierce determination in his heart. He was 100 percent resolved to battle his way back into the game. Erik missed most of the '94 season, and when he returned in '95, it was clear he was not playing at his former level. But he worked hard, spending four or five hours a day in the weight room, rebuilding his power and stamina. Week by week, his performance improved.

At our first regular season game against the Cowboys in 1995, I saw Erik for the first time since the crash. As I crossed the field to talk to him, I could see by looking at him that he was a changed man, that he had a new, more serious attitude about him. We chatted for a few moments about the crash, about the surgery, about his recovery. Then I said to him, "Now you know God saved your life, don't you?"

"Yeah," he said.

"I just wanted to make sure you knew that," I added. "God saved your life and you need to give it back to Him."

"I know, Reggie," he said. "That's what I want to do." And I believe he was sincere.

I'm told he keeps a Bible in his locker these days, as well as a sign that reads, *God places the heaviest burden on those who can carry its weight.* Make no mistake, Erik Williams is no choirboy. But he is one fine offensive lineman. If they told me right now that Erik Williams was signing with the Packers, I'd say, "All riiiight!" I'd love to play on the same team with him.

The Erik Williams I lined up against in the NFC title game on January 14, 1996, seemed to have all the physical power and mental intensity of the old, pre-crash Erik Williams. I enjoy playing against the best, and Erik is still the best offensive tackle in the game. I wanted to beat him that day.

I wanted to *win.*

"YOU WHINE TOO MUCH"

The game got off to a good start. The Packer defense was strong against the Cowboys' first drive. On their third offensive play, I bull-rushed past Erik and sacked Aikman for a big loss. Dallas was forced to punt—and we blocked the punt. We got a field goal out of that drive. The Cowboys answered with a strong drive of their own, ending in a 6-yard touchdown pass from Aikman to Michael Irvin. We were down, 7–3, but I had a good feeling that we could win that game.

A little while later, I again got past Erik with a quick inside move. I caught Emmitt Smith as he tried to find a doorway through the line of scrimmage. I hauled him down for a 1-yard loss. That hit must have shook him up good, because he didn't get back on his feet right away.

Soon afterward, on a third-down play, I was once again in the trenches facing Erik. I felt energized and confident. Dallas was playing hard, and I knew it would take a full sixty minutes of focused play to beat them—but I also knew the 'Boys from Irving were thinking the same thing about Green Bay. My senses were heightened, and my body was coiled and ready to spring like a bear trap. The steamy, sweaty smell of a hard-fought game was in my nostrils, and the roar of the fans was in my ears. I looked up at Erik as the signals were called, and I read the ferocity in his eyes. I knew he saw the same ferocious intent in mine as I grinned back at him.

The ball was snapped to Aikman. Amid the sound of shouts, growls, grunts, and clattering helmets and pads, Erik and I launched at each other. He came at me high and hands-forward, straight for my face mask. Before I could adjust, my vision was blotted out by his hands. His fingers penetrated my cage, brushing past my eyes, and gouging into my cheek. Using my arms like a forklift, I thrust him away from me, charged past him into the pocket, and forced Aikman to throw sooner than he wanted. The pass was complete—but short of a first down. Dallas had to punt again.

I looked around at the officials. Where was the flag? A face mask penalty is 15 yards, and Erik's move had been glaring and intentional. I couldn't believe the officials had missed that call.

I was mad. I was yelling. As our offense took the field, I went to the sidelines and hollered to Mike Holmgren about Erik's face mask grab. He saw the bleeding scratch below my eye, and he was mad too. When the Fox cameraman stuck his lens up close to me, I yelled at him to get that thing out of my face. A number of people watching the game on TV (including one newspaper reporter in Dallas) later claimed they read my lips and that I was swearing. Well, I was mad and I was yelling, but I certainly wasn't swearing. Some people say a minister shouldn't get mad and yell like I did. My answer to that is: (1) ministers *do* get mad and ministers *do* yell sometimes; and (2) I wasn't there as a minister, I was there as a football player, and football players *also* get mad and yell sometimes.

While I was on the sidelines, Brett Favre was on the field, working hard to get in sync with the game. He got off to a rocky start—his first five passes of the game were incompletions. After his sixth pass was picked off by Cowboys' lineman Leon Lett, the Cowboys were first and ten on our 11-yard line. Our defensive team went back onto the field and tried to defend those 11 yards, but we couldn't hold them. Halfway through the first quarter, we found ourselves in the hole, 14–3.

At that point, Brett Favre and the offensive team took the field again—and that's when something happened. It was like everything just clicked into place, and Brett suddenly became the same awesome league MVP quarterback who had played so flawlessly against the 49ers the previous weekend. On his very first play after

the Dallas kickoff, Brett launched a 73-yard missile right into the
waiting arms of Robert Brooks for a touchdown—just what we
needed. On his next drive, Brett tossed a 24-yarder to Keith Jackson
on a post pattern—another touchdown. It was incredible. Though
he had connected on only two of his first eleven passes, *both* of
them had been touchdown passes.

The game came to an abrupt halt during the second quarter.
Robert Brooks received a pass at the sideline and was promptly
run out of bounds by the Cowboys' Darren Woodson. The two
players barrel-rolled into our wide receivers coach, Gil Haskell.
Gil was knocked onto his back, and his head cracked hard against
the artificial turf at the sidelines—which, of course, is nothing but
a thin layer of rubber over hard concrete. The game was delayed
for ten minutes while the doctors applied a neck brace and placed
him on a stretcher. He was taken by ambulance to Baylor Medical
Center with a skull fracture and brain contusion—a much more
serious condition than most people realized at the time. He ended
up spending a week and a half in the hospital in Dallas and many
more weeks resting up at home before he was ready to return to
work.

Soon after the game got back under way, the Cowboys tied it up
with a 34-yard field goal by Chris Boniol; then they came at us
with a hard-fought, 11-play, 99-yard drive. During that drive, Erik
Williams watched his opportunities carefully. Most of the time, he
blocked clean—especially when I was out of the game and he was
lined up against my backup, Matt LaBounty. But every once in
a while, *pow!* He'd ring my helmet like a bell. Punching and
head-slapping is illegal, but the officials wouldn't call it.

When I went to referee Ed Hochuli and told him to keep an eye
on Erik, he just said, "You whine too much," and walked away.
Well, I don't think I was whining—and former NFL quarterback
Joe Theismann, now a commentator on ESPN, agrees with me.
"What bothers me more about the Green Bay-Dallas game," he later
said, "was the officials were unable to see that Erik Williams's
hands were all over Reggie White's face mask. Let's face it, the
officials did a [lousy] job. To sugarcoat it any other way is wrong."[2]

But that wasn't the worst thing the officials missed that day. On
one snap, my teammate, nose tackle John Jurkovic, broke through
the line and rushed for Aikman. Before Jurkovic could get to Aik-

man, Erik Williams took a running leap, diving straight for the back of Jurko's knees. Jurkovic hit the ground hard, and when Erik got up, Jurko stayed on the ground, writhing and holding his leg. The game was stopped for several minutes while the trainers talked to him and examined his knee. Finally, he was pulled to his feet and helped off the field. As he limped to the sidelines, Jurkovic pointed to Erik and cursed him out.

Once again, there was no flag on the play. Erik insists it was a legal block—a cut block to the side of the legs. But the fact is, Erik came down on the *back* of the man's legs, which is clipping—a 15-yard penalty. And both Erik and the officials know the potential for ending a player's career with a block like that. It was illegal, and the officials should have flagged it.

Our team members were furious. We knew John Jurkovic was headed for a knee operation at the least—and we all thought it was possible he had just played the last game of his career (fortunately, he recovered). From the moment Jurkovic went down with Erik Williams across the back of his knees, with no flag on the play, that game began to get ugly. Some of my teammates decided that if the officials were going to allow a street brawl on the field, then a street brawl it would be. You could sense it, like a cloud passing over the place. There was a lot more yelling, swearing, taunting, punching, and shoving from both sides. Especially in a big-stakes game, officials often adopt an anything-goes attitude, expressed by the saying, "Let 'em play in the playoffs." Well, the officials "let 'em play," and the result was summed up in the headline of *USA Today*'s review of the game: "As Nasty a Game You'll Ever Want to See."

The Cowboys scored a touchdown at the end of that 11-play drive. With just twenty-four seconds left before halftime, Dallas had a 24–17 lead. When the whistle blew, ending the half, players from both teams were clenching fists, firing hateful looks, and yapping about each other's mothers. The game was dangerously close to erupting into fistfights right on the field. In the locker room during halftime, guys were vowing payback.

We came out on the field for the second half, and our offense quickly took charge of the third quarter. A Chris Jacke field goal cut the Dallas lead to 4 points—24–20. Later, Brett Favre fired a 54-yard pass to Keith Jackson, bringing us to the Dallas 2-yard line. Another pass to Robert Brooks in the end zone gave us the lead once more. We held onto that lead, 27–24, going into the fourth quarter.

With 12:24 left in the game, the lead changed hands once more as Emmitt Smith capped a hard-fought 14-play drive with a 6-yard dash into the end zone. It was 31–27, and we were still in the game to win. Even after one of Brett's passes was intercepted by Cowboys cornerback Larry Brown, I believed we had the momentum and the power to pull it off.

On the next play after that interception, Aikman fired a pass to Michael Irvin, who was sprinting down the sideline, covered hotly by our cornerback, Doug Evans. As they ran side-by-side, Irvin reached out and shoved a forearm into Evans's chest, then grabbed the pass at our 16-yard line. It was offensive interference, as blatant as could be. Everyone in the stadium saw it—everyone, that is, but the officials. Incredibly, they flagged our guy Evans for pass interference! On the next play, Emmitt ran for a touchdown and a score of 38–27. Instead of trailing by 4, we were down by 11 with only minutes to go. We desperately tried to get back into the game, but we couldn't make it happen. When Brett threw a valiant but failed fourth-down pass at midfield with 6:36 left to play, we knew it was over. Super Bowl XXX, which had seemed so close just minutes before, slipped out of our reach.

THE DEVIL IS GONNA PAY

I was hurting bad inside as I came off the field. It was the sixth time in three seasons the Cowboys had beaten us at Texas Stadium and the third straight year Dallas had knocked us out of the play-offs. In some of those past games, we had beaten ourselves, we had made errors the other guys could take advantage of. Whenever that happened, I admitted it to myself, to the fans, and to the press. But I didn't feel we had given anything away in this game. Certainly, we hadn't played as flawless a game as we had in San Francisco the week before, but we hadn't beaten ourselves either. In many ways, Brett had played a slightly better game than Aikman; he finished the game 21 of 39 for 307 yards, compared with Aikman, who hit 21 of 33 for 255 yards.

We played a good game—and we were beaten by a great team. You have to give the Cowboys credit. They executed offensive plays exactly as they were supposed to. They restricted our running game and put a lot of pressure on Brett's passing game. Take away the swagger and glitz, the head-punching and pushing, the hype and the end-zone antics, and Dallas is still a great team, playing superb football. The day the Packers beat the Cowboys, there's gonna be nothing like it. It'll be the biggest victory of my entire career.

Losing a big game is like having a football stuck in your throat—sideways. It hurts, man. Losing eats at you. It makes you mad. It makes you cry. If you don't care enough about winning to cry when you lose, you don't belong in the game.

When I got to the locker room, I saw a lot of guys crying, including Brett. I had cried after last year's playoff loss to Dallas, but this year I was too mad to cry. There were other guys in that locker room as mad or madder than I was. One guy kicked a trash can and sent it flying like a field goal attempt. Another guy knocked over a big cooler filled with ice and Gatorade. Some of the younger guys on the team came up to me and said, "Man, I'm sorry." They hurt because they knew how bad I wanted that win—and how much I wanted to play in the Super Bowl.

My response was, "Hey, man, we're gonna get it sooner or later. I appreciate you being sorry for me, but nobody on this team has anything to be sorry for. We did a good job out there. We just couldn't make it happen this year. Let's just concentrate on making it happen next year."

When you lose a big game, time slows down. You stand in the shower, dazed, trying to comprehend it, thinking about what went wrong, what you could have done better. You sit on the locker-room bench and you ponder. It takes longer to get dressed, longer to tie your shoes. And all around you are a bunch of other guys just as dazed and deep in thought as you are.

After you get showered and dressed, you have to go out and face the press. That's hard, because you know they're going to interrogate you, they're going to ask you why you lost, and they're going to ask you a lot of really stupid questions that you are just not in the mood to answer. When I went out to talk to the reporters after the game, I sidestepped most of the questions. I just had a statement to make. "I've got a scratch under my eye from getting punched in the face," I told the reporters, "and you guys are just going to write about how we complain too much. I'm sick of it. I'm ticked off. I'm not happy about this game. But I'll tell you this: I'm very proud of this team. We will be back and we'll win a championship before I retire."

The flight back to Wisconsin was long and quiet. There was no laughter, no noise, only questions—some spoken questions, and some that just hung silently in the air. Guys would ask each other, "Remember that play in the fourth quarter? What should I have done differently?" Or, "Why did you do this? Why didn't you do that?" Brett was especially hard on himself, because of those two interceptions. I asked myself a lot of questions on the way home.

I didn't look forward to sleeping that night, because I often dream about losing. It's as if losing not only clings to you during the day, it torments you at night as well. The bigger the game, the worse the dreams. Sometimes you dream that you're back on the field, that you can't get your game going, you can't get in sync, you can't get your feet moving, the opposing line is rolling over you and you can't get to the quarterback. But the worst dreams of all are the dreams in which you win. Then you wake up and realize, "Aw, it was just a dream! We lost that game yesterday." Dreams like that make me mad.

The closer that plane got to Wisconsin, the more my thoughts turned toward Knoxville, toward Jerry and David Upton, toward the burned-out shell that had once been our church. I had to go back to Tennessee and look at the damage with my own eyes. I had to put my arms around Jerry and David, pray with them, and make sure they knew we were going to rebuild and keep moving forward.

I wasn't able to get back to Knoxville until March. My ten-year-old son, Jeremy, and I got in the car and drove over to the church. Most of the rubble had been removed, but the scorched brick walls still stood. We parked in the parking lot and just looked at the ruins of our church, not saying anything for a while. We didn't get out of the car. Jeremy was really shaken by what he saw. He didn't cry, but he was deeply affected. "Why would anybody want to do that to our church, Dad?" he asked. I said, "The devil made some people do this, Jeremy. Our church was doing too many good things for people, and the devil hates that." In my mind, I thought, *Yep, the devil sure enough did this, and the devil is sure enough gonna pay. He's gonna be sorry he ever started up with God's people.*

When I had a chance to sit down and talk with Jerry and David, I learned that the local and federal agencies investigating the crime—the Knoxville police, the FBI, and the Bureau of Alcohol, Tobacco, and Firearms—had been spending a lot of time investigating them instead of finding out who started the fire. The government had subjected both of these men to the humiliation of lie detector tests, and had wasted a lot of time and money checking their backgrounds. While I understand that law enforcement has to follow up every lead and possibility, in this case I felt they took it too far.

Why would we, as black people, write racist slurs on our church? What would be the motive for burning down our own church? Sure, people sometimes burn down a failing business in order to get insurance money—but our church wasn't failing, it was thriving. Why would we burn down our church within weeks of completing some very expensive improvements—a new balcony, a new radio station, a new daycare center, and more? As it turned out, we were seriously underinsured for the loss we suffered. There was simply no motive for anyone in the church to burn it down.

And what about the twenty-odd other churches that had burned down? What about the fact that there was already a pattern of racist firebombings throughout the South? I later found out that the authorities had treated many of the pastors and parishioners of these other churches just as badly as they treated Jerry and David. Even though the few suspects who had been apprehended in these other bombings had all turned out to be racists and vandals, even though there had never been a shred of evidence linking church members and pastors with the torching of their own churches, the authorities had persisted in making suspects out of the victims in these cases.

A few weeks later, our family flew to Hawaii, where I would play in the Pro Bowl. The Pro Bowl's always a festive time, as much a party as a football game, and we enjoyed it as usual (it helped, of course, that the NFC won). During the game broadcast, I was interviewed by ABC sideline reporter and former Steelers wide receiver Lynn Swann, and he asked me about the church bombing. "I know you're an ordained minister," he said. "Your church in Tennessee was firebombed a few weeks ago. What's happening with the investigation?"

"Personally," I said, "I'm disappointed in how the investigation is going. I'm disappointed that investigators are pointing a finger at my pastor and his brother and people in the church instead of going out and finding out who really did this. If the city of Knoxville and the police department hear me right now, I'm not happy with the way the investigation is going, because there's somebody who burned that church up, and they're not trying to find him."

"But the people in Green Bay, Wisconsin," Lynn added, "have responded to you in a tremendous fashion, haven't they?"

"Not just Green Bay, but the whole state of Wisconsin. You know, there are some excellent people up there. I can honestly say I care about the people up in Wisconsin just as much as they care about me, and they've shown how much they care by sending over $200,000, along with people from around the country. It's just been a blessing."

TRENCH WARFARE

I look back on that time, and I think, *Man, it's incredible all the things that happened to me in a few short weeks.* In that short time, I saw the best that people can do and the worst that people can do. I saw a church burned to the ground and I saw people on fire with compassion and caring. I had a Super Bowl ring almost within my grasp, and I watched it slip away. I tasted sweet victory and bitter defeat. I battled in the trenches on the football field, and in the trenches of life.

When I thought about writing this book, the title came to me almost instantly: *Reggie White: In the Trenches.* Since that moment, there's never been any other title for this book, because those three words—*in the trenches*—sum it all up for me. I live my life in the trenches. I do my work in the trenches. I serve my God in the trenches. I go to war against evil, poverty, racism, and injustice in the trenches.

In war, the trenches are the most basic form of fortification against enemy attack. Battering rams, catapults, and artillery can break down walls, but they can't get to you in the trenches. Rifle fire and machine gun fire pass harmlessly over your head when you stand your ground in the trenches. When you are dug into the trenches, you can repel any assault, you can hold your territory. Trench warfare is rugged and dirty, but wars are won in the trenches. And make no mistake: Life is warfare. You have an enemy, and he will destroy you if you do not take a stand in the trenches. You and I are together in a war against evil, against forces that are terribly real even though they can't be seen, against forces even more dangerous than a 325-pound offensive lineman or a bunch of night-creeping firebombers.

You see, life is warfare. The enemy is hate and racism. The enemy is ignorance and injustice. The enemy is the System. The enemy is the devil. I've taken my share of hits from the enemy. I've been wounded a time or two. I bet you have too. In this kind of warfare, the bones of our spirits may get broken, but they will mend. We're not giving up. We're in this game to win. We're fighters, we're conquerors, and even more than conquerors. We're gonna whip the enemy, and we're gonna beat him in the trenches.

In football, as in warfare, the battle is often won or lost in the trenches. The trenches are where the offensive and defensive linemen face each other across the line of scrimmage. The trenches are the first line of defense. When the ball is snapped, you instantly hear the grinding, thudding, clattering, clashing sound of bodies, pads, and helmets. That's the sound of battle at the front lines of the game. In seconds, the quarterback and his receivers may launch an aerial attack, or the running backs may carry the ball over the line and into enemy territory, but the battle always begins in the trenches. My job as a defensive lineman is to break through enemy lines, to invade enemy territory, to sack the enemy quarterback for a loss, to stop the enemy running backs, to thwart the enemy air attacks, to stop the enemy's drive and move the line of scrimmage back into his own territory.

In war and in football, there are rules. Invariably, some of the combatants break those rules. In football, when someone breaks the rules, the officials are there to impose penalties and enforce the rules. Sometimes they don't do their job. Bad officiating isn't something you moan and cry about. Bad officiating is just one more condition of the game you have to deal with, like playing in the other guy's stadium, or putting up with bad weather, or playing with a bad hamstring or a sore knee. You gut it up and do the best you can.

Deep in the middle of a January night in Knoxville, Tennessee, someone broke another set of rules—big-time. The officials in that case are not refs and umpires and line judges, but police officers and federal investigators. Their job is to catch the people who broke the rules and burned up a church, and to make sure that the bad guys pay the penalty for their actions. The people who torched our church are still out there somewhere. Maybe they'll get caught, maybe they won't. There's no guarantee that the officials in this case will get the job done. If they don't, we'll just have to keep moving forward, keep fighting the good fight, keep working to set people free, both economically and spiritually.

That's life in the trenches. It isn't always fair. It isn't always just. Sometimes you get punched, you get held, you get clipped from behind—and you just have to get back on your feet, bind up your wounds, line up in the trenches, and do it all over again. That's what this book is about—not just my life, but *life in the trenches.* It's about fighting the battles of life. It's about dealing with setbacks and unfair calls. It's about setting goals—and reaching them. It's about shaking up the world, and setting wrong things right. It's about making your life count for something in the big, eternal scheme of things.

Does that mean this book is gonna be all serious and solemn? No way! We're gonna have some fun!

And believe this: We're gonna talk *a lot* about football. Over the years, it's been my privilege to play with, for, and against some of the most legendary names in football. I'm gonna tell stories from my years with the Eagles and the Packers—war stories about the games, and behind-the-scenes stories about players, coaches, and owners. I'm also gonna give it to you straight about how the people running the NFL today are hurting the game, and how we could make the game greater than it ever was before.

We're gonna talk about success—success in football, success in business, success in relationships, and success in life. We're gonna talk about what success really is, how to get it, and how to enjoy it.

We're gonna talk about miracles—incredible things that have happened to me, incredible things that have happened to other people, incredible things I've seen with my own eyes. We're gonna talk about how you can start to see miracles in your own life as well.

We're gonna talk about the division between the races—how it came to be, and how to heal it. We won't just talk about *problems*. We're gonna talk about real workable *solutions* to the problems that are hollowing out our cities, grinding down our society, and holding us all—black, white, and every other color—in bondage.

This book is more than just the story of my life. I want this book to *change* your life. When you put this book down, I want you to be a different person than when you picked it up. I want to challenge you. I want to encourage you. I want to inspire you. I want to take you on an adventure from which there is no turning back.

So turn the page. Get down with me, man. Down in the trenches with Reggie White.

Chapter 2

STARTING OUT

My first run-in with racism took place when I was eleven years old. I was walking home from school with a friend, Janie, and I was teasing her. She was a classmate of mine, and I liked to irritate her now and then—kidding with her, pulling on her pigtails, things like that. She didn't really get mad; in fact, she'd usually just giggle and yell, "Stop it, Reggie!" Sometimes, she'd tease me right back.

Janie was a white girl. Understand, white, black, brown—those things didn't matter to me. I grew up in a multiracial neighborhood, and I'd never encountered racism before. Janie was a friend of mine, and my friends came in different colors—no big deal.

As we walked, I kept teasing Janie and tugging at her pigtails, and she kept giggling and pulling away and saying, "Stop it, Reggie! Leave my hair alone!"

Just then, a car pulled up to the curb next to us, and the driver, a white guy, leaned over and rolled down the window on the passenger side. "Hey, nigger, you leave her alone," he snarled, "or I'm gonna get out and kick your behind!"

I was shocked, frozen to the spot. I'd never been threatened by a stranger before—and nobody had *ever* called me "nigger." I stammered, "But I didn't do anyth—"

"You just leave her alone!" the man growled. Then he asked Janie, "Is he messing with you?"

I thought Janie would say something like, "It's okay, mister, Reggie's a good kid. He always teases me like that." Instead, she said, "Yeah, mister, he was messing with me," and she backed away like she was scared of me. I couldn't believe it.

The man scowled menacingly at me. "Well, you just keep away from her, boy, or I'm gonna kick your behind for sure!"

I didn't cause any trouble. I just straightened up and walked away, leaving Janie on that sidewalk. I went straight home, and I was mad. I didn't like being called a "nigger," and I didn't like being threatened—but I wasn't as hurt by that guy in the car as I was by the way Janie acted. I had thought of her as a friend, but she had treated me like a "nigger" too. To top it off, the next day she went and told someone at school that I had been messing with her, so I got in trouble at school as well.

I just took my punishment. I didn't try to tell the teacher I had only been kidding around with Janie, and I didn't tell the teacher that some white guy in a car had called me "nigger." And I didn't walk home with Janie anymore.

"I *KNEW* IT WAS REGGIE!"

Sure, it hurts to think back on that first encounter with racism—but for the most part, my childhood was happy and filled with good memories. The reason for all those good memories was that there was a lot of love in our family. My mother was a single parent. She gave birth to my brother, Julius, when she was fifteen, and she was nineteen when she had me. She raised us, she loved us, and she was always there for us. There's nothing more you could ask for.

Though my mother never married my father, Charles, I grew up knowing him, and he claimed me as his son. I didn't see him very much, but I was always proud of him. He was a traveling semipro baseball and softball player, and people often compared me to him when I began playing ball. "Man, you hit like your daddy!" they'd say, and I was honored to hear that.

As Bill Cosby used to say, "I started out as a child." I was born in Chattanooga, Tennessee, in 1961. You'd hardly believe it to look at my 6-foot-5, 300-pound frame today, but I came into the world weighing only six pounds. Though I started out little, I caught up fast. When I was just three months old, I weighed more than thirty pounds—more than some of my cousins who were two or three years older! My mother says I never ate baby food, just table food. At seven years of age, I looked like I was twelve or thirteen, and when I started playing tee-ball the coaches of the pee-wee baseball league couldn't believe I was that young and made my mother bring my birth certificate. I didn't like being so big, because the other kids made fun of me and called me names like "Land of the Giants" and "Bigfoot."

When I was seven, my mother married a man named Leonard Collier, and he became my stepfather. He was in the army, stationed at Fort Riley near Manhattan, Kansas, with a year to go in his hitch. So my mother gave my brother, Julius, and me a choice: We could go to Kansas with her and Leonard for a year, or we could stay in Chattanooga with my grandmother. Julius and I decided to stay in Chattanooga.

I had always been very close to my mother, and I missed her a lot during that year. But my grandmother and my aunts made sure that Julius and I had everything we needed—food, clothes, a roof over our heads, plenty of love, and an occasional whupping to keep us in line. And believe me, I needed that occasional whupping, because I could be a ratty little kid sometimes. I don't mean I was a *bad* kid. I wasn't malicious or mean. But there were a lot of us living in close proximity—my brother and my four cousins, along with my grandmother, my Aunt Jackie, and my Aunt Jeanette, so it was hard for them to give everybody attention all the time. And I *definitely* wanted my share of attention. When a kid is looking for attention, he's often not too choosy about how he gets it.

Case in point: I was a very curious kid in those days. I liked to do things just to see what would happen. One time, when no one else was in the house, I decided I wanted to see a little fire. So I got some matches and lit a little corner of the curtains. It was interesting, just watching this little bitty wisp of flame crawl up the seam of the curtains. It occurred to me that if I let it burn too far, someone would notice that the curtains were charred, so I decided I'd better knock the fire out. I was just reaching up to smother the flame with my hands when *poof!* The curtains ex-

ploded into a crackling fire! The flames roared and licked the
ceiling! I thought, *Oh, man! I'm going to burn the house down!*

I snatched up a sofa cushion and started beating at the fire.
Wisps and tatters of smoldering curtain ash floated around the
room and settled all around me. Finally, I got the fire out. Then I
lit out of that room faster than you can say, "Firebug!" I hung
around the backyard for a while after that, listening intently at
windows, trying to think of some way out of my predicament. I
couldn't think of one.

It was my Aunt Jackie who finally came in and made the discov-
ery—and what a wail of horror she let out! I was in for it—big-time.
If I had any doubts as to whom the prime suspect would be, those
doubts were quickly dispelled when I heard Aunt Jackie dial up
my mother, long distance to Kansas, and shout, "Somebody
burned the curtains! I *knew* it was Reggie! I *knew* it was Reggie!"

Yeah, it was Reggie, all right. Again, I really wasn't trying to
make trouble. I was just curious—and on some level, I'm sure I
wanted to get noticed (even if that "notice" took the form of a
whupping).

Sometimes I got in trouble with a little help from my cousins
and my brother. Like the time Julius locked me out of the house.
He tricked me into going outside, then latched the door shut and
stood at the window making faces at me. My cousin Vanessa was
in there with him, and he was obviously having so much fun
making faces at me and taunting me that she decided to join in.
Well, I got so mad at the two of them, I hauled off and put my fist
through that window. Busted glass went flying, and they jumped
back with their eyes as big and round as dinner plates. They could
see it in my eyes: I was coming to get them.

As I pulled my hand back, I looked down and saw blood drib-
bling from a small gash in my wrist. It was just a little bitty cut,
but suddenly I was more concerned about my bleeding wrist and
the broken window than I was about getting even with Julius and
Vanessa. "Get me something for this bleeding," I said, "and let me
in the house." So they scampered off and came back with a great
big bath towel. They laughed and laughed, thinking it was the
funniest thing they ever saw, me wrapping up that tiny little cut

with a huge bath towel. "You in truhhh-bullll!" they jeered. And when my grandmother got home, she proved them right. I *was* in trouble—big-time.

Though I missed my mother during the year she was gone, I had a lot of fun living with my grandmother. Sure, I fought with my brother and with Vanessa and my other cousins—but if anybody else had laid a hand on any of them, they would have had to deal with me. I loved my brother and cousins, and we were tight, we were family. Vanessa was my Aunt Jeanette's daughter; my Aunt Jackie, who lived across the street, had four kids—Denise (we called her Tuffy), Carlton, Dennis, and Christopher. And, of course, there was my grandmother, Mildred Dodds, whom we called Mother (we called my mother by her first name, Thelma). Mother, Aunt Jackie, and Aunt Jeanette worked hard, provided well for us, and took good care of us. We never lacked for anything we needed—least of all love.

LEARNING TO FIGHT

The year I lived with my grandmother is the year I learned how to take care of myself. I was not a mean kid, but I was a big kid. I had never before been in a situation where I had to fight—but during that year I often found myself being challenged by smaller kids who wanted to prove they were tough enough to take on "the big kid." Not being a fighter by nature, I was intimidated and scared by all these challenges—and I tended to give in rather than stand my ground. There was one kid in the neighborhood who bullied and terrorized all the kids. He thought it was great fun to take away my marbles. My Aunt Jackie saw what this kid was doing to the neighborhood kids, but nobody could stop him.

Then one night I had a dream that this kid came up to me and demanded my marbles again—only this time, instead of giving them to him, I laid him out cold. I woke up the next morning just brimming with confidence that I could actually go up to him and beat him up. It was an incredible feeling! First thing that morning, I dashed out of the house and went looking for him. When I finally caught up to him, I had to goad him and shove him and make him mad—because he didn't want to fight! That's when I found out that most bullies are really cowards inside. Their game is to get what they want through intimidation, not through actual fighting.

Some neighborhood kids started to gather around, and this bully saw he was going to have to fight me or be shown up as a wuss in front of the whole neighborhood. So he came at me with his arms flailing like an airplane propeller. I grabbed up a stick and began whacking at him, and I mean I wore him out. He backed off and, in a whiny bully's voice, he said, "Why don't you put that stick down and fight like a man!"

"I don't need this stick," I said, and I threw it down on the ground—and he reached right down, snatched up that stick, and began hitting me on the arm with it! And I didn't even feel it! I just grabbed that stick out of his hand and started hitting him with it again. About that time, I looked up and saw my Aunt Jackie at her screen door, hollering at me: "Whup his behind, Reggie! Whup his behind!"

Well, I whupped his behind, all right. I didn't injure him or anything, but I did teach him a lesson. Even after that whupping, he was never what you'd call a "nice kid"—but at least he didn't terrorize the neighborhood anymore.

Growing up in my old Chattanooga neighborhood in the 1960s was a lot different from growing up in the 'hood today. We got mad sometimes, we duked it out, we stayed mad at each other for a day or two, but after that we were friends again. In fact, we even had organized fighting—boxing—to enable us to work out our aggression in a safe way. If two neighborhood kids got mad at each other, they'd say, "Let's fight it out, man," and they'd go down to the Y, put on the gloves, and work it out in the ring. Nowadays, when kids get mad at each other, they pull a gun and shoot.

There were woods around the project of duplex houses where my grandmother lived, and I used to use those woods to work off my bad feelings. If I got mad or depressed, I'd grab a stick, go into the woods, and beat on a tree. Some people might say that's a terrible thing to do to a tree. Well, maybe so—but I think it's better to take out your frustration on a tree than to take it out on one another.

REMEMBERING LEONARD

I enjoyed that year, living with my grandmother, but I was even happier when my stepfather, Leonard Collier, got his discharge and he and my mother moved back home to Tennessee. They returned to Chattanooga with a little Chihuahua we named Blackie—and with a big surprise: My mother was pregnant. A few months later, my sister was born. Christie was the prettiest little baby I had ever seen. As she grew up, we made her tough by teasing her and fighting with her. I think sometimes she thought I didn't care about her, because of the way I was so tough on her—but that's just the way brothers do. I truly loved and treasured my baby sister with all my heart.

At first, I was glad to have my stepfather living with us—but soon after he and my mother moved back from Kansas, Leonard and I began to clash. He came in with some rules, and I didn't like his rules. I thought, *He's not my real dad. Who does he think he is, telling me what I gotta do and what I gotta not do?* The conflict between us continued over the next few years.

When I was thirteen, something happened that should have brought Leonard and me closer together—but instead, it split us even further apart: I got saved. My grandmother had started taking me and my brother to church during the year we lived with her, and she continued having a spiritual influence on my life over the next few years. Because of her influence, I asked Jesus to come into my life. Instantly, I was saved, I was right with God, my sins were forgiven. But you know what? There's a saying that Christians aren't perfect, they're just forgiven—and that was me. I was a long way from perfection—and one of my big blind spots was my relationship with my stepfather, Leonard.

I was judgmental and critical of him because he liked to drink, and I disapproved of drinking. Understand, Leonard wasn't a drunkard and he wasn't abusive; he just liked to drink on a social basis now and then. He was a good man, a kind man, and he had a great sense of humor. Out of love for our mother, he took us all in as his family and loved us as his own. But like a lot of teenagers, I thought I knew it all and that I had a right to judge my elders. My judgmental attitude toward Leonard's drinking blinded me to all the good qualities he had and to the love he showed us. It also generated conflict between us, because as I pointed out his flaws to him, he was sure to see the flaws I had and to point them out to me!

I look back on my relationship with Leonard and regret a lot of things I did and said, because when I judged him, criticized him, and rebelled against his rules, I limited his rightful authority as the head of our household. There were many times, of course, that I respected his authority, but all too often—over stupid stuff like taking my turn at washing the dishes or feeding the dogs—I failed to give him the respect he was due. There were even times, I'm sad to say, that he and I mixed it up with our fists.

By the time I was fifteen, our relationship began to smooth out, and I began to appreciate my stepfather. I finally realized that to be a good Christian and to show love and respect for my mother, I needed to respect my stepfather. He wasn't perfect, but he was the man in charge, and I owed him my obedience. I didn't change overnight, I still questioned him in some areas, but our relationship really began to improve about that time. As things improved between us, I began to learn from him. Realizing I had underestimated him in many ways, I began to understand him more and to respect his work ethic and the fact that he labored very hard to provide for us. Over time, we did more and more things together. He even taught me how to shoot pool and drive a car. I began to see that he really did care for me as a person.

We would joke and verbally spar with each other, and sometimes we'd team up to play tricks on my mom or my sister. At family gatherings, he'd crack up the whole family. He was the funniest person you'd ever want to know, and I think my own sense of humor, my own sense of the ridiculous, came from Leonard. Sometimes we would wrestle around the house, and he could never pin me because he was—well, he was sorta puny. But that never kept him from trying. I always enjoyed the look on people's faces when I introduced Leonard to them and said, "This is my dad." They'd stare at him, then at me, then back to him, and say, "Your dad!" Then I'd say, "Well, he's my stepdad." He and I both got a laugh out of that.

"Y'ALL KEEP LYING, I'M GONNA KILL YOU"

My grandmother, Mildred Dodds, took us kids to church and inspired us with a love for God and the Bible. Wisely, she didn't *force* us to go to church; instead, she made it seem a pleasure and a privilege to spend time in the Lord's house on Sundays and Wednesdays. My grandmother set an example for us, showing how she loved to worship God by walking five miles to church. Julius, my cousin Vanessa, and I would walk right along with her. If we missed the bus after church, we would also have to walk five miles back home. Most of us today would scream if we had to walk five blocks to get somewhere, let alone five miles—but my grandmother did it cheerfully and faithfully.

We went to an all-black church with a white pastor, Reverend Ferguson. He was one of the most sincere, authentic examples of true Christianity I've ever known—a totally selfless man who genuinely cared for people. He invested in the lives of kids, loading us all up in his van and hauling us off to the roller-skating rink or to a picnic at the park or to a ball game. He used these fun times to teach us that we have a God who wants to make our lives full and rich and joyful. By his example, he inspired me to want to serve God, to help people, and to invest myself in the lives of young people. From Reverend Ferguson, I learned that it's not enough just to talk about the love of God on Sunday mornings; you have to show people the love of God by spending time with them and getting involved in their lives.

Looking back, I realize I had some very strange ideas as a Christian teenager. I'd read my Bible and come across a passage like Zechariah 13:3, which says that false prophets who lie in God's name should be put to death. Then I'd go to school and see some kids who were lying a lot, and I'd go up to them and say, "The Bible says liars should be put to death. Y'all keep lying, I'm gonna kill you." Well, killing people is one of those things that's against the school rules—like running in the hallways or cheating on a test, only more serious. So when one of my teachers heard about it, he took me aside and said, "Reggie, you can't go around telling kids you're going to kill them."

"I wasn't serious about killing nobody," I told him, "but I am serious about the fact that those kids should stop their lying. Because I'm serious about what's written in this Book." And I pointed to the Bible that I carried around with me everywhere I went.

"I know you're serious," said the teacher, "but you still have to stop threatening to kill people—even if they don't do what it says in that Book."

"Okay," I said. "But you better tell those kids to stop their lying too."

Another example of some of the strange ideas I had back then: One time, when I was in junior high, I went to a Bible study and the leader asked me, "Have you been saved?" And I said, "Oh, yeah, I been saved two times."

A girl sitting next to me said, "What do you mean, 'two times'? You can only be saved once."

Well, that made me mad. I was like, "What do *you* know about it? You're a girl." (Okay, I admit it: I was maybe the *leeeeeeast* little bit chauvinistic in those days.)

But then the Bible study leader stepped in and said, "She's right, Reggie. Jesus died for you once. You can only be saved once, and you only *need* to be saved once." And that's when I realized that the moment I had committed my life to Jesus Christ, I had received my salvation. From then on, I knew God would always be there for me.

MOMMA'S BOY

A lot of what I am today, in terms of my confidence and my sense of security, I owe to my mother, Thelma Collier. The society we live in is constantly hammering at the self-esteem of black children. There's the racist segment of our society, which tries to tell us we are no good or we are inferior to whites. And there's the do-gooder segment of our society, which tries to tell us we can't make it in this world without the help of some handout or giveaway or government program. My mother taught me to feel secure, capable, and positive about myself. She taught me to stand on my own two feet, to believe in myself, and to go after my dreams. She made me feel special and taught me to believe that I am just as important as any other person—no more, no less.

I was nine, going on ten, when my mother returned from Kansas—and let me tell you, I instantly became reattached to her. I mean, I was Momma's boy! I was so attached to her it was ridiculous. I wanted to be around her so much that she even let me sleep in the bed with her—which was quite a sacrifice on her part, since I was such a wild sleeper. I would toss and turn and kick her, and every once in a while, when she'd had enough of getting kicked and having the covers pulled off her, she'd nudge me hard and shout, "Boy!" And I'd roll over on my side of the bed again.

My mother was a special woman. She worked from 2:30 in the afternoon to 10:30 at night, so we didn't get to see each other a lot. But in terms of her love and support, she was always there for us kids. Not only did she work hard every afternoon and evening to make sure we had a good living, but in the morning she worked hard at home, cooking and cleaning and taking care of us. Every day, she made sure dinner was fully ready before she went to work. All we had to do was take what she had made, heat it in the oven, and we had Momma's home cooking that night—even if we couldn't have Momma at the table with us.

She had a very strong work ethic, and she was diligent to pass that work ethic on to her children. Each of us had chores to do to help out around the house. She demanded our respect—but what's more, she earned it, along with our love and admiration. My mother, Thelma Collier, has always been one of my heroes.

My mother believed I could do no wrong. And even before I was saved, I was a pretty good kid—if I do say so myself. But I occasionally did things that my mother would never have believed I was capable of. For example, I sometimes used profanity. I remember one time, Julius and Vanessa wanted to prove to my mother that I said bad words, but she refused to believe it. "Oh, no," she said, "Reggie is a good boy. He don't curse."

One day, before leaving for work, my mother left instructions for me to get the dishes washed before she got home that night. Well, I figured I had plenty of time, since she wouldn't be home till after 10:30, so I went down to the recreation center to play around and have fun. While I was there, my brother called me and said, "Thelma's on her way home early, boy, so you better get home and wash those dishes." Well, I got on my bike and pedaled home as fast as I could. When I came in the door, Julius, Vanessa, and a couple other kids were sitting at the table playing cards. I hurried past them, went straight to the kitchen, filled up the sink with sudsy water, and began doing the dishes. Just as I was getting started, Julius strolled in.

"Hey, Reggie," he said, "what are you doing there?"

"You know what I'm doing here. I'm washing dishes."

"Washing dishes, huh?"

"Yeah, washing dishes."

He nodded, as if this was some deep subject he was pondering. Then he said, "Hey, Reggie, say mother-bleep." He didn't actually say "bleep," but you get the picture. I thought that was a pretty weird request, coming right out of the blue like that.

"Why do you want me to say a nasty thing like that?"

"Just say it," he said.

I looked around. Vanessa and the other kids were hanging around the kitchen doorway, watching me, and Julius was standing there, daring me. Should I do it? I debated in my mind for a few seconds, then said, "Oh, shut up, you mother-bleep!"

Instantly, they all started laughing. I figured, *Hey, I'm getting a good laugh here! This profanity thing is pretty good fun!*

Julius apparently thought it was fun too. "Reggie," he said, "say son-of-a-bleep."

I said, "Who you talkin' to, you son-of-a-bleep?"

Julius howled. "Call me a bleep-bleep!"

I said, "You bleep-bleep!"

The other kids joined in, demanding I use one of their favorite obscenities. After about five or six nasty words, it suddenly hit me: *Why are they daring me to say these things?* Suddenly, I thought I knew exactly why—and my blood ran cold. I turned around, and sure enough, there was my mother, standing right at the back door. She had heard everything.

I didn't have any excuses or explanations. I just hung my head and said, "I'll go get the belt, and you can go ahead and whup me!" I was *begging* for a whupping that day. But instead of being mad like I thought she'd be, she just burst out laughing. In fact, she thought it was so funny, she just couldn't whup me. But when she was through laughing, she gave me a stern warning. "Boy," she said, "you better cut out that bad talking." And I did. I completely stopped cussing after that.

At the time, my mother did not proclaim herself to be a strong Christian, and she was not really a practicing churchgoer, but she gave us all the love we needed. She really supported me when I started playing basketball and football in the ninth grade. Throughout my high school and college sports careers, she came to all my games, and so did my two aunts. Even when we were playing up near Nashville, more than a hundred miles away, they would drive up there to support me.

Around the time I got saved, I told my mother what I wanted to be when I grew up: I wanted to be a professional football player—and a minister. That shocked her. She could understand a kid wanting to play ball for a living, but she couldn't figure out why any young boy would want to be a *minister!* But even though she was baffled by my goal of a dual career on the football field and in the pulpit, she fully supported me. "If that's what you want to be," she said, "then work hard to achieve it—and I believe you will."

"Well, that's what I'm gonna do," I said, "and when I become a professional football player, I'll take care of you for the rest of your life." And—thanks in large part to my mother's inspiration and encouragement—that's exactly what happened.

When I was seventeen years old, I went before a group of ministers at St. John's Baptist Church in Chattanooga and gave a trial sermon on the subject of forgiveness. My mother was real proud of me. She told me later, "It was so thrilling, watching you up there preaching—it seemed like a heavenly light just shone around you." Well, that's a mother for you. I don't think the ministers judging my sermon saw any heavenly lights. But at least they thought I had done a passable job, and they gave me my minister's license. I had achieved one of my goals: I was a minister.

Becoming a professional football player would take a little longer.

Chapter 3

BIG DOG

The main reason I play pro football today is because of a man named O. J. Simpson.

For a while during my childhood, my sport was baseball. I had my sights set on a career on the diamond. But the longer I played, the worse our pitchers got. And the worse our pitchers got, the longer I had to stand out in the field, watching the other team run the bases. And the longer I had to stand out in the field, the more time I had to think, *Man, I don't know if I want to do this.*

Then, when I was about twelve years old, I was watching an NFL show on TV, and they ran a highlights film on O. J. Simpson. As I watched the film and listened to the voice of the announcer, I imagined it was me on that film, zigging and zagging, leaving a trail of would-be tacklers in my wake, thundering downfield like a roaring freight train. I imagined the NFL announcer praising the astounding gridiron performance of Reggie White. I imagined lining up against the Buffalo Bills, waiting for the snap, then tearing across that line to put a big hit on Mr. O. J. Simpson himself. I got so inspired just thinking about it that I dashed out the front door of my house and called to one of my buddies down the street. "Hey, man," I said, "did you see O. J. on the TV? Wasn't that cool? Heck with this baseball stuff, man! I'm gonna play pro football like O. J."

"Hey, I am, too, man," said my friend. "You want to be a running back like The Juice?"

"No way," I said. "You see the way he gets jumped on all the time? He's a moving target! Man, I don't want to play offense and get knocked around all the time. I want to play defense. I want to be the guy who knocks those other guys around!"

At that moment, I not only knew I wanted to play football, I even knew where I wanted to play: on the defensive line. I was totally inspired, and my baseball dreams vanished in an instant. Suddenly, I had only one objective: I wanted to be a professional football player.

Another of my heroes in those days was Dr. J—the great Julius Erving. That man was so classy, the way he handled himself on and off the basketball court. His intense rebounding, incredible jumps, razzle-dazzle ball movement, and soaring dunk shots were thrilling to watch. All my friends and I wanted to be like Dr. J. We would practice moves like his, try to dunk like he did, try to shoot like he did, even try to walk and talk like he did.

Dr. J started his professional career with the Virginia Squires of the now-defunct American Basketball Association. About the time he moved over to the NBA, I attended my first sports camp, run by the Fellowship of Christian Athletes at Black Mountain, North Carolina. Bobby Jones, who was then playing with the Denver Nuggets, was there, dunking and stuffing and going one-on-one with "the Chattanooga Choo-Choo," Anthony Roberts, a star basketball player from my hometown. Bobby talked to us kids about basketball and about living for Jesus Christ.

From then on, my heroes were O. J., Dr. J, and Bobby Jones. I looked up to these guys, and I ended up playing basketball as well as football in high school. I easily could have kept playing basketball and headed for the NBA instead of the NFL—but football was just my game. I loved basketball, I loved baseball, I even loved track and field (I came in third in the state in the shotput), but no other sport fit my strengths, skills, and personality better than football.

For one thing, as a young person, I craved attention. Perhaps it was an area of insecurity in my personality—or maybe it's just a normal part of adolescence. In any case, I saw the respect, cheers, and acclaim football players receive and I thought, *Man, that's for me.* I started at center in high school and really enjoyed the game. But even though I did well on offense, what I really wanted—even at the beginning of my high school football career—was to play defense.

PEOPLE WITH IMPACT

Sports is a great training ground for life. Almost any lesson you can learn on becoming successful in sports is a lesson you can apply to become successful in any other endeavor in your life. To succeed in sports, you need toughness, perseverance, motivation, teamwork, accountability, confidence, intense focus, a positive mental attitude, and a strong work ethic. And these are precisely the qualities you need to succeed in life. The people who pound these qualities into you while drawing out your natural skills and strengths are *coaches*. Good coaches, the ones who have a lasting effect on your life, are people you remember as long as you live. The lessons they teach you become part of the fiber of your being, and for years afterward, you can remember their names, their faces, and the sound of their voices because they had such a deep and powerful impact on your life.

The first man ever to have that kind of impact on my life was J. R. Harp, my coach in organized neighborhood baseball when I was in elementary school. I was good friends with all his sons, and he and his wife spent a lot of time with Julius and me when my mother and stepfather were at work. They would put us in the back of their station wagon and haul us to games and other events. They probably thought they were just keeping us out of trouble, but, in reality, they were investing in us, pouring their lives into us, working alongside my mother, stepfather, grandmother, and aunts to direct the course of our lives in a positive direction.

I remember coaches from my junior high days, one guy named Big Doug ("big" in his case is an understatement) and another guy named Buford. They took time with us, and we played baseball and football for them. Without being sarcastic or cussing us, they managed to get us boys motivated, taught us the basics of our games, and drilled into us the fundamentals of good sportsman-ship. They worked us hard and showed us that winning involves a lot more than fancy moves or good strategy. It involves hard work, preparation, and lots and lots of practice. They helped us see that to achieve what we wanted to achieve—winning games—we had to do a lot of things we *didn't* want to do, such as running laps and mastering the fundamentals.

Another middle school coach who played a big role in my life was Leon Tyler. He taught me the meaning and importance of discipline in reaching my goals. He was tough with us. He expected a lot of us, and taught us to expect a lot of ourselves. But as tough as he was, every boy he coached knew that he really cared. He was hard on us because he wanted the best for us—yet he was also a very patient man, because he knew that we were young and it would take time for us to learn the value of discipline. I want to publicly thank Coach Tyler for everything he did so many years ago to make me what I am today.

The coach who really impacted my life at Chattanooga Howard High School was Robert Pulliam (who now coaches at North Carolina A&T). I remember once he asked me about my ambitions. I think he expected me to say that I wanted to be a football player or some other kind of athlete. I said, "I want to be a minister." He seemed real surprised when I told him that. I don't think any high school kid had ever told him that before.

Coach Pulliam had been an outstanding defensive lineman for the University of Tennessee, so he understood that side of the game. Because he had played defense himself, it really meant a lot to me when he affirmed something in me I didn't know was there. One day after a really tough practice, he took me aside and said, "Let me tell you something, Reggie. I really believe that you could be the best defensive player to ever play the game of football."

"Really?" I asked. "You think I could be that good in high school?"

"No," he replied, "I'm not talking about high school. I mean pro football too."

Whoa! Did my head start to swell! There I was, just a sophomore in high school—and my coach was already putting up a statue in my honor in the Hall of Fame! To this day, I wonder how he saw that in me. But when he said that, he inspired me always to want to be the best.

I didn't understand at the time what Coach Pulliam was doing and what he meant—and I certainly didn't have a clue what he was *about* to do! When he told me I could be the best defensive player ever to play the game, he was talking about the *potential* he saw inside me. In order for that potential to be realized, I would have to be toughened, sharpened, strengthened, and refined. I was *good*—but I wasn't *great*. Not yet. And Coach Pulliam had a plan to bring out the greatness in me.

Fortunately for me, I didn't know what was coming.

GETTING TOUGH

Coach Pulliam saw that one of my biggest weaknesses as a defensive player was that I wasn't tough enough. The way Coach Pulliam recalls, I was "a nice, big Sunday school boy who didn't want to hurt anybody. If I told Reggie to go out on the field and really put a lick on someone, he'd do it—but a play or two later, he'd be his nice, big Sunday school self again. I couldn't be calling a timeout every other play to remind him how a football player's supposed to hit. So I knew I had to build some toughness into him."

Toughness doesn't mean meanness. When I say *toughness*, I'm talking about the ability to take punishment, to absorb the hits, to push on against pain and exhaustion, to stay focused even when the game becomes frustrating and the opponent is continually in your face. A tough player can take everything the opposing team can throw at him, and instead of giving in or giving ground, he uses that pain and fury as a motivator to propel him to even greater effort. A tough football player can take a lot and give back even more, and he does it all within the rules of the game.

That's the kind of toughness Coach Pulliam knew I needed to learn. And I had to learn it the hard way.

Our coaches at the high school—Coach Quarles, Coach West, and Coach Pulliam—were all big men. At 6-foot-2 and 280 pounds, Coach Pulliam was one of the biggest. From the day he told me about the greatness he saw in me, Coach Pulliam began to push and pressure me and to harass me on the field and in the gym. It was baffling to me, because all this rough treatment really intensified right after he had taken me aside and told me how great I could become. If he thought I was so great, why was he tearing into me this way? I mean, the things he did to me were just completely unfair!

For example, he and I would wrestle in the gym, and if I got out of his hold, then one of the other coaches would come and help him get me back down. It was those two big coaches against me, a high school kid. I didn't stand a chance! They used to frustrate me to the point where it made me cry—and then they would laugh at me and call me crybaby! I hated that, because I was cool, man, and I didn't want to be embarrassed in front of my friends. But looking back, I realize that this experience hardened me to peer pressure and the opinions of others.

Coach Pulliam stayed on me like that, pushing me, pressuring me, frustrating me for the rest of my sophomore year and on into my junior year. It was baffling to me, because I knew the coaches liked me and believed in me—but man! They sure had a funny way of showing it!

One day, during my junior year, a few of us kids were playing a game of pickup basketball against some of the coaches in the gym. We were playing man-on-man, and Coach Pulliam had personally taken charge of the job of guarding me. He had been pestering me and fouling me throughout the game—only there was no ref to call the foul, so I had to just put up with it. Finally, as I made a beautiful Dr. J-inspired move to the basket, Coach Pulliam elbowed me hard in the chest. It was deliberate, and it hurt like crazy—like someone had climbed up into the rafters and dropped a bowling ball on my chest.

That was it. I had taken that kind of stuff off Coach Pulliam for almost two years, and I was sick of it. I just slammed the basketball down, walked off the court, and started crying. Some of my friends came up to me and said, "Don't let him get to you like that, Reggie!"

"I'm getting tired of him doing me this way," I shot back. "He wrestles me, he punches me, he makes me cry, and I'm getting sick of it." I went into the locker room, sat down on a bench, and just let the tears come. I was mad and I was hurt.

A little while later, I looked up and saw Coach Pulliam walking around the corner, coming down the aisle toward me. I thought, *Finally, he's coming to say he's sorry.* In fact, years later, I found out that some of the other coaches told him he ought to apologize to me.

But when Coach Pulliam got up to me, he didn't apologize. Instead, he bent down in front of me, grabbed the front of my T-shirt, and said, "If you think I'm gonna apologize, you might as well go in there and get ready for your next whupping. Until you start fighting me back, I'm gonna keep kicking your butt." Then he straightened up and walked away. I sat there and watched him go, thinking, *Doggone it, he ain't gonna leave me alone!*

So I took up his challenge and started fighting him back. From then on, whenever we were on the basketball court and he gave me a shot with his elbow, I elbowed him back—hard. He kept wrestling me and beating me, but I kept fighting back until I won. First time I won, he wanted to wrestle me again! He said, "You gotta give me another chance!"

"Look, Coach," I said, "I don't gotta give you nothing! I've got the championship now, and I ain't gonna give it up just to give you another chance." Well, he begged me, so we wrestled a second time—this time in front of all the players—and I beat him again! From then on, Coach Pulliam recalls, I was a "holy terror."

It was years before I realized what Coach Pulliam was doing in my life: He was building toughness and confidence inside me. He knew my goal in life was to play pro football, and he knew that if I was to achieve that goal I would need to have the physical, emotional, and spiritual hide of a rhinoceros. He was pounding on me to toughen my hide—and it worked. I took a lot of pride in beating him, and I held onto that pride and self-confidence for a long time. In my senior year at Howard, I was named All-State in basketball and All-American in football, as well as Football and Basketball Player of the Year in Chattanooga. I was honored as Two-Sport Player of the Year in the nation (Patrick Ewing was first runner-up that same year).

The toughness and confidence Coach Pulliam built into me went far beyond the realm of sports. The same toughness that gets me through four quarters of a hard-fought football game has also helped me through my legal battles with the Philadelphia Eagles and the NFL, my spiritual battles against racism and church burnings in the South, and my battles in the streets of Philadelphia, Knoxville, and Milwaukee for the lives and souls of our young people. If you can build toughness in one area of your life, it will serve you well in another area. I'm not by nature a confrontational person, so the toughness Coach Pulliam built into me has helped me to be more dogged, durable, and persistent in the off-the-field areas where I might otherwise have been tempted to give ground.

About a dozen years or more after I left Chattanooga Howard High School, I called Coach Pulliam. I hadn't talked to him in years, and I wanted him to know that I appreciated the character qualities he had built into me. I said, "You know, I only recently figured out what you were doing when you were so hard on me back then, and I want to thank you for that. You were making me tough, you were building my self-confidence, and, man, you did a good job. In fact, you did such a good job, I thought you were gonna kill me!"

He laughed, then said, "You know what, Reggie? It's funny you would say that, because when you were in high school, I called the parents of all you guys and asked if I could do to them what I did to you. I asked your mother and all the other parents if I could be really hard on all you guys in order to build your confidence— and your mother was the *only one* who said yes."

I was blown away. In all those years, I had never known that my mother was in on what the coach was doing to me. As Coach Pulliam found out when he called the other parents, most parents are so protective of their kids that they want to shelter them from any rough experiences in life. But when you shelter kids from challenges they are ready for, you don't protect them—you only make them weak and soft. My mother had the wisdom to see that I was ready to become tough, I was ready to step up to the next level of self-confidence. So she let Coach Pulliam put me through the refiner's fire to burn the dross out of me and to harden the steel inside me. When Coach Pulliam told me that, I was like, *Thank God for my mother, man.*

My three main high school coaches—Pulliam, Quarles, and West—were black, and it was helpful to have black men as role models to encourage, motivate, and counsel me. I felt these men, and other coaches such as Bob Sanders, Paul Carruthers, and basketball coach Royal Jennings, truly understood me. Even though Coach Pulliam was hard on me, even though I didn't understand why he was being so rough on me, I knew he liked me and believed in me, and in many ways he was like a father to me. He was also a Christian, so I knew he would understand when I came to him with problems about spiritual matters, school, girls, or friends. It was really a kind of love-fear-hate relationship. Even after I beat him in those wrestling matches, if he got mad, I did whatever he said, no argument, no questions asked. I liked him, I feared him, I trusted him, I was mad at him, I respected him.

I played tight end my junior year. Tight end was a good offensive position for me, given my size, strength, and speed. A tight end lines up close to one of the two offensive tackles and needs to be both fast and physically powerful, since he is used both to block and to receive passes. Because a tight end is also a receiver, he has to have good hands. Though I really preferred defense, I enjoyed playing tight end my junior year.

But in my senior year, Coach Pulliam stuck me at offensive tackle. Oh, man! Offensive tackles are ineligible to receive. Their function is to be a brick wall with legs, to be bodyguards for the quarterback. I didn't get to use my quickness or my hands. Meanwhile, the guy Coach put in my old position at tight end wasn't handling the job. In practice, he kept dropping the ball when the pass came his way. Every time I saw the ball slip through his fingers, I got mad. I wanted to go scream, "I told you so, Coach! Now put me back at tight end where I belong!" During practice, I was stalking up and down the field, trying to get the coach to see how mad I was and how wrong he was. Well, he saw, all right. Sitting up in the stands, he hollered, "Reggie! Come up here!"

I thought, *Great! He's gonna move me back to tight end!*

I dashed up the bleachers and said, "Yeah, Coach?"

He squinted at me. "Your attitude stinks," he said. "Now, get back on the field and straighten up."

I was stunned. Couldn't he see that I was right and he was wrong? "But Coach, he keeps dropping the ball!"

"Right now, I don't care what he does—and neither should you. You just do your job. All these guys out here are watching you acting like a fool. I'm telling you, man, you keep it up, I'm gonna kick your behind."

Well, I did what he told me to do. When I saw Coach Pulliam was mad, I straightened up. He was a big man.

"I'M GONNA PLAY FOOTBALL"

During my senior year at Howard, I received attractive offers from a number of universities with great football programs: Alabama, UCLA, Michigan, Miami, Oklahoma, Ohio State, and—

closer to home—the University of Tennessee in Knoxville. UCLA
was one of the schools that flew me out to look over their athletic
program, and I was really impressed by what I saw. It was a multiracial campus, and the atmosphere was very congenial, very "California." The athletes of different races seemed to get along with
each other and respect each other. I liked that. In the end, though,
I decided against UCLA on the basis that California was a long
way from home. My family ties were very important to me, and I
knew I wouldn't be getting back to visit very often if I had to come
all the way from Los Angeles.

I visited the other schools and counted up all the pluses and
minuses. Last of all, I went to Knoxville and took a look at the
University of Tennessee. It was a weekend, and I got to take in a
game at UT's vast Neyland Stadium—the second-largest on-
campus stadium in the nation, a facility that gives the impression
of a hulking gray aircraft carrier docked on the banks of the Tennessee River. Man, I was impressed! As I sat in the stands, the biggest
marching band I ever saw formed a giant letter T and began playing
"Rocky Top," while fireworks soared skyward, exploding with a
gut-thumping blast. The Volunteer football team streamed out of
the tunnel, poured through that letter T, and took the field. Instantly, 96,000 fans were on their feet, cheering their hearts out,
shaking thousands of orange and white banners. The emotion was
so high in that place, it snatched me up off my seat and yanked
my heart into my throat.

That settled it. From that moment, I knew my future was going
to take me right through that same tunnel and onto that same
football field. I knew I was destined to wear the orange and white
of the UT Volunteers.

The next year, I showed up at the campus with my friend Charles
Morgan, a great athlete I had known since we played on the same
team in junior high. Charles had originally planned to accept a
football scholarship to the University of Miami, but I had talked
him into rooming with me at UT. Arriving on campus, we reported
to the athletic dorm to receive the room assignment we had been
promised as an incentive for signing with Tennessee. At the infor-
mation desk, however, they told us we had been assigned to different rooms. There had been some kind of mix-up, they explained,

and now that all the rooms were assigned, there was no way the assignments could be changed until the following year.

We were angry and disappointed. We had been best friends for years, two guys from Chattanooga who had never really been away from home before. Being split up caused us to lose our sense of security and connection with home. Just a couple weeks after school started, Charles quit school and went home. I often wondered after that whether I should have talked him into coming to UT. He was such a talented athlete. Could he have had an NFL career if he had followed his original plan and gone to Miami? I'll never know—but I'm sure of this: If we had been allowed to room together, he probably would have stayed in school. I believe we would have supported each other and gotten each other through.

It was both exciting and intimidating to be at Tennessee, "Big Orange," a school where football is not just a tradition, it's practically a religion. Over 170 UT Volunteers have gone on to play pro football, and the school even has its own Hall of Fame Football Museum. General Robert R. Neyland, the founding coach of the Volunteers, is almost as legendary in Tennessee as Vince Lombardi is in Wisconsin. In a head coaching career that extended from 1926 to 1952, Bob Neyland racked up a record of 173 wins, 31 losses, and 12 ties—and his Volunteers once went 17 consecutive games without being scored on! Now, that's a tradition!

I had stepped up to the next level of my football career. That was the exciting part. The intimidating part was that I was now playing with the *really* big boys! In high school, my size had always intimidated the other guys. Now I was playing in a league where there were *plenty* of guys who were roughly as big as me. I could hold my own, certainly, but I wouldn't be as dominating a force as I had been in high school. Even so, I clearly stood out in a crowd, and because of my size, my classmates and teammates began calling me Big Dog, my nickname ever since.

My first day of college football practice, I absorbed more physical punishment and verbal abuse than in a month of high school football. If Coach Pulliam hadn't pounded some toughness into me when I was in high school, I'm not sure I would have persevered through the first few weeks of college football—especially the time a huge linebacker named Lamont Holt Jeffers accidentally blindsided me while I was trying to get to the ball carrier. His helmet torpedoed my ribcage, and I was slammed to the ground, gasping for breath. I had to be carried off the field on a stretcher— and this was only practice!

That night, I called my mother and told her about the pounding I had taken that day. "Thelma," I said, "I can't take any more of this. I'm gonna have to give it up."

Of course, I didn't know then that she had been in cahoots with Coach Pulliam when he was trying to toughen me up. She wanted me to be tough, too, because she wanted me to achieve my goals in life. "Reggie," she said, "remember what you told me before you left home?"

Yeah, I remembered.

"You told me," she continued, "'As long as God blesses me with the ability to play football, I'm gonna give it everything I've got and I'm never gonna give up!' You remember telling me that?"

"Yeah," I said. "I remember."

"So what are you going to do, Reggie?"

I sighed. "I'm gonna play football."

BUILDING ENDURANCE

After I settled in and decided that nothing was going to stop me, I began to focus on my goals. I wanted to make All-American. And what's more, I wanted to be the Southeastern Conference (SEC) Player of the Year. Those are high goals and good goals— but looking back, I realize that I was so focused on my personal best that I was not as focused as I should have been on the team best. I also wasn't focused on the conditioning and training that would enable me to achieve those goals. The result was that I got hurt a lot during my junior year at UT.

The principle is simple: Which is harder to break—a cable made of braided spaghetti or a cable made of steel? I'm not saying my muscles and ligaments were made of spaghetti—but they weren't made of steel either. I wasn't working out like I should. The result: A sprained ankle in the game against the Duke University Blue Devils. Then, a couple weeks later, I sprained the other ankle in the game against 'Bama's Crimson Tide. Then an elbow injury. Then a pinched nerve in my neck.

The local press took notice of all my battle wounds—and literally added insult to injury! "Reggie White can't take it," they said, "because he's a Christian."

Because I'm a Christian! As if the Jewish Carpenter who went uncomplaining to the cross was not tough! As if the Christians who chose to be burned alive or fed to lions rather than deny their faith weren't tough! As if Coach Pulliam—a Christian coach who pounded me relentlessly in high school—wasn't tough! Man, I can't think of anything in this world that makes you more tough, more tenacious, more purposeful, more doggedly determined than having Jesus Christ in your life.

I wasn't injured because I was a Christian. I was injured because football is a punishing game and my body was not as tough as it needed to be. I had been wanting to become the best without paying the price of becoming the best. To achieve my goals, I'd have to harden and toughen my body. That meant more time in the weight room, grunting and straining and sweating. The weight room is no fun, but that's where you turn spaghetti into steel. That's where you build the kind of body that can take enormous punishment without popping a hamstring or pulling a tendon or tearing a muscle. I had not been taking weight training seriously. That was going to have to change.

During my senior year, I invested much more time building my strength and bulk with weight training, building my speed with sprints, and building my endurance with laps around the track. I saw my power and durability increase dramatically—and my game really improved. But wouldn't you know it, the press jumped on me again! "What's this? Reggie White can't have a great year in football! He can't make the hits! He can't make the sacks! He's a Christian!" You can't win with those guys.

Later, when I began playing pro ball with the USFL, I experienced more injuries—a sprained ankle and a broken rib. Two months after I began playing with the Philadelphia Eagles, I broke my rib again. It was around that time, in 1985, that I saw the televised game in which Redskins quarterback Joe Theismann's career was ended when the Giants' Lawrence Taylor sent him out with a broken leg. That really scared me. I thought, *Man, my career could be ended in a whiff, just like Joe's!* And Joe Theismann was in pretty good shape when he took that hit. I realized that being in good shape was not enough. I needed to build a shell of hardened armorplate around my tendons, bones, and joints if I was going to enjoy a long career. To stay healthy enough to play football, I would need to step up my work ethic to the next level— or maybe the level after that. In my rookie year with the NFL, I made up my mind that I was going to be in better shape than anybody else in the game. I'm convinced that's the reason I've been able to avoid career-busting injuries these past twelve or more seasons in the pros.

Discipline is the key to longevity in this game. I believe as a Christian I've got to work just as hard or harder than anybody else in order to stay great. To this day, I maintain a daily discipline of weight training, both in season and off.

BIG ORANGE

Just off the Neyland-Thompson Sports Center at UT is a street called Johnny Majors Drive. That street is named after the head coach who coached me through four seasons at the University of Tennessee. Back in 1956, Majors was a crew-cut football hero who led Big Orange to an undefeated regular season and an SEC championship title. That same year, he won the SEC Player of the Year Award—the last Tennessee Volunteer to win that honor (I planned to be the next). When I played at UT, Coach Majors was a statewide legend, a man who could have had the governor's job for the asking. Every football fan in Tennessee wanted to shake his hand or buddy up to him, and every teenage boy in Tennessee wanted to play for him. I was lucky. I *did* play for him.

Coach Johnny Majors demanded perfection from his players. And if you managed to give him the perfection he demanded, he'd turn right around and demand *more!* He studied each team on our schedule with exacting care, then spent hours preparing us and practicing us for any situation they might throw at us. Throughout my four years at UT, I don't recall a single game in which the opposing team took us by surprise. We were always well prepared for any eventuality, because Coach Majors had done his homework, and he demanded we do ours.

Like the local media, Coach Majors originally thought that the Christians on his team wouldn't work as hard, wouldn't hit as hard, wouldn't play as hard to win as the other players. Somehow, he had gotten the notion that if a player loves Jesus, he's going to go easy on the other team. There were a number of Christian players wearing the orange and white of the Volunteers during the time I played at UT. After I had played a couple seasons there, Coach Majors took some of us aside and told us that the Christians on his team were the best, most hardworking players he had—and the hardest-hitting players as well.

Another key to our preparation as a team was our defensive coordinator, Larry Marmie. He was a great motivator for our defensive line. Unlike many coaches who threaten or cuss their players to get them going, Coach Marmie inspired our best efforts through positive motivation. Sure, he could holler at us when the occasion required—all good coaches do. But he would much rather draw out our best performance by making us believe in ourselves than by shaming us into action. All of us on the defensive line just loved Coach Marmie, and we were ready to go to war for him at any time.

My first three years at UT, our team was last in the SEC in total defense; then Coach Marmie came aboard as defensive coordinator. By the end of my senior year, our Big Orange defense had gone from worst in the conference to best! I closed the season with fifteen sacks and more than a hundred tackles. I believe the performance of the defensive squad in general—and "Big Dog" Reggie White in particular—can largely be credited to the excellent coaching of Larry Marmie.

As a result of the great season I had in my senior year, the same press corps that earlier criticized me for not being tough enough voted me the Southeastern Conference Player of the Year—the fulfillment of my goal. I was also a finalist for the Lombardi Trophy for outstanding college lineman of the year (Dean Steinkuhler of Nebraska took that top honor). I had the privilege of playing alongside—and building lifelong friendships with—teammates like Willie Gault (now with the Oakland Raiders), Fuad Reveiz (now a kicker with the Vikings, and a guy I often team up with on various Christian service enterprises), Tim Irwin (also of the Vikings), Raleigh McKenzie (center for the Washington Redskins), and Lee Jenkins, who was a great cornerback in those days (these days, he's a great stockbroker, and he takes good care of my money).

The Tennessee fans are a lot like Packers fans: fanatically loyal
and totally committed to the game of football. Just as there is never
an empty seat for a Packers home game, Tennessee fans fill Neyland
Stadium to capacity for every home game. On six Saturdays every
season, 96,000 screaming fans stream onto the UT campus, and
Neyland Stadium becomes the fourth largest population center in
the state of Tennessee. Win or lose, those fans cheer their team on
with a passion that shakes the playing field and rattles the skyboxes. Even though I've gone on to wear the silver and red of the
Memphis Showboats, the green of the Philadelphia Eagles, and
the green and gold of the Packers, I still have a deep and lasting
affection for the Big Orange of Tennessee.

SHOWBOAT YEARS

From 1983 to 1986, a new professional spring league, the United
States Football League (USFL) competed with the NFL. Great players like Herschel Walker, Jim Kelly, Steve Young, Doug Flutie, Anthony Carter, and Kelvin Bryant were attracted to the new league,
which paid more and allowed more freedom than the NFL at that
time. Exuberant behavior that had been banned by the NFL—like
sack dances and end zone shimmies—were not only allowed but
encouraged in the wildly colorful USFL. The NFL grumbled over
having to pay more money to keep its players from jumping to
teams with names like the Baltimore Stars, the Arizona Outlaws,
the Birmingham Stallions, the Jacksonville Bulls, the Los Angeles
Express, the Michigan Panthers, the Houston Gamblers, and Don-
ald Trump's New Jersey Generals.

Me? I was chosen in the first round of the '84 USFL draft by the
Memphis Showboats. Even though I was a few class hours shy of
finishing my four-year degree, the Showboats made me an offer I
couldn't refuse. So I left school to play pro ball.

(A brief aside about school: Throughout most of my school
career, I had been satisfied making Bs, Cs, and even Ds. I wanted
to make As, I had the capacity to make As, but I just didn't put
the time in. I later went back to school and finished the degree I
had started just to prove to myself that I could finish strong and
make grades as good as anybody. And I *did* prove it. I made As
and earned a bachelor of science degree in human services in

1990. To any young person who is considering leaving school—
and especially to any young athlete considering leaving early to
play in the pros—my advice is to finish school, even if you have
to take classes on a reduced basis in the off-season. I can't tell you
what a great sense of accomplishment and confidence it brings not
only to achieve in sports but to achieve in school, and to finish
the academic journey you have begun.)

Some people thought I was crazy to pass up a chance to play in
the NFL in order to join the USFL. Fact is, those of us who signed
with the USFL were taking a chance. When I turned pro, the USFL
had been in existence for scarcely a year. All of us in the USFL
knew that the NFL was not one bit happy about a whole new league
competing for the NFL's fans, advertising dollars, and players, all
of which drove up costs and drove down profits for NFL owners.
If this shaky, fledgling league folded, would the NFL take us in—
or would we be blackballed from pro football?

But playing with the USFL's Memphis Showboats allowed me
to stay close to home. It also gave me a chance to play for the
Showboats' head coach, Pepper Rogers. I knew his reputation, and
that alone was a great inducement. Also, the money was very good
(or would have been, if I had gotten all the money I signed for).

My transition from college football to pro football was easy: As
soon as the college season ended, practice with the Showboats
began. I was finally a pro. My dream was coming true in a big
way. I would not only be playing professional football, I'd be playing close to home where my family and friends could come watch
me play.

Playing in the USFL was great. I've never experienced anything
like it in the NFL (though playing for the Packers comes close in
many ways). It was a much less strict and structured place to play
football. One reason the USFL was such a fun league to play in
was that it was run by football people, not by accountants and
lawyers like today's NFL. It was a warm, congenial, *family* atmosphere. Our entire team, players and coaches alike, were a family.
In fact, we included our families in many of our team activities.
As a team, we ate together, practiced together, and even spent
leisure time together.

Another nice thing about playing in the USFL was that all the
games were played in the springtime when the weather was nice

(compare that with playing on the famed "frozen tundra" of Lambeau Field in the dead of winter!). And then there were the fans—a more boisterous, fun-loving group of people you never met in your life. There was one group of dedicated Showboats fans who sat together in the end zone under a banner proclaiming them to be "The Boat People." They wore sailors caps and life preservers and were the rowdiest bunch of football nuts you ever saw in your life.

The laid-back style of the 'Boats reflected the personality of Coach Pepper Rogers. Everything about Coach Rogers was laid-back—his wildly mismatched clothes, his unruly hair, and his shoes worn without socks. He had a laid-back way of talking, a laid-back style of coaching, and a friendly, inspiring style of motivating his players, which contrasted with the loud, raucous, and even abusive style of many other coaches. As a football strategist, he was rambunctious, unpredictable, and daring—sometimes pulling a running or passing play out of a hat in punt situations. The other teams never knew what to expect from Pepper and his Showboats.

I made a lot of warm, close friendships with people I keep in touch with to this day—people like fellow players Walter Lewis and Calvin Clark; John Banazak; and our defensive line coach, Chuck Dickerson. As much as any other coach I've known, Chuck taught me the importance of defensive technique.

Coming out of UT, I had a lot of raw power, speed, and one basic move: the bull rush. The bull rush is simple: You just run over your man and keep going till you get to the ball carrier. But Chuck showed me how to add finesse to my power and speed. He taught me many of the moves I have used throughout my career—the spin, the rip, the club. (The rip is a kind of uppercut, delivered under the offensive lineman's arm to get his hands off you.) I use an adaptation of the club that Raiders defensive end Howie Long perfected. When the offensive lineman steps out and comes at me with his hands up, I get him underneath his armpit and throw him to my outside. It's a quick move, and you usually see the guy flying. That's why it's so awesome, because if you can pick a guy up off his feet and throw him across the field, you intimidate him. A newspaper interview with Larry Allen of the Dallas Cowboys shows what it's like from an offensive lineman's point of view:

Larry Allen isn't easily shaken. Only 23, he has been stabbed 12 times, shot at and menaced by street gangs and drug dealers. But Allen's first encounter with the brute force known as Reggie White was something he never will forget.

"One second I was blocking him," Allen recalled, "the next second, I was flying through the air, thinking, 'What is this?' I never had that feeling before."

Allen is a 6–3, 327-pound rookie tackle with the Dallas Cowboys, a second-round draft pick from tiny Sonoma (Calif.) State. He was forced into the starting lineup five weeks ago when Erik Williams was lost for the season in a car wreck. Despite his inexperience, Allen held his own through four games. Then he faced White, the former Eagle now with Green Bay, last Thursday at Texas Stadium.

Playing with one good arm, White still tossed Allen aside like a rag doll on his first play from scrimmage. Allen landed flat on his back as White rushed in to level quarterback Jason Garrett. The play was rerun several times in slow motion on TV with Fox commentator Pat Summerall noting, in awestruck tones, that White used only his right arm to send the enormous Allen flying.[1]

Chuck Dickerson and John Banazak really taught me a lot about pass rush technique while I was with the 'Boats, as did Dale Haupt, my defensive line coach with the Philadelphia Eagles. I owe a lot of my success to these great coaches.

For three years, the USFL struggled to survive while competing unsuccessfully against the powerful NFL for lucrative network contracts. (USFL games were carried on the ESPN cable sports network but not on the bigger networks such as ABC and NBC.) Finally, the USFL filed an antitrust suit against the NFL, seeking $1.69 billion in damages. The USFL won the suit—and was awarded a single measly dollar in damages. (If that was winning, what would it have been like to *lose*?) Mired in debt, the USFL was forced to suspend play in 1986 while attempting to mount an appeal and win a real damage award. But it was not to be.

Like a lot of players, I saw the end coming months before the USFL crashed and burned. I got out while the getting was good.

Chapter 4

INCREDIBLE
WEALTH

had just turned twenty-one when I went into the USFL. My first check from the Memphis Showboats was a signing bonus of $240,000. It really shocked me to hold that check in my hands— I had never seen that much money in my life! That's a substantial amount of money to place in the hands of a twenty-one year old who had never had much money to speak of before. What usually happens in such a situation is that a lot of that money ends up getting wasted. And that's exactly what happened with me.

I spent money. I gave money away. I sank a lot of money into a condominium, paying more than it was worth and more than my money advisors told me it would cost. People took advantage of me because I didn't know very much about handling large amounts of money. By the end of my first year with the 'Boats, I was $50,000 in debt!

FALLING IN LOVE

In January 1985, as I was preparing to begin my second year with the Showboats, I married a wonderful, beautiful lady named Sara Copeland.

When Sara and I first met, she was a sixteen-year-old college freshman at East Tennessee State in Knoxville. I was a nineteen-year-old sophomore at UT, and I saw her coming into the dorm one day. She was with friends who were college freshmen at UT, so I assumed she was about eighteen years old. If I'd known she was a sixteen-year-old freshman, I would have been scared off for sure! But even though I wasn't introduced to her and didn't know her name—I only saw her walking through the dorm—I was instantly attracted to her, because she was beautiful. Oh, man, she's beautiful!

That was in 1982, the year we had the big World's Fair in Knoxville—the Energy Fair. Not long after seeing Sara at the dorm, I was at the fair, and wouldn't you know it—there she was again! She was working at a booth, and something was tugging inside me so bad, I just wanted to go up and talk to her. Problem was, there was another guy there in the booth, and they were talking and laughing together. I thought, *Oh, man! She's got a boyfriend!* Well, you'd expect a beautiful girl like her to have a boyfriend. So I just left it alone and didn't say anything to her.

I didn't know then that she was a Christian. Fact is, she had only recently gotten saved, so she had all the fire and excitement of a new believer. She was constantly telling other people about Jesus. In fact, she was talking to a girlfriend of hers, Lisa Chapman, about God so much that she was getting on that poor girl's nerves! Lisa was also a friend of mine, and knowing that I was a very dedicated Christian, Lisa thought Sara and I would be a good match for each other. So Lisa told Sara, "I want you to meet this wonderful guy. He's a Christian, and I think you'd really like him."

Sara agreed to meet me, so Lisa called me up one Saturday and said, "There's a girl I'd really like you to meet. She's a Christian and she's really beautiful. I told her how nice you are, and she'd like to meet you. Can I introduce you to each other?"

Well, I don't know how I knew, but I just knew that Lisa was talking about Sara! Even though I didn't know Sara's name, I knew without a shadow of a doubt that Lisa wanted me to meet this beautiful girl. I said, "Tell you what. Why don't you tell her to come to church tomorrow and I'll meet her there?"

So she came to the First Apostolic Church in Knoxville and we met for the first time. After church, we went out to eat at Bojangles. I wish I could say it was love at first sight for Sara like it was for me, but the fact is, I didn't make a great first impression on her. I found out later she thought that this hulking 6-foot-6 football player was too big for her! At the same time, I was thinking, *Man, this girl is beautiful—what would she ever want with a guy like me? She's so slim and graceful and I'm so big and I walk kinda goofy.* But I wasn't going to let a little thing like that stop me. I was instantly, completely, hopelessly in love with Sara, and even if she didn't know it yet, I absolutely knew she was going to be my wife.

We spent the afternoon together. Later that month, I visited her at ETSU, and she did her homework while I ate pizza and stretched out and had a nap. Then I went back to the dorm and thought, *This is all right! I think she likes me!* Later that week, I got a nice letter from her, in which she wrote, "I don't know why God had us to meet, but there must be some reason He put us together." I thought, *Whoa! She does like me!*

The following week, I went to visit her and asked her to be my girlfriend. She said, "Well, I've got a boyfriend."

I was shattered. I thought, *Oh, man! She led me on!* So I left her alone for a while and we stayed friends. I called her off and on for the next few months, and I pursued her for a while, but the relationship didn't seem to be going anywhere. We stayed buddies. I told her everything like I would a buddy, and I accepted our friendship as that.

I finished school and went on to the USFL. I was living by myself in my overpriced condo in Memphis. I couldn't get Sara off my mind. I couldn't let go of the feeling I had that she was going to be my wife. Finally, I decided I hadn't talked to Sara in a while and it was time to give her a call. On the phone, I asked her how she was doing and stuff, and she asked me how I was doing and stuff. She said she didn't have anything going for the weekend, and I said, "You want to come with me?" So she came to Memphis and I showed her around. While we were in the car, I thought, *I gotta make my move.* I reached over and took her hand—

And we've been in love ever since.

A MIRACLE MARRIAGE

We had decided to get married in July of 1985, after Sara's graduation in May. But when she went home over Thanksgiving 1984, I began to sense that God was moving us to get married in January. She couldn't figure why God would want her to change her plans. In order for us to marry in January, she'd have to transfer to Memphis State, which meant she'd have to make sure all her credits would transfer from Knoxville to Memphis. Education was a number one priority with Sara, and she didn't want to take any chances messing up her graduation plans. So she said to God, "January is just six weeks away. If You want me to get married in January, You have to take care of all these details. You have to take care of the wedding plans. You have to make sure my credits transfer."

Sara has never been a procrastinator, so as soon as she got off the prayer line with God, she got on the phone line with Memphis State. She talked to three different people in the senior office to make sure her credits would transfer. They said, "Oh, no problem, Miss Copeland. Both the school you are transferring from and school you are transferring to are semester schools, both in the Tennessee state university system, so you'll be able to transfer and graduate on time."

Well, that was taken care of—but there was still the wedding itself, with a lot of details to be tied up and a lot of problems to be solved. One big issue for Sara was the wedding dress. She had her heart set on one particular dress, which she had been saving up for—but she knew she wouldn't have all the money saved up by January. One day, as she was browsing at the wedding shop, she saw the very dress she wanted hanging on a clearance rack for—get this!—over 90 percent off the price she had originally been told it would cost! It was a size larger than she needed, so it was easy to tailor it down to a perfect fit. "Now, that," she told me, "was a miracle."

Then there were the invitations. Now, you might think what I'm about to tell you is crazy, but this is exactly what happened— another miracle. Sara was sitting in my condo, writing out the wording of the invitations so she could take them to the printer, but she couldn't think of the church's address. Just then, the TV, which had been turned off, popped on! A commercial was running—a promotional message for our church! Our pastor was on the tube, telling the viewers, "So come worship with us at the First Apostolic Church, 5020 Pleasantridge Road." The very address she needed for the invitations! Sara just about came unglued! She was a young Christian, and nothing miraculous had ever happened to her before. She thought she was going crazy, but she didn't have time to think about it too long. "Thank You, Lord!" she said, scribbling the address on the invitation. Then she rushed out to the print shop where another miracle occurred.

The printer told Sara it would take four weeks to get the invitations printed. "Can't you get them done any sooner?" Sara pleaded. They said they'd do the best they could, but it looked like four weeks was the minimum. Two days later, the printer called Sara. The invitations were done, and they were perfect.

Sara says, "There were other ways that the Lord just cleared out all the obstacles to a January wedding. At first, the place we wanted for the reception was booked—but then a cancellation came up for the very time we wanted. It only cost a third of what it would have in July because it was wintertime instead of summer. There were many other details that just clicked into place.

So Sara thought, *Okay, God, You must really want me to marry this man.* She is a very independent, strong-willed person, and she says that if we hadn't gotten married in January, we probably wouldn't have gotten married at all. Another six months would have been enough time for the devil to come in and mess up our relationship. Sara, in her independence, would have said, "Forget it. I'm not getting married. I don't have to go through with this. I want to keep my freedom." So we believe it was God's will for us to get married in January—and He showed His will to Sara very plainly through miraculous circumstances.

THE THRIFT OF A GOOD WIFE

At the time, a few people said Sara married me to get her hands on my money. Nothing could be further from the truth. Fact is, Sara saved me from bankruptcy. She came in and totally reorganized my finances. She was very open and vocal about some of the problems she saw in this area, and I didn't want to recognize that people I trusted to handle my professional football earnings were mismanaging my financial affairs. I mean, here was this twenty-year-old woman telling me she knew more about my business than my business advisors! And to make matters worse, she was right!

Today, thanks to the skill and wisdom of my wife, Sara, we not only have more money than I ever would without her, but we have been able to give away more money to good causes than I ever could have without her. She has taken my lavish, naive generosity—which was almost my undoing—and transformed it into very wise and carefully targeted generosity. Because of Sara, the wealth I earn on the football field has been multiplied and used to bless the lives of many other people. God sent her into my life for a lot of reasons—and one of those reasons was to save my finances.

Sara was incredibly knowledgeable about money when we got married. At twenty-one, she received her degree in marketing and management, but long before she had that degree, she had an enormous amount of financial insight and experience. Sara's father had his own business and taught her the value of work, saving, and money management. From the time she was in grade school, she had chores to do, including cooking the family dinner one night a week. At age twelve, her father paid her to keep the books for his dry-cleaning business.

By the time Sara was only fifteen years old, she had six thousand dollars in the bank—money she had earned not only working for her father but also running a paper route, working at a hardware store, and working at the tennis courts. She saved her money and used her earnings to buy her own clothes and school supplies. In school, Sara worked just as hard, earning excellent grades and entering college when she was only sixteen years old. She put herself through school and helped out her sister while at college.

To this day, Sara is still an incredibly hardworking woman. You hardly ever see her sitting down—she's constantly in motion. Sure, we could easily afford a nanny to take care of the kids, but Sara won't have it. In addition to all her work for the church, her work in support of my ministry, her public speaking schedule, and all of our traveling, she also home-schools our two children, Jeremy and Jecolia. Is this woman amazing or what?!

Now, perhaps, you can see why I feel so lucky to have found a wife like Sara!

FORGIVING DEBTORS

Sara learned at an early age to value money—but not to love money. Her father is a very generous and giving man, and you can see these same qualities in Sara: a strong work ethic, self-reliance, business savvy, and genuine compassion.

One time, when Sara was young, her family's next-door neighbor came to her father asking for a small loan to help them through a difficult time. "All I need is twenty-five dollars," said the neighbor lady, "and I'll pay you back as soon as our check comes in." Sara's father lent his credit card to the neighbor, and the lady promised she would only charge a twenty-five-dollar item on it. Instead, she ran up charges of over two thousand dollars—and she had absolutely no intention of repaying it. Sara's father could have sued—but he decided just to pay the bill and forget it.

Though Sara's dad managed his business well, he was certainly not wealthy. That two-thousand-dollar loss was very painful and caused Sara's family some financial difficulty. But ultimately, Sara recalls, the neighbors suffered a series of trials and problems, whereas her family overcame their financial difficulties and were richly blessed in many ways by God. "When people do you wrong," she says, "you don't have to fight the battle. My father believes in the scriptural principles of 'Forgive us our debts, as we forgive our debtors,' and '"Vengeance is Mine, I will repay," says the Lord.' That neighbor lady set out to do something terribly wrong against my family, but it came back to hurt her, and our family was blessed."

Would Sara have forgiven that debt the way her father did? No way! But is she generous and compassionate? You bet! While doing a tremendous job of shepherding the White family resources, she has also been instrumental in seeing that much-needed financial assistance flows out to literally hundreds of people. She is a beautiful model of that sensitive biblical balance between financial accountability and openhanded generosity.

A BILLION-DOLLAR GOAL

Let's face it: I get paid very well for what I do. Some would say I get paid too well.

When I signed with Green Bay, a lot of reporters and sports commentators focused much more on the money I was getting than on what this new relationship would mean for Reggie White or the Packers or the fans or the game of football. They made a big

deal about me being the then highest-paid player in the NFL, and
they called me "The $17 Million Man." On the NBC *Today Show,*
Bryant Gumbel asked me, "How do you justify getting paid that
kind of money? What do you say to a man in the sanitation department making twenty thousand dollars a year?"

I wish I had thought to respond, "Hey, Bryant, that's a good
question. Tell you what, you go first. You tell that sanitation engi-
neer why you are justified making $1.5 million, and then I'll tell
him why I'm justified making what I make." On another occasion,
I was asked the same question by Brent Musburger of CBS Sports,
a guy who makes something like $1.2 million a year with little
chance of getting hurt.

The fact is, no one should ever have to apologize for earning a
dollar or a million dollars as long as he comes by it honestly. The
football business happens to be a business that brings in tons of
money. A football player is an entertainer, much like a pop star or
an actor. I don't remember Bryant Gumbel asking Jack Nicholson
to justify making $60 million for a few days' work on the *Batman*
movie. It's just understood that entertainers make a ton of money.
Sports figures happen to occupy another corner of the entertainment industry, and we get paid accordingly. It's not right or wrong,
fair or unfair, it's just the way it is. If the players didn't get paid
so much, where would the money go? To the owners, most of
whom make many times what a player makes, even after paying
all those big salaries. Is Bryant Gumbel going to go interview the
owners about how much they are making? I don't think so. The
fact is, the money is there to get and we get it, end of story.

Now, once we get it, we are morally responsible for what we do
with it. We are accountable before God. I believe even those who
don't believe in God and who refuse to acknowledge God with
their lives and finances will ultimately have to give an account to
God. Some guys who make millions use it responsibly. I know
quite a number of sports figures who give large amounts of money
to churches and charitable organizations, who set up foundations
to help kids, who use their money to run sports camps and inner-
city programs. I also know a number of sports figures who can
easily put a million a year up their noses. It's not wrong to earn
tons of money, but the way you spend it can be very beneficial to
a lot of people—or very destructive to yourself and others. Once

God blesses a man or woman with resources, that man or woman should bless others.

Another thing people need to understand is that a million dollars is not a lot of money.

"Say what?!"

You heard me right. A million dollars is not a lot of money. And I'll tell you why. First of all, taxes. When I signed with the Green Bay Packers, I got my first year's salary plus a big signing bonus—but that was also the year Bill Clinton got his retroactive tax increase passed, so half of everything I made went to Bill Clinton and his buddies in the Congress. I ask you: Who do you think would do a better job of wisely spending all that money? Reggie White? Or Bill Clinton and Newt Gingrich? Hey, you know the answer.

One of the ministries I'm involved in is the Knoxville Community Development Bank, a nonprofit organization that invests in the people of the inner-city community with low-interest loans for personal needs, business start-ups, and home mortgages. This bank does not lend money at 12 to 18 percent, like profit-making banks. It lends at about a point and a half over prime—usually closer to 7 or 8 percent—and the goal is to help people who deserve an economic opportunity but who might not be able to get a loan from a conventional bank. Our bank does not have depositors, does not offer checking and savings accounts, and does not issue credit cards, so it needs to have a substantial amount of start-up capital in order to make loans and meet overhead. By "substantial," I mean a minimum of about five million dollars.

I wish I could have fully funded the bank out of my own resources; in fact, I wish I had the money to start fifty or a hundred such banks all around the country. I make a lot of money, but I don't make that kind of money. I could only help put a million dollars in the start-up pot, and it was very hard to get anyone else in the community to step up and boost the funding to the needed levels. So, unfortunately, the bank is operating on a severely undercapitalized basis, and a lot of people who could have been helped and who deserve to be helped are being turned away. When you are trying to do something good for a lot of people, a million dollars just doesn't go very far.

Like I said, I make a lot of money, and many people believe I have an endless supply of it. That belief became evident about three years after my stepfather was murdered on December 19, 1992 (I will write more about him later). I made a statement that was picked up by the press, expressing my disappointment with the fact that the police had failed to solve the case. "The Chattanooga police said they were doing their best," I said, "but a murderer is still on the loose. I'm tired of hearing how they're doing their best." A police lieutenant with the Chattanooga police responded with a public statement addressed to me that "sweetening the reward with some of your fat salary wouldn't hurt." First, I don't see that it's my job to open my checkbook and solve crimes; that's what the police are paid to do.

Second, that statement expresses the attitude of a lot of people: If you're a professional athlete, then you must have a bottomless wallet. Well, the Lord has blessed me, and I think Sara and I have been good managers of what God has given us, and one of the ways we try to be good money managers is by not putting money in every outstretched hand we see. Whenever I write a check, I try to make sure it is an investment—not necessarily an investment that will bring dollar returns to me, but one that will bring some kind of major return in someone's life, or a return for the furthering of God's plan.

I look at it this way: What is a better way for us to go as a society—to tear down and take away from those who have created and acquired wealth, or to create opportunities so that more people can become wealthy? Is it better to push down the rich or to lift up the poor? The reason I am involved with the Community Development Bank, and the reason I want to see this concept spread to more cities across the country, is that I want to create more opportunities for more people. I want to make it possible for inner-city entrepreneurs to create wealth, to become taxpayers and employers who will in turn create still more jobs and opportunities for others, and on and on and on. I want to generate hope in places where there has been no hope.

I'll tell you something else that may surprise you. One of my goals in life is to become a billionaire. That's right, I said *billionaire* with a *b*. I'm not sure how I'm going to do that—especially since the companies we have started, such as Big Doggie Records, are losing money while they are investing in people's lives. On top of that, our accountant is constantly upset with us over the amount of money we give away. But that's my goal. I'm sure God would not approve of us spending a billion dollars on ourselves or hoarding it, nor would He be pleased if money became the thing that we wanted in life above all else. But I don't believe there is anything wrong with a person wanting to generate a billion dollars or more of income, with the goal of using that wealth to help others.

The ability to value money without loving money is surely a delicate balance—but Sara and I have asked close Christian friends to watch our lives and hold us accountable to seek that balance always. I believe this world needs more Christian billionaires who will use their God-given resources as a tool to make a difference in the world. God knows that Sara and I will always use God's blessing in our lives to bless other people—to impact their lives, to give them opportunities, to give them hope.

FAR ABOVE RUBIES

I don't have a billion dollars today; I don't have anything near that. But I am a fabulously wealthy man. No, I'm not talking about the money I make playing football. The most incredible wealth I possess cannot be invested in real estate or in the stock market or in government bonds. My greatest wealth is my wife, Sara, who is worth more to me than all the rubies in the world.

Every morning when she begins her day, Sara spends time meditating in Proverbs 31, a passage that describes in detail what God intends a woman and wife to be. Sara has written a set of goals for her life that she refers to on a regular basis. These goals—this vision for her life as a wife and mother—were based on this passage of Scripture.

Some people might say, "Oh, the Bible was written by a bunch of old men. That's just some sexist man's image of what women ought to be like." Wrong. That passage, according to Proverbs 31:1, was written by a woman, the mother of King Lemuel, and it could actually be called a "manifesto of biblical feminism." It describes a virtuous wife like Sara as hardworking, industrious, and productive:

> She seeks wool and flax,
> And willingly works with her hands . . .
> She also rises while it is yet night,
> And provides food for her household.

Like Sara, the woman of Proverbs 31 is money-wise and a shrewd investor:

> She considers a field and buys it;
> From her profits she plants a vineyard.

Like the virtuous woman of this passage, Sara looks after her own health, works out at the gym, and keeps herself in great physical shape:

> She girds herself with strength,
> And strengthens her arms.

This woman is also compassionate and caring, and she demonstrates her caring with action—as Sara demonstrated when she served as chaplain in a state mental hospital when we lived in Philadelphia:

> She extends her hand to the poor,
> Yes, she reaches out her hands to the needy.

There is a reason Sara is in great demand as a public speaker— a reason that has nothing to do with the fact that she's married to Reggie White. Sara has something important to say, because she has patterned herself after the virtuous woman of this passage:

> She opens her mouth with wisdom.
> And on her tongue is the law of kindness.

A woman like Sara doesn't have to go around acting vain and doing things to get people to notice her or flatter her. Secure and self-confident, she goes about her life, doing the things God has given her to do—and praise just naturally comes her way. As Proverbs 31:28 says,

Her children rise up and call her blessed;
Her husband also, and he praises her.

And that's how the kids and I talk about Sara.

God has been good in helping us to work out the issues and problems in the early years of our marriage, helping us to grow closer and closer to each other day by day. We've been fortunate to have a number of Christian friends who have mentored us, counseled us, and helped us to deepen and strengthen our marriage communication—people like Brett and Cynthia Fuller, R. V. and Frances Brown, and Rice Brooks from Washington, D.C. A good marriage doesn't just happen; it takes a lot of hard work. These good friends have helped us to understand better our roles and responsibilities in a marriage, so that we can work at the job of marriage more productively.

Sara is a great support to me in everything I do. Before the games, she gives me prayer, encouragement, and confidence. After a big win, she shares my triumph. After a loss, she is patient with me and comforting, and she helps me to restore my emotional edge. If I need to work through a tough problem or hurtful emotions, she keeps the house quiet so I can pray and meditate and work it through. Every day, she works hard to mold our two children, Jeremy and Jecolia, so that they will grow up to be responsive to God's calling on their lives. She also encourages me and holds me accountable to be the man God has called me to be.

Do we have the perfect marriage? Hey, who's kidding whom? Nobody has a perfect marriage. But one thing we do have is a wide-open, two-way line of communication. I'm willing to be confronted and corrected. So is Sara. I'm willing to listen. So is Sara. I'm willing to admit it when I'm wrong. Sara's willing to admit it when I'm wrong too. (Just kidding!)

I've never known a woman who better fulfilled the description of ideal womanhood found in Proverbs 31. The reason she fits that Scripture passage so well, I believe, is that she lives daily in that passage and always keeps its principles in front of her as the goal of her life. The passage closes with these words:

Charm is deceitful and beauty is passing,
But a woman who fears the Lord, she shall be praised.[1]

That's my wife, Sara—an incredible treasure worth far more than rubies. She not only does a good job of looking after my treasures on earth, she is my treasure and my wealth—and her own works praise her.

Chapter 5

BUDDYBALL

Early in my second season with the USFL, I became concerned about the league's future—and my survival. I was certainly being paid well to play for the Memphis Showboats—but what good is a fat contract if the league folds up and blows away? Also, I looked at the talent in the NFL, and there was no question that the level of play was a notch or two higher than in the USFL. I began to wish I could prove myself against the best guys in the top league.

I called my agent, Patrick Forte, and said, "I want to play in the NFL. What can you do for me?"

"Reggie," he said, "by the fourth game of the fall season, I'll have you in an NFL uniform."

I entered the NFL supplemental draft in the spring of '84. Usually, a supplemental draft is for college players who are graduating early or choosing to forfeit their remaining eligibility. Because of the shaky condition of the USFL, however, there were a lot of USFL players in this draft who, like me, were looking to move to the NFL. The Philadelphia Eagles selected me as their first-round pick. I was fourth pick overall—the New York Giants had first choice and took Gary Zimmerman, an offensive lineman they later traded to the Vikings. I turned out to be a lot better than Giants' head coach Bill Parcells thought I would be. Bill (who is now with the New York Jets) is a good friend, but I've never let him forget that he could have had me on his team. And I've never forgotten that if I had played with the Giants, I'd have gotten two Super Bowl rings with them.

The Eagles bought out the rest of my contract with the Show-boats and signed me to a four-year contract. As predicted, I suited up in Eagle green for the fourth game of the fall season—a game against the New York Giants. Even though we lost 16–10, I gave the team its money's worth, with ten tackles and two and a half sacks in my first NFL outing. I also batted a pass that was inter-cepted by Herm Edwards for a touchdown. My goal in that game was simple: to be the best. I figured, Hey, I'm a Christian! I'm serving the best, so why shouldn't I be the best?

Having played the spring season with the USFL and the fall season with the NFL, I had packed thirty-five professional games into a single year—and when the year was over, man, I was ready for a break! Despite missing the first four games of the season, my fellow NFL players voted me Defensive Rookie of the Year—a great honor, being applauded by your peers. I also made the first team NFL All-Rookie Team and Honorable Mention All-Pro. Over the next dozen years, I would be elected every year to the Pro Bowl, another great honor. But perhaps the hardest honor of all to bear (literally) is being named to the All-Madden Team. "Big John" Madden hands out a trophy that is a solid chunk of rock with a polished brass plaque on it—and let me tell you, that sucker's heavy!

I was thrilled to be in the NFL, but I had no idea what lay ahead. My years with the Eagles were destined to be the stormiest, most troubled years of my career.

BUDDY RYAN, MY RELENTLESS FRIEND

My first season with the Philadelphia Eagles, we finished with 7 wins and 9 losses—certainly not a record to write home about. Head coach Marion Campbell was let go, and Buddy Ryan, who had been defensive coordinator for the Chicago Bears, was hired to take over. I was excited that Buddy was coming to coach us, because I knew he had an extremely aggressive style of defense. I had heard a lot of good stuff about Buddy from my friend, Bears linebacker Mike Singletary. With Buddy coaching the Chicago de-fense, the Bears had finished the season with 15 wins and 1 loss and had beaten the New England Patriots in the Super Bowl, 46–10. Mike also told me what a great player's coach Buddy was—a guy who relentlessly pushed you to be the best, but also a good friend, the kind of guy you would gladly go into battle for.

I remember when we had our first minicamp, Buddy was a little nervous. He wore those famous white shoes of his, the same ones he'd been wearing since the 1960s; I guess he'd just get them repainted every few years. First day, he came up and asked me (and I remember this, because Sara was pregnant with our first child, Jeremy), "How's your wife?"

I said, "She's doing good."

"When's the baby coming?"

"In May."

"Well, you make sure you spend plenty of time with your wife," he said, "because family's the most important thing. This is a great game, but family's number one." I was real glad to hear him say that, and I knew it was genuine; it was not put on. I had just gotten my first glimpse of Buddy Ryan, the player's friend. The man really cared.

Going from minicamp to the first day of training camp, we all got to see the relentless side of Buddy Ryan. It was mid-August in the stadium at West Chester University where our training camp was held. The temperature was ninety-some-odd degrees and humid as a sauna, and we were all stewing in our juices under our pads. Buddy came out and began to put us through our drills—and let me tell you, he was like a whole different Buddy Ryan. It was like he came in mad at everybody! He hollered at us and he worked us and he didn't let up. I thought he was about to kill us. He had us running sprints and doing endurance runs; then he'd have us line up and hit. Just when we thought we'd had about all we could stand, he'd yell at us to do it all over again. A bunch of guys just dropped from dehydration and heat prostration.

During a break in that hot, sweaty, bone-grinding training camp, Buddy came up to me and said something that shocked me, something that I'll never forget. "Reggie," he said, "I just want you to know that you're the best defensive lineman I've ever seen. You do some things I haven't seen guys do before." He had never seen me in a game, only in practice—and he had coached some of the top All-Pro and Hall of Fame defensive linemen in the game, including Dan Hampton, Richard Dent, and the Purple People Eaters of the '69–'71 Vikings—Carl Eller, Alan Page, and Jim

Marshall. That was a high compliment he paid me, and I believed he meant it, because I knew God had given me some talent and that I could use it by being the best at what I do.

To this day, I don't know if Buddy was trying to motivate me or humble me, but coming on top of all the heat, hustling, and hollering I had endured in that training camp, those words blew into my soul like a cool breeze, creating a bond of respect and appreciation that I feel for Coach Ryan to this day. I also took that compliment as a challenge to be worthy of the praise, and I worked harder for that man than for any other coach I had ever played for up to that time. That year, my second year in the NFL, I had eighteen sacks.

Over the next few days, the reason for the intensity of Coach Ryan's training camp soon became clear. He was purifying the Eagles team like ore in a smelter, using heat to burn away the dross. If a guy couldn't take the hard work and the heat of training camp, he wouldn't be able to deliver a winning performance in a game. Coach didn't want anyone on the field or on his bench who wasn't committed to winning and to doing everything it takes to win. It was the first time in my career—including high school, college, and the USFL—that I had ever seen ball players just up and quit. Some of those guys had been in the league one or two years, pulling down hefty paychecks—yet they were throwing down their helmets in disgust, saying, "I don't need this!" I remember one guy saying, "Shucks, my dad's rich. I'm going home!"

At the end of training camp, the Eagles organization was smaller, but tougher and leaner. Still, the weeding-out process had been grueling and painful for everybody who suited up in an Eagles uniform. Buddy blasted some of our guys in the media, and we wondered why he did that. There was a lot of anger and resentment and bewilderment flowing through the team in the first few weeks of Buddy's tenure as head coach. Those of us on the team couldn't understand what the man was doing, because he had gotten rid of a lot of very talented players. Later on, however, I realized he was trying to get his own guys, he was trying to build a team that was loyal to him, a team with a work ethic of pure tempered steel, a team that would play four crushing quarters of football without giving up, a team that was as relentless as Buddy Ryan.

For some reason, God always put me with coaches who were hard-nosed, tough, and even mean at times—and I sometimes wondered, *God, why don't You put me with a coach who is a little more low-key?*

But the Lord knew what I needed. I always thought when I was younger that I was putting out 100 percent, but these tough-guy coaches kept finding another 5 or 10 percent inside me that I didn't know I had. By revealing these extra, hidden reserves of energy, stamina, skill, and strength to me, coaches like Buddy pushed me to a higher level of performance as I matured and took on more and more self-responsibility. Eventually, I matured to a point where coaches didn't have to push me, they'd see me pushing myself. They'd point out my mistakes, then let me go out and play because they'd see that I always got going when I needed to.

I have a lot of respect for tough coaches, and Buddy is one of the toughest. He was demanding but fair. There was only one thing I ever asked of my coaches, and Buddy and Johnny Majors and all my coaches respected that request: I asked that they not curse at me, and they didn't. I always told them, "I can take anything— screaming, hollering, making me work till I drop—but I can't take someone cursing at me." Buddy would curse around me, and I accepted that, but he never got in my face and swore at me—and that's all I asked.

We had a very strict regimen during training camp, in which we not only trained together but stayed together and spent our off-hours together as a team. We were going into battle together, and the idea was that we needed to stay focused on our game and our teamwork, and we needed to build camaraderie. So we worked, ate, relaxed, and stayed together as a team during training and before every game. One night during training camp, Sara came to West Chester and was staying in a hotel overnight, so I wanted to ask Buddy if I could take a one-night break from the team and spend the night with my wife. I walked down the hall to his office and knocked on the door, but Buddy wasn't there. Some of the other coaches were hanging out, and they shouted, "Hey, Buddy! Reggie White wants you!"

You could hear Buddy yowling and growling from way down the hall. "Reggie White!" he said. "I've been coaching for over twenty years! And I've been cussing ever since I was in the

National Football League! I've been cussing since I was a high
school coach." Just then he came around the corner and stamped
into the office, his face all red and his forehead creased. "Reggie
White," he said, looking me right in the eye, "I've cussed every
day of my life and I can't stop cussing now!"

I said, "I ain't coming at you to stop cussing. I just want to ask
you if I can stay overnight with my wife."

He stopped in his tracks and he looked stunned. "Oh," he said
mildly, "Sure, okay, go ahead."

SEARCHLIGHTS, POWER, AND SPEED

Buddy Ryan is a master of misdirection. Before the opening
exhibition game against Detroit, he laughed it off when reporters
asked him if he was going to use the famous 46 defense he had
employed so successfully in Chicago. "No, we won't use the 46,"
he said. "We'd embarrass ourselves! We couldn't play the 46
against ourselves, much less the Lions." So what did Buddy call
as the defensive play in our very first series against the Lions? The
46! For that defense, Buddy switched me from end to nose tackle—
and when I lined up over the center, there was no stopping me.
Man, we buried the Detroit offense.

The 46 defense is a big-blitz, high-stakes scheme. Other teams
have used it, but Buddy Ryan devised it in the mid-'70s and refined
it through the '80s, using it effectively with the Bears to win the
'85 Super Bowl. Designed primarily as a pass defense with an
eight-man front, the 46 is also very effective in shutting down the
running game. The 46 has its problems, though. It forces cornerbacks to single-cover, which can expose you to the big play. When
the opponent knows you're going to the 46 a lot and plans around
it, he can get a lot of passing yardage past you.

It's a complex defense, especially when you are first learning it
and trying to integrate it with the eighty or so other defensive
schemes you have to memorize. But it works well for a versatile,
hard-blitzing lineman like myself, who can quickly adjust to a
given situation and either rush the passer or drop into the coverage
against the run.

The 46 was just one of a lot of new defensive strategies Buddy
Ryan brought to the Eagles. Buddy liked moving me around to

different positions on the defensive line. His idea was to intimidate as many guys as possible in a game. It worked pretty well, too. Today, Coach Mike Holmgren likes to do this same thing with the Packers defense—shift things around and scare as many of the other guys as we can.

Of course, there were a lot of players I lined up against who just couldn't be scared. I quickly gained a rep as one of the best defensive players in the NFL (in fact, a 1989 *Sports Illustrated* poll of players gave me 38 percent of the votes for best D in the league, over three times as many ballots as any other player). Being perceived as the best is like having a big bull's-eye painted on your chest. They double- and triple-teamed me on every play—and that's okay, that's expected. If they threw two or three tight ends at me, it just meant the run was coming my way. That's what I had worked so hard for: To be the best, and to be in the other guy's crosshairs for four tough quarters of football.

The thing a defensive lineman has to watch, more than anything else, is the back of his legs. With every snap, you've got 300, 600, maybe even 900 pounds of raw beef aiming to land on you. Could come from your blind side. Could come from a cut block from the side, or a chop block from the rear. Could just happen when you get "caught in the wash" beneath a tangled pile of bodies, pads, and helmets. Any play can be a career-buster. Guys who survive long-term in the trenches have to have an ability to detect danger and adjust instantly. I don't know if that's an acquired ability or a God-given gift in my case—maybe a little of both. Fact is, it's not something I analyze or could verbalize or could teach to somebody else. It's just something I do. We call it "keeping the searchlights on"—always being aware of what's going on around you, always being tuned in to the shifting, whirling action at your sides and your back, not just the man you're going for.

One time, in a game against the Giants, Buddy again had me at tackle, over the center, Bart Oates. Next to Oates, at left tackle, was Jumbo Elliott—all 6-foot-7, 305 pounds of him. Oates snapped the ball and immediately came at me, hands high, standing me up. At the same time, Elliott somersaulted so that his feet were flying at me. It was a bizarre move, but it could have been absolutely brutal. When two offensive linemen come at a defensive player, one high and one low like that, it's called a crop block. It can take out a guy's knee—for good. Fortunately, I snatched my knee back in time. The rules on the crop blocking scheme are screwy, because it's legal on a running play, illegal on a passing play, and the officials rarely call it on any play. All you can do is be careful and watch your knees.

Later in that same game, I lined up against 275-pound tackle Doug Riesenberg on another running play. At the snap, he blocked me while Giants fullback Marice Carthon came down low with his legs barrelling into my ankle like a bowling ball rolling straight at a ninepin. I had to jump backward to get out of the way of Carthon's legs, then spin to break away from Riesenberg. A whole bunch of bodies ended up in the wash—but not mine. I was still standing when the play was over.

But you know what? I don't remember any of that happening. I only know it happened because I saw it on the game film later. The fact is, everything happens too fast to think. You can't say to yourself, *Uh-oh, Riesenberg's got his hands on me,* and, *Oh-my, here comes Carthon, diving for my ankles. I better move here, I better spin there.* By the time you've completed the thought, you're on the deck, waiting for the stretcher to arrive. It has to be instinctive, it has to be reaction, there has to be a continual awareness coupled with the ability to respond to shifting conditions without even having to think. That comes with hours and hours of experience, practice, and drill—plus a little something extra that, I believe, I was blessed to be born with.

To me, that little something extra is a combination of ingredients—searchlights, power, and speed. In training camp, they clocked me at 4.69 in the 40—pretty fast for a 285-pound guy. That kind of speed along with a powerful set of hands are what makes it possible for me to bull-rush a Mack-truck-size offensive lineman into his own backfield. And power? I believe that was God-given, too. I did some lifting in college, but I never really got serious about weight training until I joined the Eagles. Even so, I was bench-pressing 425 pounds my first day. The thing is, you should never take the natural abilities God gives you for granted. They are a gift from God, and you need to appreciate them, build on them, nurture them, and use them for His work—or they'll not only be wasted, they'll waste away.

In '85, my first year with the Eagles, I had 13 sacks in 13 games. In 1986, I had 18 sacks and 133 tackles (96 unassisted). In 1987 (a strike-shortened year), 21 sacks and 76 unassisted tackles. Those were great stats, the kind of stats that got me elected to the Pro Bowl year after year—plus 1987 Pro Bowl MVP. Sacks are fun, man. There's nothing like throwing a quarterback down for a big loss. But there's a whole lot more to being a great defensive lineman than sacking the quarterback. You have to play the run as well as the pass. The defensive ends I respect and emulate the most are the ones who play both the run and the pass—players like Howie Long of the Raiders and Charles Mann of the Redskins.

One form of defensive production that never shows up in the stats is the "quarterback hurry." You have to be able to put on the pressure and force the other guy to make costly mistakes—to fumble, to release sooner than he wants to, to ground the ball when nobody's open, to throw interceptions. When you hurry the quarterback, the fans and the guys in the announcers' booth usually don't notice—but it can make a big difference in the final score. When the scribes pronounce judgment on a quarterback because he "couldn't get in the rhythm" or "he couldn't get his game going," often it's because a very good defensive player was keeping him off-balance, forcing him to rush his game.

Another form of defensive production involves tying down your opponents' offensive line. When I was being double- and triple-teamed, that just meant I kept one or two extra offensive linemen busy—and that opened up lanes for my linemates, like Clyde Simmons, Jerome Brown, and Mike Pitts. If I wasn't getting the sacks and tackles, they were.

THE BEST OF GAMES,
THE WORST OF GAMES

The era of "Buddyball" in Philadelphia was one of the most memorable and controversial in NFL history—and one of the most memorable and controversial games of that era was the '87 season opener against the Washington Redskins on their home turf at RFK Stadium. I lined up against Ed Simmons, who had played his first NFL game just one week before. Simmons was helped out on double team efforts by tight end Glenn Dennison. My goal was to hit hard, early, and often, to take Simmons's confidence away.

Just three minutes into the game, I got past Simmons and caught 'Skins QB Jay Schroeder as he was looking to unload a pass. The hit sprained Schroeder's shoulder. He played one more snap, then walked off the field, holding his shoulder. The game had been a quick one for him, and he would sit out another game or two before he would suit up again.

Normally, sidelining your opponent's starting quarterback that early in the game should put you in good shape to win. After all, the 'Skins backup quarterback had only thrown one pass the entire previous season! Doug Williams had earned a reputation as a wild-armed ball-thrower in Tampa Bay, as well as in two different USFL franchises, before joining the Redskins. As it turned out, however, ol' Doug didn't plan to let the Philadelphia Eagles just walk all over him. In fact, he was about to have one of the best games of his career. When he took over as quarterback, Washington was up, 3–0.

By the second quarter, the game was tied at 10. With less than two minutes left in the first half, we drew a 15-yard penalty for unsportsmanlike conduct with a hideout substitution—a fake-punt pass from kicker John Teltschik to William Frizzell, leaving us in a fourth-and-27 situation. Time to punt, right? Well, somehow there was a disastrous miscommunication between Buddy and our special teams coach, Dan Neal. Buddy apparently thought it was obvious that the run was off and a punt was on. The special teams guys apparently thought they got a sign from Buddy to try another fake. So the order was given for another fake punt—a call so out-landish you wouldn't see a bunch of kids try it in a game of sandlot touch ball. Sure enough, Teltschik came up 17 yards short of a first down. Washington took over the ball and scored the go-ahead touchdown almost before you could blink. It was 17–10 at the half. Believe me, Buddy was cussing up a storm over that play, though he later took full responsibility for the miscommunication.

Just ninety seconds before the end of the half, as the Redskins launched a running play, I was just a little late off the ball—and Simmons and Dennison were right on time. They pounded me to the turf—about the only time that happened in the whole game—and I was hurting enough I decided to just stay on my back for a little while, checking out the gray, soggy skies over Washington, D.C. As I lay there, fifty-two thousand Redskins fans roared their approval that I had been knocked on my back. I mean, they were really nasty about it. Nice folks, these Washington fans. It's hard to blame them. They were still mad, no doubt, about what I had done to Schroeder.

I guess that kind of fan behavior—verbally kicking a guy when he's on the ground and possibly seriously hurt—is supposed to hurt your fighting spirit. It just revs me up. I knew I wasn't hurt bad, so I got back on my feet, slapped on a grin, lined up again, and finished the half. The crowd was pretty quiet after that.

Four minutes into the third quarter, Doug Williams completed a 57-yard pass to Ricky Sanders, which—when followed by a dive by Reggie Branch—put the 'Skins up 24 to 10. Our quarterback, Randall Cunningham, answered with an 80-yard drive, ending in a two-yard rollout to the left, which made it 24–17.

On Washington's next possession, with only eight seconds left in the quarter, Doug Williams took the snap and went back for the pass. I easily slipped past Simmons and got to Williams, hitting him on his blind side, the back side. His arm came out as he went down, and there was his hand clutching the football right in front of me. I snatched the ball, tucked it into my arms, and took off running. Our goal line was 70 yards away. At first, I didn't want to look back, I just wanted to keep sprinting. But after twenty or thirty yards, I glanced behind me and saw a running back tailing me. I knew he wasn't going to catch me. Man, it felt good. As I jogged into the end zone with that football in my hands, I looked up to the sky and thanked Jesus. I saw Sara in the first row, almost jumping over the rail—and she was pregnant.

That was my first touchdown in the NFL and my second as a professional football player (I had scored with a 30-yard run on a fumble recovery when I was with the USFL Memphis Showboats, playing against Birmingham). That touchdown tied the game at 24, and I was jumping and shouting and praising God—but the exhilaration of that moment would soon be eclipsed.

On the very first play after a 54-yard Washington kickoff return, Doug Williams found Art Monk with a 39-yard touchdown pass. Somehow, we had left our linebacker, Seth Joyner, alone to cover Monk—a Pro Bowl wide receiver. We should have had another defensive back covering Monk on the left slot. It was heartbreaking to watch Seth running after Monk, knowing there was no way the Redskin receiver would even slow down till he'd crossed the line. Like the fake-punt disaster in the second quarter, this was the result of a costly miscue. The Redskins went up 31–24, and capped it off with a field goal to win 34–24.

A game like that is full of hard lessons about football and about life. We had some great individual performances in that game. I had a 70-yard touchdown run, 5 tackles, and a sack for 8 yards. Our fullback, Mike Haddix, had one of his best games, running for 60 yards on 14 carries, plus 24 yards on 3 pass receptions. Randall Cunningham racked up some great stats, hitting 21 of 36 passes for 269 yards and a touchdown, plus 39 yards on the ground. I mean, the highlight film of that game showed the Eagles turning in a winning performance—but we lost.

Fact is, in football and in life, individual performances don't win games. Only teamwork wins. In football and in life, you have to communicate with each other, you have to have everybody on the same page. That's true whether you are on a football team, or on a church team, or on a business team, or whether you are part of a team called the United States of America. It's even true when the team you are on is the entire human race. We have to communicate with each other, we have to work together, we have to unite together—or disaster will result.

We had a chance to win that game, and we just let it go. Randall and the rest of the offensive side pretty much did their job that day. But on the defensive side, we failed to keep Washington from putting points on the board. We let the other guy pass too much. We had the game in our hands, we should have won it, but we didn't. We didn't play sixty minutes of football that day.

When you have a game like that, you remember it. You don't dwell on it, but you don't forget it either. You take the lessons, you take the emotions of the loss, and you harness them so that you have a better game your next time out.

It's my custom to go out to mid-field after a game and shake hands with the other team, and sometimes kneel and pray with them. This time, everybody on both teams came out after the game and shook hands. For most of the guys, it was a show of union solidarity. For weeks, the NFL Players Association had been talking to league ownership about a new contract, and the negotiations weren't going well. Talk of a national strike was in the air. Many fans, who see how much football players make and who don't understand all the issues in the player-management relationship, view the players as a bunch of crybabies who just want more money. So when we shook hands out in the middle of RFK Stadium, a chorus of boos went up from the stands.

It was an omen of things to come.

FROM THE YARD LINES
TO THE PICKET LINES

A strike is a symbol of failure—a failure to communicate, to understand one another, to care for one another, to respect one another. None of us on the Eagles were enthusiastic about going out on strike. Despite the season-opening loss, we were having a good season. We wanted to play football. But the NFL owners were treating us unfairly, and we intended to call them to account.

A lot of people thought the players were just sticking up the league to get more money. Well, money was an issue, but not the main issue, and certainly not the only issue. There were also matters of player security, pensions, severance pay, and other benefits. But the real sticking point was freedom—free agency, the freedom of player movement, the freedom to pursue opportunities. What the players demanded was unrestricted free agency, with no compensation to the teams losing players. We didn't want to hurt management, but we had endured a situation that was the equivalent of highly paid servitude. No other American sport had as restrictive a policy as the NFL. America was founded on the concept of freedom, and all we wanted was to be treated like other Americans. Once our contract was up, we wanted to be free to make a new agreement in our own best interests, without outside restrictions.

One of the biggest problems I had was with the attitude of the owners and their representatives. It was always management's choice, management's strike, not ours. Our job was to play football, not carry picket signs. But at every turn, it seemed that their intent was to humiliate and belittle the players, the very people who made them rich. They played mind games with us and offered vague proposals without hard numbers. They waged a vicious PR campaign and continually tried to pit the public against the players. Jack Donlan, chief negotiator for the NFL Management Council, was on TV day after day telling the public things that we, the players, knew were not true.

It finally came down to the simple fact that the only leverage we had as players was to strike. Management wouldn't listen to anything we said, they wouldn't come to the table, so we had no choice but to trade the yard lines for the picket lines.

Just before the national strike, Coach Ryan called the team together in the locker room. I thought he was going to try and talk us out of striking. Instead, he said to us, "If you go out on strike, you go out together. If you come back, you come back together. I don't want one guy coming in. If one guy comes in, everybody comes in. If one guy wants to come in and the rest don't, then that one guy should stay out with his teammates." When the strike was over, Buddy wanted his players to be as tightly bonded as the day they went out. He had worked hard for over a year to temper and refine us into a powerful fighting unit—and he didn't want the strike to tear down what he had built and what he was still in the process of building.

On Wednesday, September 23, 1987, talks broke down and the strike began. You might have thought most of us would just be sitting around looking at each other, waiting for the strike to end. Fact is, for most of us, the strike was a very busy period.

We all did some picketing, of course, but we also worked out to stay in shape so we'd be ready to play when the strike was over. Some of us also found work to bring in a paycheck. Kenny Jackson spent more time running his restaurant—Kenny's Deli Corner in Camden, New Jersey—and he even hired some of the striking Eagles as waiters for minimum wage plus tips. Strong safety Andre Waters did some substitute teaching and coaching in Camden. The Eagles' number one draft pick, defensive tackle Jerome Brown, sold shoes at the Pro Shop in Cherry Hill. Cornerback Roynell Young and I spent a lot of time doing community work with inner-city youth in Philadelphia; it didn't bring in any money, but it was productive, satisfying work.

The NFL Management Council, made up of NFL ownership, decided to put on phony football games with scab players—and they decided that the games would count toward league standings. In other words, we had to live with a bunch of strikebreaker players coming into our locker rooms, putting on our uniforms, playing on our field—and when the strike was over, their performance on the field would largely determine whether we got into the playoffs and the Super Bowl or not.

Every day, Buddy Ryan had to coach these replacement players, and he didn't hesitate to say on his weekly radio show and to the press, "This is not my team." Eagles owner Norman Braman pressured Buddy, both publicly and privately, to stop bad-mouthing the replacement games, to quit encouraging the players to remain unified. In my mind, Mr. Braman was trying to get Buddy to lie for him, and that made me mad. Buddy had a right to be his own man and to speak his own mind—and as it turned out, not even Mr. Braman could keep him from doing just that. Buddy Ryan is gonna be Buddy Ryan, no matter what anybody says.

Eagles management and the rest of the NFL owners continued to charge NFL ticket prices for these sub-NFL games. But then, what did the owners really care about most? The fans? The integrity of the sport? Or the money? On one occasion, Norm Braman—a millionaire Cadillac dealer from south Florida—told the press, "You talk about the constitutional rights of football players. I talk about the rights of the fans . . . who are responsible for the success of this game."[1] If Mr. Braman was so all-fired concerned about the rights of the fans, why didn't he and the other owners come to the table and negotiate in good faith?

I appreciate the fans. I wouldn't be anywhere without the fans. But I don't agree that the fans are solely responsible for the success of the game of football. Last time I checked, I didn't see a lot of fans coming to the stadium to look at all the other fans or to look up at the owners in their skyboxes. Unless I'm mistaken, the fans spend most of the game watching the action on the field.

Fact is, despite the efforts of the owners to drive a PR wedge between the fans and the players, the Philadelphia fans were overwhelmingly supportive of our cause. City councilmembers John F. Street and Lucien E. Blackwell joined us on the picket line to show their support. Mayor Goode also voiced his support and tried to find a legal way to keep Mr. Braman from using a city-owned facility—Veterans Stadium—as a chopping block for union-busting.

We picketed in a very friendly, laid-back way, chatting with the fans and signing autographs while explaining our position. Sure, there were a few tense and even ugly moments when we confronted the busloads of scab players face-to-face as they went into Vet Stadium to practice. But we always cooperated with police and avoided blocking traffic. There was never any violence—though I admit there were some very heated exchanges! You could tell those scab players were stung by it all and that they hadn't realized what they were getting into when they agreed to play our games in our place.

At an October game between the scab-Philadelphia Eagles and the scab-Chicago Bears, there were almost as many protesting fans (about three thousand) as there were picket-line-crossing spectators (about four thousand). The protesting fans crowded the ten entrances into Vet Stadium, making it hard for the replacement-game fans—many of whom had been given free tickets by the Eagles organization—to get in. Around a hundred tractor-trailer rigs circled the stadium, blowing horns and tying up traffic. There was some shouting and some shoving, but all in all, it was a peaceful protest. At the end of it all, the scab-Bears won, 35–3.

Less than two weeks after that game, the strike collapsed. It had lasted twenty-four days, and surrendering to management was a bitter pill to swallow—but in Philadelphia, Norm Braman and team president Harry Gamble were determined to make it even more bitter for us. We went to the locker room to suit up for practice; we were scheduled to play Green Bay the following Sunday. Mr. Gamble was waiting for us. He told us we would not be allowed to play Green Bay—unless we wanted to stick around and be paid training camp per diem. He said we had missed the reporting deadline set by the NFL Management Council. The NFL, he said, was "concerned" that we could not be in shape to play Sunday, so we would not be paid our regular NFL salaries. We had swallowed hard, ended our strike, and come in to play—and management had decided to give us another humiliating kick in the hindquarters. They imposed a lockout. They were determined not only to win but to make their victory as bitter for us as possible.

That says a lot, I think, about the mindset of the Eagles management in those days.

We ended up sitting out Green Bay and focused on getting ready for Dallas the following Sunday. The replacement team went out and lost a third straight game for us, all of which went on our record. Sometimes, I wish Buddy Ryan had supported the replacement players a little bit, because if the replacement team had won just a couple of those games, we would have gotten into the playoffs. But Mr. Braman and the rest of the Eagles management didn't seem to care if we won or lost. They still got their money from the TV rights, regardless of how sorry those games were.

John Spagnola, the Eagles tight end who served as the player representative for the club, would be cut from the team a year later—an act of management vindictiveness, in my opinion. We had lost the strike, we had lost one battle—and the owners had rubbed our noses in it. But the war wasn't over. The end of the free agency war was still five years away—but I would be on the front lines of that battle, and we would win!

Chapter 6

AN EAGLE
IN THE STORM

In late October 1987, we were back together as a team. We had all been working out, and the team was in great shape. The first day of practice, Buddy ran us ragged, doing up-downs and running and hitting. He was real pleased with the condition we were in and happy to have his team back. Now we were ready to play football.

Of course, Coach Ryan couldn't resist getting a dig or two in to management. At a press conference later that season, he demonstrated his contempt for what he called "the Scab Team" by staging a "Scab Ring Ceremony." Without any advance warning, Buddy called Joe Woolley, our director of player personnel, and George Azar, assistant to team president Harry Gamble, in front of a roomful of reporters. These two men had been in charge of recruiting the replacement team, which had lost all three games during the strike. In front of all those cameras and microphones, Buddy presented those poor guys a pair of gigantic championship-type rings—the infamous "Scab Rings." I felt sorry for Joe and George—they just did the job they were paid to do. I think everybody in that room was embarrassed—except Buddy, of course. It was a typical Buddy Ryan gesture—outspoken, uncouth, and totally honest.

Before the strike, a lot of guys had been resentful toward Coach Ryan. Buddy had blasted some of his players on his radio show, in the papers, and face-to-face, and they hadn't understood his reasons for doing that. He had cussed us and ridden us hard in practice after practice. After the strike, however, everybody understood what Buddy was all about, and they gained the utmost respect for him. They finally understood that Buddy was trying to build team unity. As one sportswriter put it, "This is pro football, and Ryan brings a military approach to the job and doesn't want any disbelievers in his trenches."[1] It seemed like, once the strike was behind us, Buddy didn't ride us as hard. He didn't yell at us and cuss at us so much. It was as if he saw that the experience of the strike had pulled us together and finally made us a team.

Before, during, and after the strike, Buddy Ryan was totally loyal to us players. There were many situations where he backed the team and stood up to ownership—and that took guts, because a coach lives and dies at the pleasure of the owners. Eagles owner Norman Braman probably never understood and certainly never appreciated how much Buddy did for ownership by standing up to them. I don't think he ever forgave Buddy for his loyalty to the players during the strike. But when Buddy closed ranks with the players, he did so for the good of the entire organization, including Mr. Braman. He did it to make us a winning team.

Coach Ryan was like a father figure to a lot of us. He treated us with respect. He had fun with us and he made it fun to play the game. We worked hard, but we had fun because of Buddy, and we all love him for that. A lot of us on the team grew up without fathers, and Buddy seemed to be a special friend to guys like us, and he treated us like sons. His wife, Joani, reached out to Sara and me. He is one of the great coaches of the game, and I'm proud to say that Buddy Ryan is a true friend of mine.

Buddy Ryan can be loud, gruff, tough, earthy, profane, and unpredictable. But he and Joani are two of the most sincere, honest, and caring people you'd ever want to know. Sara and I love these two special people with all our hearts.

FEELING SICK AT THE SUPER BOWL

The '87 season had been marred by the players' strike, and even after the strike ended, it was a rocky time for my relationship with the Eagles organization. My contract was up for renegotiation—

and I was not happy with my contract. Sure, I was happy to be in Philly, I loved the fans and the team, I loved Buddy Ryan, and I really wanted to finish my career in an Eagles uniform. But I was not happy with my deal. I knew I was not making as much money as other guys, and I thought my '85 signing bonus had been too low—I had gotten a bigger bonus in the USFL! But I let it go, and for my first few years with the Eagles, I never expressed any dissatisfaction.

When I first signed with the Eagles in 1985, I really liked Mr. Braman. I considered him an honorable man, and I felt he had made a real effort to get me to play in Philadelphia. My agent at that time, Patrick Forte, had called me about a month after the contract had been signed. "Reggie," he said, "the Eagles want to hire me to work in the front office. What should I do?"

"You're asking me?"

"Well," he said, "it's sort of a conflict of interest, you know—me representing you in a negotiation with the Eagles, then getting hired by the organization. I just didn't want you to get the wrong idea—and of course, I won't be able to represent you anymore. I just wanted to make sure it was okay with you if I take the job."

"Take the job," I said. "Instead of being on the road all the time, you'll be with your family. Take the job."

So he took it. After Patrick left, Jimmy Sexton and Kyle Rote, Jr., represented me. I later had reason to believe that while Patrick Forte was negotiating on my behalf, he was already pursuing a job with the Eagles. Whether or not that is actually true is something only Forte himself and the Eagles management know—but it would certainly account for a number of problems in my contract that I didn't even know about when I began negotiations in 1988.

I had been developing a sour feeling in my stomach about Mr. Braman for some time—a feeling that intensified with the way he treated Buddy and the team during the strike. Early in '88, something happened that really set my teeth on edge. Mr. Braman invited Sara and me to share a skybox with him and Mrs. Braman at Super Bowl XXII—part of the "wining and dining" stage of the contract negotiation. The big game that year was at Jack Murphy Stadium in San Diego, where the Washington Redskins beat the Denver Broncos.

I'll never forget sitting in that box with him, trying to watch the game while he sat there comparing the plays on the field with the way the Eagles played football. He criticized our play calling, he criticized our coaching, he criticized our players. He'd say stuff like, "How come we never throw to the tight end like that?" He was very negative and sarcastic, and I was getting pretty sick of it.

Once, when I commented on some holding of a defensive player on the field, he said, "You know, Reggie, you're always complaining about holding. You think people are holding you all the time."

"Yeah," I said, "they do hold me all the time." He just kind of shrugged and turned away.

I leaned over to Sara and said, "We're leaving at halftime."

"Why?" she said.

"Because I'm about to say something I might regret for the rest of my career."

Then I leaned over to Mr. Braman and said, "I'm feeling a little sick. I think Sara and I are going to go back to the hotel."

"Oh, that's too bad," he said. "Well, you know, I really want to get a deal done. Why don't you, me, Kyle, Jimmy, and Sara get together when we get back to Philly?"

"Sure, Mr. Braman," I said. "We'll do that."

Over the next few weeks, we got ready for the negotiations. I told my agents, Jimmy and Kyle, what I wanted, and it was pretty simple: An extension of my contract, a signing bonus, and a compensation package on par with what the other players were getting paid. But then came the shocker.

Kyle called me and said, "Pull your contract out." So I pulled my contract out. He said, "Is paragraph 17 marked out on your copy of the contract?"

I looked, and said, "No. It's right here."

"Well," he said, "you've got an extra year."

"What do you mean, 'an extra year'?"

"You've got an option year in your deal. Didn't anybody ever tell you that?"

"No, Kyle. Nobody told me nothing."

"Didn't Patrick Forte explain it to you?"

"No. You explain it to me."

It turned out that my contract gave the Eagles the option of playing me for a fifth year at just 10 percent more than my fourth-year salary. In other words, this clause stacked the deck in their favor.

At the end of our four-year deal, they had the power to cut me loose for free, or to hold me to another year for cheap. Either way, I lose.

But there was more. I found out that Patrick Forte had violated NFL Players Association rules by collecting his entire negotiating fee up front instead of receiving it over the life of the contract. Even more hurtful, he had advised me to cancel a life insurance policy I had taken out to protect my family; the Eagles contract, he told me, already included a policy of more than a million dollars, so I didn't need a policy of my own. So I canceled that policy, not knowing that the Eagles organization—not Sara—was the primary beneficiary. If I had died while my first contract was in force, the Eagles would have gotten the million, and Sara and my newborn son, Jeremy, would have gotten a mere $80,000, paid out over four years.

I was mad, because neither the Eagles nor Patrick ever sat me down and explained to me what an option year was. Patrick didn't represent me as he should have. He swears up and down he explained to me and Sara about that option year, but I never would have accepted such a clause if I had known about it. I was also mad about the insurance thing. The Eagles management was so concerned about what they would lose if I died, and they had me paying money out of my contract to cover them—but they had no concern whatsoever for my wife and child.

I felt I had been cheated, and I wasn't about to get walked on anymore. We attempted to set up a meeting for the contract negotiations with Mr. Braman. We would agree on the dates and buy our plane tickets (we had to fly out from Knoxville), and then Mr. Braman would abruptly cancel the meeting and we'd be out the money for the tickets. He did this to us several times, and I became convinced that this was just Mr. Braman's style, to play irritating mind games.

On one occasion, I talked to Mr. Braman on the phone—he was at his home in Miami. In the course of the conversation, he tried to tell me I was making good money and I should be happy with my contract. I was making more money, he claimed, than most Pro Bowlers.

"Mr. Braman," I said, "don't insult me like that. There are guys backing me up making two times the money I'm making."

"But Reggie," he said, "you're a Christian. You shouldn't make demands like that. You shouldn't care so much about money."

I had an answer for him—but I decided to hold it in until we got together face-to-face.

Finally, we met in Philly. Before we started the meeting, I said, "I want to say something first before Kyle and Jimmy get started. Mr. Braman, on the phone the other day, you told me I shouldn't ask for so much money because I'm a Christian. Let me tell you something: I work just as hard as the wicked man does. I deserve just as much as he gets. If I'm the best at my position, then I'm going to demand what I think I deserve, whether I'm a Christian or not. So that's out the window right now. I don't even want to hear that."

I didn't want to sign a multiyear contract that bound me to play at the Eagles' pleasure, yet allowed the organization to cut me after a year or two. My agents raised the issue during the meeting. "We want a guaranteed contract," they said.

"I'll guarantee your contract!" Mr. Braman countered loudly. "Next year! I guarantee you'll be playing next year!"

The thing that infuriated me about those contract talks was that, through it all, Mr. Braman treated me like I was dumb. For him to treat me like a "boy" who didn't know when my chain was being pulled made me mad. Mr. Braman also insinuated that I didn't deserve more than what I was offered because I wasn't in the leading class of defensive players in the NFL. Meanwhile, most of the sports reporters around the country were calling me the best defensive player in the NFL.

"This is ridiculous," Jimmy Sexton grumbled as we left one round of talks. "Braman's not even in the same universe as the rest of us."

Soon afterward, I came out publicly and challenged Mr. Braman's commitment to winning. "If the Eagles front office isn't committed to the high goals of excellence and competition I share with Coach Ryan, Randall Cunningham, and other members of the team, then they should come out and admit it publicly," I said.

"If Mr. Braman just wants to raise ticket prices to increase the profit line instead of improving the team, then he should admit to that too."

Clearly, the talks were not going well. Fact is, it would turn out to be the longest negotiation in NFL history—over a year and a half.

THE WINGS OF EAGLES

We got the 1988 season off to a bad start, losing three of our first four games. Buddy pulled me and Randall Cunningham into his office and said, "I stood up for you guys in the strike. My job is being threatened. I need you all to stand up for me right now." And we did. Randall and I talked to the other guys on the team, and then we all played our hearts out for Buddy. And we started winning. We won nine of our next twelve games, capping it off with an NFC Eastern Division championship win over the Dallas Cowboys, 23–7. A sports editorial in the *Philadelphia Inquirer* recognized all the ingredients that had turned a losing season into a division championship: heart, cohesion, unity, belief in ourselves, and belief in Buddy Ryan:

> In winning their conference for the first time in eight years, the Eagles have yet to prove that they are a team of destiny. . . . But it would be a mistake to bet against a team that plays with such heart. . . . Led by their Pro Bowl representatives, quarterback Randall Cunningham and tight end Keith Jackson on offense, and lineman Reggie White on defense, today's Birds have proven to be one of the most exciting Eagles teams ever. And one of the most cohesive. It didn't matter whether the fans—or the sports writers—did or didn't have confidence in them, the players obviously believed in themselves. And in their coach.[2]

We didn't go to the Super Bowl that year. Our championship dreams vanished in the mists of what came to be known as the "Fog Bowl," when Mike Ditka's Chicago Bears beat us 20–12 at Soldier Field on New Year's Day 1989. The first half of the game we played in sunshine. But when the fog rolled in, it was like a blanket of thick smoke from a forest fire. At times, visibility was only 10 to 15 yards, and the football was just a faint blur. I can't say the fog cost us the game: it was as foggy on Chicago's side of the line as it was on ours. Some people thought the game should have been called on account of the weather, but Buddy had a quick answer for that: "This is football, not baseball."

At one point in the game, referee Jim Tunney—the official who made the decision to keep playing—came into the Eagles huddle. He asked Randall, "Can you see the goalposts at the other end?" Randall looked downfield and saw nothing but a wall of gray. "Nope," he said. Then Tunney said, "Can you see the thirty-second clock?" Again, Randall said, "Nope." Tunney shrugged and said, "Well, don't worry about a delay-of-game penalty. We won't call it today."

It was a game we played with a lot of heart and intensity, but we missed a lot of opportunities. Randall passed for 407 yards and led the team inside Chicago's 20-yard line nine times—but without a touchdown. We moved the ball, but we dropped it a lot too, including a bobbled pass in the end zone. We were penalized seven times for a total of 60 yards. I put a hit on the Bears starting quarterback, Mike Tomczak, which sent him out of the game with his arm in a sling (though I might have done the Bears a favor; Tomczak had already thrown three interceptions, and his replacement, Jim McMahon, ended up having a very big game). In the end, all 12 of our points were scored by the big toe of our kicker, Luis Zendejas, with his four field goals.

It was, without a doubt, the weirdest game I ever played in. When we had first arrived in Chicago for the game, Buddy had the team bus circle the stadium and honk its horn to let everybody know we were in town. After the game, I went to Buddy and said, "Man, we shoulda circled the stadium seven times like Joshua did in the Bible, not just once. If Joshua brought down the walls of Jericho, maybe we could've brought down the walls of Soldier Field."

A loss to Chicago wasn't the way we wanted to end the season— but there was no denying it had been a great year. It had taken him three years to do it, but Coach Ryan had finally built the team he wanted. His first year coaching the Eagles had produced a 5–10–1 season. We ended the second year with 7 wins and 8 losses. His third year, 1988, we were 10 and 6. Clearly, Buddy's loyalty to his players inspired the best effort from his team, and we kept getting better and better.

NO YES-YES

In the course of my long negotiation with Eagles management, I had to file a lawsuit against Patrick Forte for "breach of contract, negligence and breach of fiduciary duty." I didn't want to do that, but I had to in order to get them to step up to the plate. Mr. Braman contended he was unaffected by the suit against Patrick. "The lawsuit doesn't concern us," he told the press. "It doesn't involve the Philadelphia Eagles. The lawsuit involves Patrick Forte and Reggie White." Fact is, the suit was a big headache for the Eagles management. If I won, I could go on to dissolve my contract with the Eagles and the bogus option year that had been slipped in on me, and I'd be a free agent. If I lost, the relationship between me and the team would be irreparably ruptured just as the team was moving into the winning column. If Eagles management settled the contract dispute, then my lawsuit would be moot, and I would drop it. So the Eagles, despite what Mr. Braman said publicly, were very concerned about that suit.

By this point, I was so tired of being exploited and patronized in the press by Mr. Braman that I was more interested in being traded than in signing again with the Eagles. The only reason I was willing to come to terms with the Eagles was Buddy Ryan. I would endure a lot of Mr. Braman's nonsense in order to play for a coach like Buddy, and with teammates like Randall Cunningham, Jerome Brown, Mike Quick, Kenny Jackson, Keith Jackson, Andre Waters, Keith Byars, Clyde Simmons, Seth Joyner, Eric Allen, Mike Golic, and the rest. Yeah, I would endure a lot—but I had my limits.

The longer the Eagles organization stalled the talks, the more it cost them. My bargaining position was strengthened week by week as other defensive players—such as Washington linebacker Wilber Marshall and Buffalo Bills defensive lineman Bruce Smith—signed deals that topped the Eagles' offers, and increased my market value. A little respect on the part of Eagles ownership, a little willingness to make a yes-yes deal instead of playing mind games and one-upping and trying to rub my nose in it, would have gotten my signature on a contract a lot sooner and would have saved the organization a lot of money. Mr. Braman's arrogance was a very expensive luxury—but I guess he figured he could afford it.

As negotiations dragged out, I attended some informal workouts but stayed away from minicamp, the voluntary preseason workouts at West Chester and Vet Stadium, and the August exhibition game against the Browns at Wembley Stadium in London. I know Buddy was very concerned that he wouldn't have me in the trenches for the start of the '89 season. Our first five games were scheduled to be the toughest: Seattle, Washington, San Francisco, Chicago, and New York. But Buddy understood the principle I was fighting for, and I felt I had his support. I was absolutely prepared to sit out the season, if that's what it took.

I was hopeful that the public would understand that I wasn't trying to take the Eagles for everything they had. I was just asking for what I thought was fair. Finally, in late August, we settled on a deal. I got what I wanted—three years guaranteed with a signing bonus, not the six years without a guarantee that ownership had continually tried to push at me. After the three years was up—free agency. Once the contract was signed, we quickly resolved the suit against Patrick. Because of that hidden option year in my original contract, I was technically a holdout and subject to fines, but we resolved that by working out a deal between myself and Harry Gamble that I would make a $35,000 donation to Fellowship of Christian Athletes.

I played with the Eagles for four more years. I was happy to be playing with the guys. I was happy to be playing for Buddy. But I didn't think management was committed to winning. Several others, such as Mike Quick, were going through contract hassles around that time, and none of them thought management was really committed to winning either. If the ownership is willing to pay for top talent, then ownership clearly wants to win. If not . . . Well, you can draw your own conclusions.

My few years in Philadelphia had been stormy, on the field and off. Throughout that time, one of my favorite verses of Scripture was:

> But those who wait on the Lord
> Shall renew their strength;
> They shall mount up with wings like eagles,
> They shall run and not be weary,
> They shall walk and not faint.[3]

I thought of "mounting up with wings like eagles" whenever I suited up and put on that shiny-winged Eagles helmet. There were times when I felt like an eagle in the storm—and the skies were getting darker and more threatening all the time.

THE END OF THE BUDDYBALL ERA

Buddy Ryan's fifth and final season as head coach of the Eagles ended with the playoff game against Washington on January 5, 1991. The last time we had played the Redskins, just two months before, we completely dominated the game, winning 28–14. We had whupped them so bad that ten of their players were medically sidelined in the course of the game, and both their starting and backup quarterbacks (Stan Humphries and Jeff Rutledge) were benched. The 'Skins coach, Joe Gibbs, had to send in a rookie running back as an emergency backup quarterback.

Maybe that previous win made us overconfident as we went into the playoffs. This was our third trip in three years, and we had been knocked out in the first round of the previous two outings. This time, we all believed that Buddy was going to coach us all the way to the Super Bowl. Man, were we ever wrong!

In front of 65,000 Philadelphia fans in our own Veterans Stadium, the Washington Redskins proceeded to hand us our heads. The game started out well enough. We took a 6–0 lead on two field goals by Roger Ruzek. Then, with less than six minutes left in the half, Washington went ahead, 7–6, with a touchdown pass from Mark Rypien to Art Monk. Just before the half, Washington's Earnest Byner fumbled at our 5-yard line, and our rookie cornerback, Ben Smith, snatched up the ball and ran 95 yards for a touchdown—or so we all thought. The officials ruled the ball dead on the ground and took away Ben's touchdown. That call threatened to set off a riot in the City of Brotherly Love. The Redskins took the ball over again and kicked a 20-yard field goal for a 10–6 lead at the half.

In the second half, the Washington zone defense just shut down our offense. We couldn't get the ball into the end zone to save our lives. Late in the third quarter, the Redskins kicked another field goal for a 13–6 lead. At that point, things got a little crazy.

A lot of people said that Buddy "hit the panic button" at that point. No way. Buddy Ryan does not panic. But he does sometimes do some very strange and unpredictable things. In this case what he did was send offensive coordinator Rich Kotite over to Randall Cunningham, who was standing on the sidelines while the defensive team was on the field. "Randall," said Rich, "Buddy says Jimmy is going to take the next series." In other words, Randall would sit on the bench while Jim McMahon went into the game. ("Jimmy Mac" McMahon was our Super Bowl-winning backup QB, recently acquired from the Bears.)

You have to understand, Randall was having his best season ever. In 1990, he had passed for 3,466 yards and 30 touchdowns. As a scrambler and broken field runner, he was almost without peer and had finished the regular season only 26 yards short of the NFL rushing record for quarterbacks. Even though we had not yet penetrated the end zone in this game, we were only down by one touchdown with more than a whole quarter left to play. From Dick Vermeil in the ABC broadcast booth to Mr. Braman in the owner's box to the fans in the stands to the players on both sidelines, everyone was asking the same question: "What's wrong with Randall? Why did Buddy Ryan take him out and put in a backup?"

Maybe he wanted to fire Randall up and motivate him (Randall went right back into the game after Jimmy Mac's brief series). Or maybe he thought Jimmy could bring some new spark that could ignite our offense. Whatever Buddy planned with that move, the result was that Jim McMahon threw three incompletions, and then we punted. A short time later, Washington's Rypien threw another touchdown for a 20–6 lead—and that's where the score stood till the final gun.

Mr. Braman was seething. "Only seven points behind," he growled to a reporter, "and Ryan embarrasses Randall before a national television audience!" A few days later, he fired Coach Ryan. The era of Buddyball in Philadelphia was over. I heard about the firing on my car radio when I was back home—but it didn't come as any great surprise. The professional relationship between Buddy Ryan and Norm Braman had been rocky for years.

Yes, we had lost playoff games three seasons in a row—but you have to have three winning seasons just to make it to three playoffs. Under Buddy, we had won 31 games over the last three seasons.

Only three teams—San Francisco, New York, and Buffalo—had won more. Buddy had spent five years taking the Eagles from being an aging, lackluster, bottom-of-the-barrel team to a young, exciting, improving, winning, world-class team. Dumping Buddy Ryan meant starting over again and rebuilding. It was a dumb thing to do. Coach Ryan summed it up himself when he said, "I've been fired before, but usually for losing. I've never been fired for winning before." Our tightly wound tight end, Keith Jackson, was even more blunt: "Get this down," he told reporters. "The owner is stupid. He don't have no brains, that's for sure."

I was not happy about the loss of Buddy Ryan. I was not happy about a lot of things in the Philadelphia Eagles. I didn't think it could get any worse than this.

But it did get worse. A lot worse.

Chapter 7

WINS—AND DEEP LOSSES

Buddy Ryan had spent five years unifying our team and hardening us into a dominant, aggressive fighting force. In one devastating stroke, our unity was destroyed. Our aggression was turned inward. We became a divided team. The drive and forceful personality of Buddy Ryan had held us together and channeled the rambunctious energy of our team. Without him, the team was directionless. We were falling apart.

We felt it coming even before Buddy was fired. Just one day after the playoff game, the team gathered at the facility so we could clean out our lockers and collect the tips for the locker-room and training-room staff. It was a bad day for me, a real sad day.

Coach Ryan was there to give us a season-ending talk. He told us to be proud of our record and reminded us of all the critics who had written us off at the beginning of the season. He didn't say anything about the possibility that he would be fired, although we all felt it in the air, hanging over us like a shadow. Somehow, I think we all knew this was the last pep talk Buddy Ryan would give to the Philadelphia Eagles. The only reference he made to the flap about benching Randall was when he said, "Remember, guys, the coach decides who plays. I'll see you all next season."

Everybody handled their emotions in their own way. I remember being pretty quiet that day. I just stuffed all my belongings in a big sack, then hugged everybody and said my goodbyes. Jerome Brown, our big loud defensive tackle and team clown, joked and hollered and tried to keep everybody's spirits up. Our center, Dave Alexander, mostly talked about the new baby he and his wife were expecting any day. Our kicker, Roger Ruzek, wore black and sat and stared like he was at a funeral. Tight end Keith Jackson was making up raps while he piled his stuff into boxes. Linebacker Seth Joyner was sitting around, talking about things that went wrong in the game, saying we could have won it. He was real mad and felt that a lot of guys on the team had not prepared themselves to win.

Randall wasn't there, so a lot of guys were griping about him. The gist of the gripes went like this: "Randall's a great quarterback, but he's got to cut out all this 'I have to win the game' stuff. He has to learn that we're a *team*." "Randall shouldn't have said that stuff about Buddy on TV." "So he was out for three plays. Why does he have to tell the world how insulted he is?" That kind of stuff.

"Whether people say it was the panic button or not, something happened yesterday," Randall had told the TV cameras. "First time it ever happened in my career—high school, college, or pro. A few people said, 'If Randall can't move anything past the pass protection, how can Jim McMahon do it? He's not as mobile.' It's kind of insulting, when I think about it. But I've got to be professional about it. I've just got to keep going. I'll do whatever it takes. I'll give all I have for the players and the owner and the coaching staff because that's just the way I am."

I'll tell you, I was mad at Randall. And I got more mad in the next few days, after the word came down that Buddy was fired. Randall and I had always been very tight throughout our years together on the team, and Randall had always been a big supporter and defender of Buddy Ryan. But after the playoff loss, I became convinced Randall had something to do with getting Buddy fired. Buddy was not a guy you could easily control—and Mr. Braman liked to have control over the people who worked for him. I worried that the things Randall had said in the media had given Mr. Braman just the excuse he needed to fire our brash, uncontrollable, game-winning coach.

REGROUPING FOR BATTLE

When Coach Ryan was fired, Mr. Braman named offensive coordinator Rich Kotite to be the new head coach of the Eagles. Richie is a great motivator and a solid strategist, though not as much of an innovative and driving force as Buddy. Personally, I had hoped that the job would go to our defensive coordinator, Jeff Fisher (when he didn't get the job, he took a position with the coaching staff of the Rams). I knew Randall had publicly voiced a preference for Rich Kotite even before Buddy had officially been fired, and I wondered if Randall had been involved in lobbying the front office to have Richie promoted to the head coaching slot. In my heart, rightly or wrongly, I blamed Randall for all that had happened since the playoff loss to Washington.

Randall and I got together at the Hilton Hawaiian Village in Honolulu before the Pro Bowl on February 2, 1991, and we had a long talk about all that had happened over the past few weeks— the game, Randall's comments to the media, Buddy's firing, and the hiring of Rich Kotite as the new head coach of the Eagles. I told him that he was The Man, he was the team's leader and field commander, but that I felt his ego sometimes got in the way of his leadership role. I told him I felt he sometimes lost sight of the fact that the Eagles are a team, not just a quarterback, and that a lot of the guys got upset when he grabbed the team's successes as his own. He defended himself against the things I said—and I can't blame him for that, because I was pretty hard on him. He said he had only talked in the media about Rich Kotite's potential as head coach because he had heard rumors about Rich being in line for the top coaching job at the Cleveland Browns.

Randall was insistent on one point: "Man, it wasn't my fault that Buddy got fired. I didn't go and ask Braman to fire Buddy. It was something that had been coming for a long time, and it would have happened sooner or later." And I was equally insistent: "You have some fault and it looks like you got Buddy fired. I don't think you did it intentionally, but I think that's the result of the things you did and said, and I think you ought to admit it."

Our talk was personal, painful, and frustrating for us both. After we talked, we were even more divided than before. I knew that, somehow, we had to work out our feelings and our attitudes to a point where we could accept each other and work together again. Somehow, we had to regroup—not only Randall and me, but the entire Eagles team—in order to get back to the job of winning football games and going after a championship.

When I got back to the mainland, I called Rich and asked if he would set aside the first of two April minicamps for a team gripe-and-regrouping session. I felt we needed to get everything off our chests if we were ever to be able to put our arms around each other and go into battle together. I told Rich that, while I respected him, I loved Buddy like a father and his firing had hurt me and a lot of the other guys very personally. But when you lose a member of your family, you still have to find some way to pull yourself together and go on. We needed to do that as a team. Rich agreed and proceeded to set aside a minicamp where all of us on the team could work out our issues and feelings. None of us knew if we could resolve everything in one meeting, but it was a place to begin.

So we got together at the Eagles facility and had a wide-open, no-holds-barred meeting. No subject, no complaint, no personality was out of bounds. We cleared the air, big-time. Randall wasn't the only subject we discussed in that meeting. Fact is, the guys had a lot of issues and gripes. It had been easy to keep a lid on all those problems and dissensions while Buddy was around to keep us focused and while we were all working toward the goal of winning. But the firing of Coach Ryan had caused all these different issues to break to the surface. They needed to be dealt with, and we dealt with every one of them.

It was a tough session. Man, it was tough! There was a lot of anger—but a lot of laughs too. We didn't come out of there all agreeing with one another, but we did leave committed to one another as men and as teammates. Whatever our differences, we had to agree on our purpose: *Winning*. Rich gave us a short talk about preparation and about camaraderie: "We've got forty-five guys, and we've got to pull together, practice together, live together, and play together. If we do that, man, we're gonna be all right."

A lot of us thought it would take at least two or three meetings to get everything aired, but we managed to do it all in one session. We all grew a lot that day. And when it was all over, we went out to a hotel and watched the NCAA basketball championships on a big-screen TV.

I have to give credit to my friend Randall Cunningham. That was a hard session for him, and he took it like a man. Despite the hard time he and I went through together in the early part of 1991, I would never take anything away from Randall Cunningham. He is a man of real character and dedication to his team. He is a great quarterback because he has an intense work ethic, he is committed to the game and to winning, and he is merciless in criticizing his own performance. I always have and always will consider it a privilege to have played the game of football with him.

Since that time, I've told Randall that I love him, man-to-man. I don't know if he believes that, because the hurt of that time we went through was so intense—but it's true. Randall, if you're reading this, I want you to know that I respect you, man.

WOUNDED EAGLES

It's a good thing we made the effort to clear the air, because the '91 season turned out to be a very tough one for us all. If we hadn't pulled ourselves together, I don't know how we would have made it through.

We started the season in great shape. The previous season, Randall was getting sacked at least two or three times a game, so we drafted 6-foot-5, 320-pound Antone Davis, a huge, yet amazingly quick, offensive tackle from the University of Tennessee, to give the man more protection. Antone and I spent a lot of preseason time working out together. Since we're both from UT, we had a lot to talk about. To keep our defense on track, Rich hired defensive coordinator Bud Carson, the mastermind of Pittsburgh's legendary Steel Curtain defense of the 1970s.

Rich's practice sessions were a lot different from Buddy's—less of the strenuous can-you-take-it stuff, less hitting, more noncontact drills, more weight training, more endurance training, more mental preparation, more fun. Rich didn't scrap everything from the Buddy Ryan era. He kept up many of Buddy's traditions, including the annual training camp game of Izzy-Dizzy—the relay race where you put your forehead on the end of a baseball bat, spin around the bat in circles till you are dizzy, then try to run to the far end of the field without falling down.

Rich Kotite brought a more disciplined (and, some said, more cautious and conservative) style of football to the Eagles. He wanted us to play aggressive but cool—no more desperation plays, no more dumb penalties for late hits and piling on. Under Buddy, we had gained a rep as the "bad boys" of the NFL, the "Gang Green." Rich took strides to clean up our image and our play. We still used Buddy's 46 defense, but Bud Carson modified and adapted it to give us less blitzing and better coverage in the corners to guard against the big play—again, a more cautious and disciplined approach to defense than the daring and exciting (but occasionally disastrous) Buddy Ryan approach.

We had a great preseason schedule and won most of our games. Randall was at the top of his form in the preseason, completing over 76 percent of his passes and averaging more than 6 yards per carry on the rush. He had been responsible for about 70 percent of all offensive yardage the previous season, and he was poised to have a terrific year in '91. Mr. Braman had ordered Rich Kotite to take the Eagles "to the next level"—and it was looking like we were going to do just that. On the first day of September 1991, we went to Lambeau Field in Green Bay for our first game of the regular season. On the very first play of the second quarter, the unthinkable happened.

As Randall Cunningham dropped back to pass, a 247-pound rookie Green Bay linebacker came blitzing right up the middle, past our center, David Alexander. That rookie linebacker's name was Bryce Paup, and it was his very first game in the NFL. A split second after Randall released the ball, Paup hit him with a flying tackle to his left knee. Randall went down on his back with torn medial collateral and posterior cruciate ligaments—and he was done for the rest of the year! He spent the rest of the year having his knee rebuilt and watching games from the sidelines.

You might think we'd have lost that game. No way! We all stepped up our game and showed the Packers that, even without our starting quarterback, we play and win as a team. With very little warm-up time, Jim McMahon turned in a beautiful backup performance, completing 17 of 25 passes, including two for touchdowns. Keith Byars caught eight passes for 111 yards—including one that he caught lying flat on his back in the end zone after a Packers safety slapped it up in the air!

Switching between the left and the middle, I bothered Green Bay QB Don "Majik" Majkowski all day, sacking him three times, knocking down two passes (one for an interception), and forcing a bunch of fumbles, including one that I recovered. In the end, we won that game, 20–3.

In many ways, that season opener was a foretaste of the entire 1991 season. We went through four starting quarterbacks that year: Randall, who was out in the first game; Jimmy Mac, who got hurt early in the season; Jeff Kemp (son of former congressman and HUD secretary Jack Kemp), who ended up getting a concussion; and rookie Brad Goebel. We could hardly believe the bad breaks raining on our offense that year. It was frustrating, because our defense was so outstanding that, if we'd had Randall leading the charge, I have no doubt we would have won it all in '91.

Our defense was so strong that some sportswriters compared the '91 Eagles to the '63 Bears—a team whose QB, Billy Wade, was continually laid up, who had no offensive rushers in the top twenty, whose offense ranked tenth out of fourteen NFL teams, yet who finished with a 11–1–2 record and a championship because of their invincible defense. I don't know that our defense was *quite* in that class, but I don't think it's an idle brag to say that we were pretty awesome.

We tromped the Cowboys, 24 to zip, sacking Troy Aikman 11 times on his own turf (Clyde Simmons led that charge with 4½ sacks) and forcing three interceptions. We held the Dallas offense— the number one offense in the division—to 90 yards total, and we allowed Emmitt Smith only 4 yards rushing in the first half. That was the worst offensive production in the history of the Dallas Cowboys.

We went on to beat the Giants twice. We beat the Oilers in their own backyard. We staged an incredible comeback in Cleveland. Sure, we had a few bad games too: an embarrassing rematch with Dallas in our own stadium, a 23–0 blowout in Washington, a sorry Sunday outing in Tampa Bay. But given the fact that our season was littered with wounded quarterbacks, given the fact that we had to battle our way back from a 3 and 5 deficit, I think our 10 and 6 record at the end of the season was very respectable.

We didn't go to the playoffs (just one more win would have gotten us a berth), but we achieved a lot against long odds, ending the season with the number one defense in the league. Number one in the NFL against the rush, number one against the pass. The entire year, we never allowed 100 yards rushing to any ball carrier, nor 100 yards to any receiver. We had four players with six or more sacks—Clyde and I each with 13, Jerome Brown with 9, and Seth Joyner with 6½. There was a chemistry to the Eagles front four that made it a very special group to be a part of.

Clyde was our fighting spirit—quiet but consistent. He was dependable, steady, and he played hard. His play often rallied us in tough, come-from-behind situations because he was a tough, come-from-behind guy—a late-round draft-pick player who made a first-class rep for himself in the NFL and in the Pro Bowl.

Seth was our intensity, our fire, our anger. He was thoughtful and analytical, and he agonized over losses, picking them apart in order to understand how to perform better next time. He was hard on his teammates at times, but never any harder than he was on himself. He was our accountability, our truth.

Jerome Brown was our emotion, our sense of fun. He was our talker, our hollerer, our jokester, our heart. He lifted us and drove us and powered our defense with his wide-open-throttle approach to the game and to life.

And me? I was the Minister of Defense, the Rev. It was my job to put the fear of God into the guys on the other side of the line.

The four of us linemen, plus cornerback Eric Allen, were named to the NFC Pro Bowl team that year. Even without a trip to the playoffs, we finished the season happy because we capped it with a big win—a glorious, nail-biting, gut-wrenching 24–22 win over the NFC East champion Redskins, who were 14 and 1 until that game.

The most incredible moment in that entire incredible game came in the waning seconds of the last quarter. A long pass had given the Redskins a first down just 9 yards from the end zone. We were desperately trying to fend them off and preserve our slim 2-point lead. It looked hopeless. On the first down, Jerome Brown bull-rushed right through Redskin linemen Jeff Bostic and Mike Schlereth, then yanked Ricky Ervins, the Redskin running back, to the ground for a loss. On the second down, Jerome battled clear

After twelve years in the NFL,
I finally realized my dream:
a Super Bowl championship!

Can you believe that lean dude is me in fourth grade?

But, man, did I grow by high school! My senior year was blessed by several awards: High School All-American, High School All-State, Top Player in Tennessee, Player of the Year for Chattanooga.

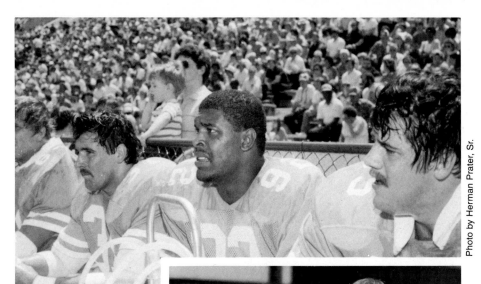

The lineup on the bench at an Orange and White Game, the University of Tennessee.

And the guy who organized that bunch of guys: my friend and mentor—then Tennessee coach Johnny Majors.

I love to pose for these photos—
College Player of the Year Award in 1983.

In the tunnel before a Memphis Showboat game.

Photo by Herman Prater, Sr.

My pastor and best friend—
Jerry Upton and his wife, Janice.

Celebrating the day I married Sara
with my stepfather, Leonard Collier,
my mother, Thelma, and my sister,
Christy Collier, January 5, 1985.

Photo by Herman Prater, Sr.

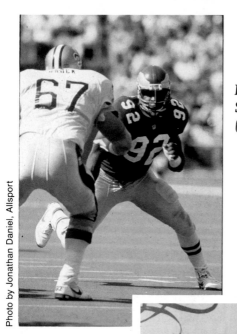

Photo by Jonathan Daniel, Allsport

Rushing offensive Saints lineman Stan Brock in October of 1991 (Saints 13, Eagles 6).

"Look, audience, am I as strong as Dad?"—I cohost a radio show in Philadelphia with Neil Hartman, and my son, Jeremy, in 1991.

Sterling Sharpe and I at the Reggie White and Friends Football Clinic in Chattanooga, Tennessee.

Wearing the Jerome Brown #99 armpatch at the Eagles opening game of the 1992 season.

Photo by Jeff Hixon, Allsport

My dad, Charles White, and I at the Pro Bowl in 1992.

Me and my daughter, Jecolia (five years old), on a date in 1993.

Above: *Friends and family: (front row) Jeremy White, Denisha Tillison, Jecolia White, Nicholas Tillison, (back row) Reggie, uncle Ronnie Dodds, Chuckie Spruce, Mike Wilson, uncle Lemone Wilson.*

Below: *Sara and her family—sister Liz Taylor, cousin Dana Garcia, aunt Feli Shelsher. At back, her sister Maria Dozier.*

*Sara's parents—Charles and Maria Copeland—with their girls—
Sara, Liz, and Maria and their grandkids—Shari, Kiera, Wesley,
Jecolia, Jeremy, and baby Morgan.*

Going through drills at one of my football camps.

The 1994 Reggie White and Friends Football Clinic in Chattanooga with safety Ronnie Lott.

Photo by Herman Prater, Sr.

Bull-rushing Erik
Williams at the October
1995 Packers-Cowboys
game.

Photo by Al Bello, Allsport

Running back John
Mackey of the Baltimore
Colts and I congratulate
each other at the Mackey
Awards banquet in
Chicago, Illinois, in July
1996.

The longest-running rivalry in the NFL affects every Bears/Packers game. Here, I get a piece of Erik Kramer.

This was before I hurt my hamstring at the Bengals-Packers game in December 1995 (Packers 24, Bengals 10).

Here I get the first of my Super Bowl record three sacks of New England's Drew Bledsoe in the Superdome.

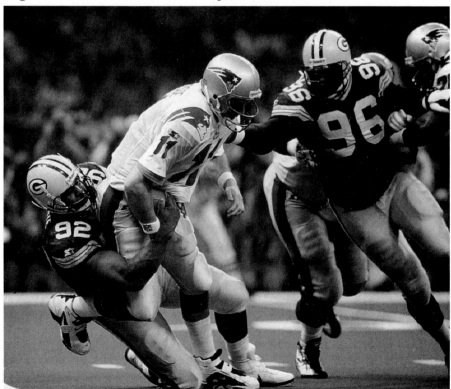

Investigators comb through the burned-out remains of my church in Knoxville, Tennessee, in January 1996, looking for clues to arson. Almost immediately after, the church and ministry were overwhelmed with love and support.

Giving my son, Jeremy (seven years old), a "pep" talk about hustling at my camp.

Sara and I ministering with our close friends, Pastor Isaiah and Gloria Williams of Jesus People Ministry in Miami, Florida.

Still in love and best friends after twelve years!

At the Super Bowl!
Go, gooooo Packers!

of Bostic and Schlereth in time to bat down a pass that was rock-
eting straight for the end zone—again, we dodged the bullet,
thanks to Jerome. On the third down, Jerome was a wild man,
furiously bull-rushing the middle of Washington's offensive line,
enabling me and Mike Pitts to sweep past their offense and sack
Jeff Rutledge for a 12-yard loss.

We had stopped the Redskins cold. I jumped up and looked for
a big pot-bellied defensive lineman with the number 99 on his
back. I didn't have to look far. Jerome was leaping up and down,
war-whooping and laughing like a kid on a roller coaster. I ran
to him and chest-bumped him, whapped him on the helmet,
then hugged that big, beautiful earth-mover of a man around the
shoulders.

I had no way of knowing that I had just lined up alongside
Jerome Brown for our very last Eagles game together. A few months
later, he would be gone.

FALLEN EAGLE

Jerome Brown spent Thursday, June 25, 1992—the last day of
his life—in his hometown of Brooksville, Florida, north of Tampa.
That afternoon, he and his twelve-year-old nephew, Wesley Au-
gusta "Gus" Brown, were driving in his shiny green '91 Corvette.
Jerome stopped the car at a Chevy dealership garage to check on
a '73 Impala that was being rebuilt for him. Gus waited in the car.
Jerome joked around with the mechanic who was doing the rebuild
and chatted with the manager about a big fish fry he was planning
to host for the town before the season began. Then he went back
out to the Corvette, climbed behind the wheel, revved the engine,
and drove out onto Hale Avenue.

The car could do zero to sixty in just over four seconds—and
knowing the way Jerome loved to drive, that's probably just what
he did. The streets were a little rain-slick, and Jerome probably
had the engine racing before he got it completely nose-forward and
straightened out. Somehow, the car slewed out of Jerome's control,
crossed the road, clipped a tree, corkscrewed through the air, and
landed in a heap against another tree. Jerome, a man who seemed
so big and invincible on the football field, was killed instantly. So
was his young nephew—a boy who had planned to be a preacher

when he grew up. Police said that no drugs or alcohol were involved in the accident. Jerome was twenty-seven years old.

I was at the Billy Graham Crusade when I got a message that Jerome had died in an accident. I asked, "Are you sure?" It was being called an "unconfirmed report," but it looked pretty bad.

I was sure it couldn't be true. Jerome Brown killed? No way! Not that big, wild, happy child of a man! So I got the number of the hospital in Brooksville and called. A nurse answered, and I said, "This is Reggie White, one of Jerome Brown's teammates. How's Jerome doing?"

"I'm sorry," she said simply. "He died."

People can say what they want about Jerome Brown: that he was loud, crude, profane, outrageous, reckless. Yes, he could be all those things at times. But he was also straightforward and loyal, he loved people and kids, he was one of the most caring and generous people I've ever known. He was also one of the funniest. His face was always lit up with a big smile. He was always having fun and spreading joy wherever he went. He was a prankster. He was crazy. He was a friend, and I miss him.

I remember what defensive tackle Mike Golic said the night Jerome died, when we all got together at a meeting room in Veterans Stadium: "Forget all of the football. He was a great friend. If you leave this game with a handful of friends, you're lucky." Jerome was a great football player—one of the best defensive linemen ever to play the game, the Eagles' number one draft choice in '87, NFC defensive rookie of the year in '88, the anchor of our awesome '91 defensive line (150 tackles, 9 sacks), a two-time Pro Bowl star, a leader on the team. But more important than all his stats, his fame, and his achievements on the field is the simple fact that Jerome Brown was a great human being.

There were many things Jerome loved—playing football, racing motorcycles, driving his cars, hunting and shooting, playing with his ugly old rottweiler dog. But what Jerome loved most was kids. He loved his own two sons most of all, of course, but he really loved *all* kids, and he loved to be surrounded by them—I think because he was such a big fun-loving kid himself.

Just a month before he died, Jerome hosted the First Annual Jerome Brown Football Camp at Hernando High School in Brooksville, where he used to play football and baseball (they called him "Freight Train Brown" back then). He invited a bunch of us Eagles down for three days of barbecue, collards, sweet potato pie, golfing, and card playing—and then he roped us all into helping out with his camp. So three hundred kids from all around Brooksville got to meet and talk to Reggie White, Randall Cunningham, Wes Hopkins, Seth Joyner, Clyde Simmons, Mike Pitts, Keith Jackson, and Ron Heller. He had me give the kids talks about values and clean living and having Jesus in their lives. And he got us all to do a bit of coaching and instruction. The whole thing was chaotic from an organizational point of view, and Jerome seemed to be on the verge of a nervous breakdown every day of the camp. But it was nonstop fun and excitement for the kids, and I know that every one of those kids had his or her life changed by Camp Jerome.

Most people don't know all the wonderful, generous, thoughtful things Jerome Brown did for so many causes and individuals, because he was never showy about it. He quietly gave a lot of money to the Josephine Street Church of the Living God, the church where he grew up and sang in the choir when he was a boy. If anybody needed money or the shirt off his back, Jerome would give it. When people were down on their luck or just passing through, he would let them sack out in his condo, rent-free and hassle-free, for as long as they wanted. If anybody needed someone to talk to or needed some help muscling a refrigerator down a flight of stairs, Jerome would do it.

He once raised a lot of money to pay the hospital bills for an eleven-year-old girl who was paralyzed in a traffic accident. Another time, he pulled a truck driver out of an overturned tractor-trailer. Still another time, he got a family out of a burning house. Although he was the team clown and always wanted to be the center of attention, he never asked for recognition or repayment for the kind things he did for people. He didn't have a big ego. He had a big heart.

Few people know about the great courage of Jerome Brown. To this day, Brooksville is very much a segregated community, a place where the Ku Klux Klan holds an annual rally. A few years before he died, Jerome became a local hero—at least, among the black community in Brooksville—when he and some friends rigged a pair of monster speakers on top of his Ford Bronco, drove over to the rally, and blasted out the Klansmen with rap music! I mean, he broke up that meeting before they even got to light the cross!

Jerome provided a lot more for the team than hits, tackles, and sacks. When the team got too tight, he kept us loose. When it was time to knuckle down, he got serious and we all got serious. When the team was wearing down, he fired us up. If he thought winning was going to our heads, he'd bring us back to earth: "Hey! You blankety-blanks aren't so great!" If we were lagging or sagging, he'd say, "C'mon, you blankety-blanks! We're a team! Stay focused!" He was the personality of the Eagles. He injected passion into our game by hollering at us and cussing at us but also by making the plays when we needed plays made. He would get excited, and that emotional energy would just crackle through the team like a burst of electricity.

Buddy Ryan knew exactly what he was doing when he drafted Jerome. Although many of us didn't realize it at the time, Jerome was really the emotional core of our team, and all the attitudes, the intensity, the unity, the fearlessness that Buddy built into the Eagles during the five years he coached us, he built around Jerome. Jerome was the on-field reflection of Buddy Ryan's personality and philosophy of football. That's why Buddy and Jerome were so close. Emotionally, Jerome held a team full of ambitious, contentious, ego-driven personalities together—which is exactly what Buddy Ryan wanted and intended. Without Jerome, I don't think Buddy and Rich Kotite could have succeeded in making us the winning team we ultimately became.

One of the ways Jerome charged up the team was by his example when he played hurt. He didn't like to practice much and he was hurt a lot, but he played anyway. He'd go out all strapped up, his shoulders shot full of cortizone and painkillers, and he'd have himself a great game. It fires up a team to see a guy playing through the pain.

Jerome could be brash, loud, and disrespectful, just like Buddy Ryan, which is why Mr. Braman was never very fond of either of them. I used to get real mad when Mr. Braman criticized Jerome in the media and objected to paying him what he was worth. Jerome made a lot of sacrifices and played his heart out for the Eagles, yet the team management continually raked him for his "work habits," for gambling on the team plane, for not controlling his weight. Jerome was stung by that kind of public criticism, and he really tried to discipline himself. He bought workout equipment and hired a nutritionist so he could stay in shape during the off-season, and when he reported for the first game of the '91 season, he was twenty-five pounds lighter than when he left.

Did Jerome *really* cuss out the assistant coaches from time to time? Was he *really* wild and unpredictable? Did he *really* lose thousands of dollars playing high stakes boo-ray on the team plane? No question. But was he completely committed to the team? Was he a true team player, a humble servant, a guy with a genuine "we" attitude, not an "I" attitude? Absolutely.

Jerome was a great big mischievous kid. Like most kids, he was eager to please. He didn't like being mad at people, and he didn't like having people mad at him. I never knew him to hold a grudge. After Coach Ryan was fired and Rich Kotite took over, Jerome and Rich got into a lot of conflicts with each other. They were critical of each other and they argued a lot. But just before the first game of the '91 season in Green Bay, Jerome came up to Rich while we were in the tunnel getting ready to take the field. He grabbed Rich Kotite in a big bear hug and lifted him right off his feet. I think Rich was probably scared at first—being in a bear hug with Jerome Brown would scare anybody!—but then Jerome set him down and said, "Coach, let's let bygones be bygones, and let's win us some games together." That really touched the heart of Coach Kotite. They didn't have any more problems after that—not big ones anyway.

Once Jerome was asked what he liked best about playing defense. "Two things," he said. "Hitting quarterbacks and . . . uhhh . . . hitting quarterbacks." I'll always remember Jerome's big grin, his loud, infectious laugh, his crazy hats, his nonstop chatter, his practical jokes. Off the field, he loved to dash full-speed at a fan or a reporter like he was going to put a full-powered, bull-rush hit on him. At the very last instant, he'd screech to a stop, grin real wide, and say, "Got any candy?"

See what I mean? A big kid.

"DON'T LET HIS DEATH BE IN VAIN"

The day Jerome died, I was scheduled to speak at a Billy Graham crusade at Veterans Stadium. I had spent many tough, grueling

hours playing football in that stadium, but I had never done anything as difficult as what I had to do that night. Tears were rolling
down my face as I got up before a crowd of fifty thousand people
and said, "Today, I lost a dear friend. Jerome Brown was one of
the greatest men I ever knew in my life." And I proceeded to tell
his story. Amazingly, though my voice was choking with grief, I
was able to get through it without totally breaking down.

The following week, my teammates and I gathered again in
Brooksville to bury our friend. Mr. Braman and Mr. Gamble were
there too. So were hundreds of school kids, most of whom had
just been to Jerome's football camp a few weeks earlier.

The Josephine Street Church was too small to contain the 1,500
mourners, so the funeral was held at the mostly white First Baptist
Church, which had loudspeakers in the lawn area and closed-
circuit TV to accommodate the overflow crowds. Preacher
Brown—that is, Rev. Theodore N. Brown, Jerome's uncle—did the
service.

Jerome's mother and father, Willie and Annie Bell Brown, are
two of the godliest people you ever knew, and they asked me to
get up and speak at the funeral. "Every time a life ends," I said,
"there's a purpose. If we don't grab on to the purpose, we lose the
whole plan." I wasn't sure what the purpose was in Jerome being
snatched away from us like that, but I trusted God. He always has
a purpose and a plan, and He doesn't make mistakes.

In some ways, I'm not sure Jerome would have liked the service.
He never liked long-winded preaching, and this service was two
hours long. But I think he would have enjoyed everything that was
said and the songs that were sung. I think he would have especially
enjoyed the sight of so many black people and white people sitting
together, praying together, and hugging one another.

It was the finest, most joy-filled funeral I've ever been to in my
life. Jerome's mom and dad were dancing in the Spirit and the joy
of the Lord. If you think it's strange that grieving parents would
dance at the funeral of their son, I don't blame you for being
surprised. But these are people who have a strong trust in the
living God. They understood the finality of death, but they knew
that the power of death is nothing at all compared to the power
and the purpose of the Lord Jesus Christ. When Christians gather

to remember and celebrate a life that has been completed, sadness and joy mingle together.

After the service, a smaller group of us went out to the cemetery to commit our friend's body to the earth. Jerome's pallbearers were all men who had lined up with him on the Philadelphia Eagles football team. It was stifling hot and humid out there, and we were all drenched in sweat as we carried the bronze casket to the grave. Preacher Brown said a few more words of comfort to those who were gathered around, and each of us, Jerome's teammates, re-moved our ties and draped them over the casket. Then we stood together, our arms about each other and wept. None of us wanted to leave our friend there. Finally, I bent down beside the casket and knocked on the bronze lid with my ring. Then I said one last prayer to God for my friend Jerome. "Please," I said, "don't let his death be in vain."

Jerome's nephew, Gus, was also buried that day, in a light blue casket, in a plot next to Jerome's.

A couple things happened at the funeral that disturbed me. I saw a lot of women in sexy, short dresses who looked more like they were going to a cocktail party than a funeral. I don't think they were invited, nor were they part of the community. I think they were there to pick up guys. I don't know how people can do a thing like that at an occasion like a funeral. It was also disturbing to me that people approached us, Jerome's teammates, and wanted our autographs. Our friend had just died, and they seemed to have no concept of what we were going through.

A question sticks in my mind to this day: Did Jerome know the Lord? I hope to God he did. His life was a bundle of contradictions. His wild way of living and his profanity surely are not consistent with a life lived in the power of Jesus. Yet he was more kind, more generous, more openhearted, more honest than a lot of churchgo-ing people I know. He had a reputation as the least reverent player on our team, and he often poked fun at me and the other Christians on the team, especially in the first couple years that we played football together. At the same time, he also told me very seriously that he admired me, that he would like to live his life the way I live mine, that he wanted to follow God at some point in his life—but just not yet. Beginning with the '91 season, I saw him maturing a great deal, behaving less outrageously, less rebelliously; his bear hug with Rich Kotite was just one example of that.

God alone knows the state of Jerome's heart when he died. No one has the right or the power to judge his relationship with the Lord. If there is one lesson to take away from Jerome's life and death, it may be this: Jerome thought he had all the time in the world. He had no idea, as he slid into that bucket seat and turned the key in the ignition, that he was living the last few seconds of his life. We're all just like Jerome. None of us knows the hour of our death. We don't live or die according to our own schedule. We should never take chances with eternity. We should never wait until some future time to get right with God. We should get right with Him today and stay right with Him today, while we have time, while we have life.

TIME TO REGROUP—AGAIN

Every day I suited up, I was reminded of Jerome. His locker was right next to mine, and we left it exactly as he had left it—with his helmet and pads, some socks and shirts and shoes, even his old knee wrap and his crazy old fishing hat inside. We taped some pictures of Jerome on the locker, and I looked over at his grinning face every day. His jersey, with the big number 99, was hung in his dressing stall. Those of us who lined up with Jerome—guys like Seth, Clyde, Mike Pitts, and I—had an awfully hard time dealing with his loss as we moved through training camp and headed toward the regular season. The heart had been ripped out of our team, and we all knew it.

Over the years, I've tended to be one of the quiet players on the line. I tried to inspire the team and get things going by the intensity of my play. But Jerome, our big talker, was gone, so I began to call out encouragement to the other players on the field. I couldn't cuss or scream or make guys laugh like Jerome could, but I tried to fill the hole that Jerome left—at least a little. Some of the other guys did too. But nobody could get guys going the way Jerome did.

Randall Cunningham, the Scrambling One, came back with his knee in a brace, saying he felt ready to scramble for the '92 season. (We had six other quarterbacks on the roster—just in case.) Running back Herschel Walker joined the team to provide additional offensive energy. Except for the huge hole at defensive tackle and in our hearts, it looked like we were ready to take on another season.

During summer training, most of us players blackened the silver eagle wings on our green helmets as a symbol of mourning for Jerome. Others wrote a black 99, Jerome's number, over the wings. We had planned to wear the blackened wings throughout the season in his memory, and Mr. Braman and NFL Properties (the merchandising and logo-licensing arm of the league) approved the plan—but NFL commissioner Paul Tagliabue nixed the idea. I considered that a slap in the face of our team and Jerome's memory, but we agreed instead to wear commemorative patches on our uniform—the Eagles 60th anniversary logo, but with the number 99 substituting for the number 60.

At our opening game against the New Orleans Saints, September 6, 1992, more than sixty thousand people jammed Veterans Stadium. You could feel the emotion that charged the air in that place. NFL Films produced a video tribute to Jerome that was shown on the big scoreboard screen. Then Seth Joyner got up and gave his own tribute to Jerome straight from his heart—no notes, no preparation, but a lot of tears. "I just want to talk for a second about Jerome Brown—not the football player, but the man," he began. And then he talked about what a great, caring, giving, big-hearted man Jerome was. "God has His reasons why," Seth concluded, "and who are we to question His reasons? We're gonna miss you, Jerome. We love you, brother. We love you forever."

Jerome's parents were there. They had become like a mother and father to all of us on the team. So after Seth stepped down, I called Mr. and Mrs. Brown over and presented them with a framed jersey, number 99. "Jerome's memory will always be with us," I said, presenting the memento to Willie and Annie Bell Brown, choking on my words. "One of the things that's being done today by the Philadelphia Eagles is that the number 99 will never be worn again."

There was a long, thunderous wave of applause and cheering. And then we proceeded to beat the Saints in a close, emotional contest, winning 15–13.

We got the season off to a good start. Four games into it, we were 4 and 0, and we were on top of our game in a big way. The fourth game of the season was a home game against Dallas. On the very first snap, I broke through the line and chased Troy Aikman all over the backfield, forcing an intentional grounding call. At the final gun, we had a sweet 31–7 victory. After that game, the sportswriters were talking about how, for the second year in a row, even without the presence of Jerome Brown, the Eagles defense was utterly invincible.

But the very next week, at Arrowhead Stadium in Kansas City, we became "vincible." We got "vinced," big-time. The Chiefs had open receivers and long passes everywhere. What did we have? Busted coverage, play after play. They continually faked the run, drawing our defense in with play action, then lobbing the ball over our heads. I wish I had a dollar for every time I heard somebody say "I thought you had him" in that game. It was embarrassing. We got out-game-planned from the beginning—and we could have gotten it back, but we didn't. There's no doubt in my mind that we lost that game in our minds, in our emotions, because we didn't have Jerome there to help us get our focus back.

It seemed our best games were the ones in which we were the most aware of what Jerome would say and do if he was with us. In one late-season game against the Vikings, Seth Joyner intercepted a pass and returned it 24 yards for the winning touchdown. Beyond the end zone, some fans held up a big banner that said JEROME IS WATCHING. Seth ran up in front of that banner, stopped, and snapped a touching salute to Jerome's memory. We closed the season 11 and 5—certainly a good record, but I couldn't help wondering what we could have done if we'd had Jerome with us. It had been a season of a lot of wins—but also many deep losses.

ANOTHER DEEP LOSS

Just after Thanksgiving 1992 I said to my wife, "Sara, I need to call Leonard. I'm gonna sit with him and tell him how much I love him and care about him. Maybe he and I should go fishing."

"But you don't fish," said Sara.

"I know," I said, "but Leonard likes to fish. I want to do something he likes to do. I want to take him out fishing. We can sit and talk and remember some good times, and I can tell him I'm sorry about a few things and just let him know I really care about him."

I never got the chance to do that. On December 19, 1992—coincidentally, my thirty-first birthday—Chattanooga police officers walked up to a parked car at the St. Elmo Recreation Center. Inside the car, they found the body of my stepfather, Leonard Collier. He had been killed by a hammer blow to the head, and police believe he probably stopped to help a (supposedly) stranded motorist. In all probability, the person he tried to help was the person who robbed and killed him. He was forty-four years old. The police questioned a number of suspects, but to this day, no one has been charged with the crime.

It was about six months later that Michael Jordan's father, James Jordan, was murdered under similar circumstances near Lumberton, North Carolina—and hearing that story in the news unleashed the pain of Leonard's death inside me all over again. I think I know how Mike feels. Losing someone you care about to a natural death is hard enough. But when someone you love is murdered, the loss is magnified by the cruelty and senselessness of it. Why should a good man like Leonard have to give his life to put a few measly dollars in someone else's pocket?

I don't have many regrets in my life, but I do have one: I wish I hadn't been so judgmental of Leonard. I wish I had spent less time when I was a teenager telling him, "You shouldn't do this. You shouldn't do that." I should have accepted Leonard for who he was. And I wish I had told him I cared for him one last time before he died.

WINNING THE FREE AGENCY BATTLE

The 1992 season was the season that brought free agency to the NFL. The battle for free agency had begun five years earlier with the aborted NFL players strike. The players' cause got a big boost in September of '92 when an eight-member jury in Minneapolis delivered a verdict striking down the NFL's "Plan B" or limited free-agency system on the grounds that it violated antitrust laws. It meant the possibility of much greater freedom and opportunity for all players, including myself. I wanted to stay in Philly and finish my career as an Eagle if Mr. Braman and the organization were truly committed to winning; if not, free agency would make it possible for me to play for a team that really wanted to win, that really wanted me, and that was willing to pay my fair market value.

The Minneapolis verdict didn't make free agency automatic. Rather, it cleared the way and set the stage for a series of lawsuits that would force the NFL to agree to a collective bargaining settlement in the players' favor. Keith Jackson filed the first suit, along with Garin Veris of the Patriots, Webster Slaughter of the Browns, and D. J. Dozier of the Detroit Lions. Clyde Simmons and Seth Joyner also filed a damage suit against the league. Keith ended up winning his freedom and signing with the Dolphins. Suddenly, instead of making his Eagles base salary of $350,000, he was getting $1.5 million a year in Miami—his true market value as a player.

My agent called me and said, "The Players Association wants to use you as a plaintiff against the league. Are you willing?" I instantly agreed. I became the lead plaintiff in a class action on behalf of hundreds of players throughout the league. For the first time since joining the NFL, I began to feel I was no longer a slave to the owners. I believed the suit would affect players already playing the game, plus players in years to come.

Some people were concerned that my career would be hurt, that owners would try to blackball me. I wasn't worried because (1) my destiny was in God's hands; (2) I had money saved up so that I could get by even if I was blackballed; and (3) I was confident of my abilities and my value to a team.

I remember how John Mackey, tight end of the old Baltimore Colts, stuck his neck out for players' rights in the 1970s, and it would be nice if the next generation of players would remember what I and others did for players' rights in the 1990s. Mackey paid a great price for what he did, and I suspect his union activism was a big factor in slowing his induction into the Hall of Fame. I think it's a travesty that we players have not done more to honor him and thank him for the sacrifices he made. I look at what Mackey did and I think, *Man, I had it easy.* I didn't have to do anything, the lawyers took care of everything and just kept me informed of what was going on.

The NFL owners got together in October of '92, trying to craft a settlement with the players. There was a lot of dissension among the owners. Some teams, like the 49ers, the Cowboys, the Redskins, and the Raiders, truly wanted to win and were willing to spend the money to do it. The owners who screamed the loudest about free agency were the owners of the notoriously tightwad teams—the Eagles, the Bengals, the Steelers.

My lawsuit uncovered some facts that made Eagles players and fans feel all the more exploited. We learned that while Mr. Braman was claiming there just wasn't any more money in the till, while he kept pleading poverty and raising ticket prices, while the Eagles ranked tenth in the league in dollars spent on player salaries, he was running the most profitable franchise in the entire NFL—*and* he was paying himself a salary of $7.5 million a year! The Eagles would occasionally pay top dollar to bring in a free agent like Herschel Walker, but there were guys who had been wearing Eagle green for five, six, or more years, giving up their bodies to win for Philadelphia, and yet they were financially exploited, forced to sit out of training camp in order to get the club to sign them to a contract that was far below the player's market value. Plus, there was all this insulting nickel-and-dime stinginess, with Mr. Braman charging his players for things like socks and pads which all other NFL teams supplied to their players without charge.

Throughout the fall of 1992, NFL owners dickered and bickered and footdragged through negotiations with the players. My lawsuit was heard in November, and the judge in the case held off handing down a decision for weeks in hopes that the owners and the players association could come to an agreement on their own. Finally, just before Christmas, the owners and players arrived at a complex 200-page tentative settlement agreement that ended the five-year-long labor war that began with the players' strike of 1987. The deal gave us what we had been fighting for all along: unrestricted free agency. It also gave owners a shorter NFL draft (seven rounds instead of twelve) and the salary cap concept, borrowed from Major League Baseball and the National Basketball Association, to pro-tect teams from runaway bidding wars.

It was a compromise agreement that Mr. Braman fought tooth and nail until he no longer had any choice. It's not hard to under-stand why: Free agency meant he either had to pay a lot more money or see the breakup of the best defensive line in the NFL. Mr. Braman fought so hard, in fact, that in April of '93, the other NFL owners petitioned the U.S. district court to punish him for trying to scuttle the agreement. In the end, Mr. Braman lost the battle. To this day, I don't think he realizes just how much he lost or how unnecessary it was. I believe he could have had it all—a unified, loyal, dedicated team; a championship; bigger profits.

I have a lot of friends on a lot of teams, and I've had many opportunities to compare notes about the working conditions. I began to notice that there were some teams where the players loved their coaches, their organization, their owners. I talked to guys playing for teams like the 49ers and the Redskins, and they never wanted to play anywhere else. You couldn't pay them enough to leave. Why is that? Obviously, it wasn't a matter of money. It was a matter of being appreciated. Those players wanted to stay where they were because they received the affirmation of the front office on a regular basis. At contract time, management negotiated in a straightforward way, not with stalling tactics, confrontation, and mind games. Those players rewarded their ball clubs with loyalty, outstanding performances, championships, and ticket sales.

For several years, I tried to bring this to the attention of Mr. Braman. I sat in his office and told him, eye-to-eye and man-to-man, that it hurt the team that he only came into the locker room to congratulate us after a win, that he ignored us when we lost. I told him that it hurt his defensive players that he would come into the locker room and only talk to the guys on the offensive side, that he would never come to our side of the locker room and shake our hands and say hello to us. You may think that's a small thing, but I truly think it could have made a big difference in our morale and our fighting spirit, to know that the team owner cared about us as people, not just as assembly-line workers in a touchdown factory.

For me, personally, it got to the point where I couldn't even wear one of my Eagles T-shirts around the house. Like most guys who played with that team, I just didn't feel like I was a part of the organization. Yes, I played my tail off and, yes, I cared about the other players and my coaches. But once I went home, I wasn't an Eagle. I didn't want any part in the Eagles system and the way it treated people. I couldn't take being part of the atmosphere that hung over the Philadelphia Eagles organization.

I don't think Mr. Braman ever understood what it was all about—the '87 strike, the lawsuits, the battle for free agency. Keith

Jackson, Seth Joyner, Clyde Simmons, and I were not a bunch of greedy, spoiled athletes who wanted to bankrupt the man who signed our paychecks. If the man had dealt with us on the basis of win-win, mutual respect, and trust instead of on a basis of confrontation and I-win/you-lose, he could have built a tradition of winning *and* a healthy bottom line.

And, perhaps, he would have gotten a Super Bowl ring or two.

TIME TO MOVE

We capped a painful '92 season with a humiliating postseason loss to the Dallas Cowboys. It was the most exasperating, embarrassing playoff game I remember playing in as an Eagle. The Cowboys crushed our offense, baffled our defense, and even kicked the tar out of our special teams. Randall only managed to pass for 160 yards, and there was a long stretch from the late first quarter till the end of the third where we only managed to get one first down. Our defense allowed Troy Aikman to lob two touchdown passes and let Emmitt Smith get away with 114 yards and a touchdown. It was the most depressing four quarters I ever spent inside a stadium.

The '92 Dallas Cowboys were a great team, a talented team, a tough team—but we had beaten them before. We had beaten them *bad* before. Something was missing this time: *emotion*. We were playing our hearts out—but we were playing without our heart: Jerome. We might have lost even if he had been there but I believe we wouldn't have lost so bad, not 34–10. He wouldn't have let us. Fact is, if we'd had Jerome there, I think we might have won it all.

Before the Dallas game, I knew that if we didn't go all the way to the Super Bowl this season, it just wasn't going to happen in Philadelphia. Not without Jerome. Not without Keith Jackson. Not with the halfhearted desire to win that I saw coming from the fourth-floor suite. The championship dream was sinking in Philadelphia, and I wasn't about to let my dreams go down with it.

I had spent eight years in Philly, reaching and straining and getting pounded into the rug for something that just wasn't gonna happen. I loved the fans. I loved my teammates. But eight years was enough. It was time to move on.

Chapter 8

"REGGIE, THIS IS GOD..."

One game in the '92 season made a big impression on me—the November 15 game against the Green Bay Packers at Milwaukee County Stadium. In fact, it would be fair to say that something happened in that game that changed the course of my career: I ran full-tilt into a twenty-three-year-old country boy named Brett Favre.

There were more than fifty thousand fans braving the 17-degree windchill to watch the 4 and 6 Packers play the 6 and 4 Eagles— and hardly anyone figured the Packers to win. Brett, the Packers' 6-foot-3, 230-pound rookie quarterback from Kiln, Mississippi (pop. 1,261), was leading an offense ranked sixteenth in the NFL, and he was playing only his seventh professional football game. I had never heard of him before. Hardly anyone had ever heard of him. It looked like one of those David-and-Goliath mismatches— but as the story of David shows, it's often risky to bet on Goliath.

Thirteen minutes into the first quarter, I put a hit on Brett that sent him crashing to the turf with a separated left shoulder. Packers coach Mike Holmgren wanted to take him out of the game, but Brett refused to leave. So the team doctor shot him with painkiller and sent him back in. Three plays later, he threw a 5-yard touchdown pass to Sterling Sharpe for a 6–3 Packers lead. All in all during the first half, he threw a perfect 11 completions of 11 attempts. I wondered, *Who is this guy?*

Brett's a right-handed passer, but don't underestimate the pain of trying to throw a football with your right arm after the ball-joint, tendons, and muscles of your left shoulder have been yanked from their moorings. I could see the pain in Brett's face every time I rushed him, and after absorbing every tackle, he had to struggle to get back on his feet. By the start of the second half, his left arm had seized up so bad, he couldn't even lift it, much less hand off to that side. Even so, he wound up completing 70 percent of his passes for 275 yards and two touchdowns after playing forty-seven minutes with a dislocated shoulder.

Another thing that impressed me almost as much as Brett's grit and determination in that game was that he played so cool and smart. He was as confident and composed as any seasoned veteran quarterback. He frustrated our defense by taking a short three-step drop and chucking the pass underneath our coverage. He released the ball so quickly and dunked it so short that I couldn't get close enough to hurry him. He read our zones with unerring accuracy. Even when we knew what he was going to do, we could do nothing about it.

In the end, the sixteenth ranked offense in the league slipped past the number one defense in the league, and the Packers won it, 27–24. Right there, I knew that this Mississippi country boy had all the stuff of a championship quarterback. In fact, that win over the Eagles started the Packers on a six-game winning streak; they finished the season 9 and 7, and just missed a shot in the playoffs. Brett ended the year with a 64.1 percent completion record—even better than Bart Starr's season best (63.7 percent) in '68. At twenty-three, he was the youngest quarterback ever invited to the Pro Bowl.

When I left the Philadelphia Eagles and began looking for a new home in which to play football, the vivid memory of Brett Favre playing straight through the punishment I put on him stuck in my mind.

BROKEN TIES

After the Dallas playoff game, I was determined not to come back as an Eagle. Some of my teammates and I went out to lunch to talk about it. Eric Allen, Clyde, Seth, and Wes Hopkins all asked me not to leave. I said, "I can't hold on. I don't believe these guys on the fourth floor want to win."

"If Braman pays you the money you want," they asked, "would you come back?"

"I don't think they could pay me enough to come back," I said. "Mr. Braman could top the best offer by a couple million, and I wouldn't come back, because I just don't think the organization is committed to winning."

Soon after that lunch meeting, I got a call from Mr. Braman, and he promised he'd make an effort to re-sign me. I was pleased and surprised to hear that, because I was getting the impression he wasn't interested in keeping me. I thought, *Okay, let's see what he's gonna do.* I didn't hear anything from him for two weeks. Next thing I knew, I heard a news report in which Mr. Braman said to reporters, "I think Reggie White's ties with the Eagles are over." That was the way he was.

There was a big grassroots effort to keep me in Philly. Radio WIP held a big "Rally for Reggie" at JFK Plaza to show their support and to demonstrate how much the people of the city wanted me to stay. Mayor Rendell and fifteen thousand other people were there. That public outpouring of love was a real blessing. The organizers of the rally wanted me to appear at the rally, but I just couldn't go. I know exactly what would have happened: I would have gotten so emotional that I probably would have made an emotional decision about my future. I did send a note to the rally that was read to the people, expressing how much I appreciated their love for me and my family.

I was sorry to leave Philadelphia because the people of the city loved me, but I had made it clear to Mr. Braman that I wanted to be a part of a championship organization. Loudly and clearly, Braman had made it plain to me that he did not intend to do what needed to be done to build the Eagles team to that level. And, through his statement to the media, he had made it clear he had no more interest in keeping me in Philadelphia.

How could I stay?

Then there was Rich Kotite. Near the end of the '92 season, I had told him of my doubts about staying with the Eagles for another year. He responded, "Reggie, I assure you that you'll be back here next year. I'm going to fight to keep you with the Eagles." The season ended. Weeks passed. Rich Kotite never called me. Mr. Braman made his announcement that my ties with the Eagles were over. Rich still never called. He hasn't called me since. I was disappointed in that, because I always gave Richie everything he ever asked of me. When he couldn't control guys and needed help, he'd bring me in the office and ask me to help him, and I would do it. Anything he asked me to do, I did it for him. In the end, I felt he turned his back on me.

It was clear to me that my ties with the Philadelphia Eagles were indeed broken, just as Mr. Braman said. I didn't break 'em. The fans didn't break 'em. My teammates didn't break 'em. The media didn't break 'em. Those ties were broken by Norm Braman and the Eagles organization.

GOD, FAMILY, AND THE
GREEN BAY PACKERS

They called it "The Reggie Tour," and the press had a lot of fun, following me around from city to city, trying to predict which team I was going to go to. Art Modell sent his private jet to pick up Sara and me in Knoxville and take us to Cleveland. He put us up in a $400-a-night suite in the Ritz-Carlton and had roses waiting in the room for Sara. We toured the Browns' $12 million facility— which was not only more luxurious than the facility in Philly, it was almost as luxurious as our two-room suite at the Ritz-Carlton! I was amazed at how nice and polite everybody was, even in the locker rooms. (I later found out that Modell had banned all cursing from the place while I was there.)

While we were there, I got calls from Cleveland mayor Michael White and from the great Jim Brown, who played fullback for Cleveland from '57 to '66. Jim had been very active in programs helping inner-city youth, and he told me that Cleveland would be a great base for an inner-city ministry. Mr. Modell also pledged the organization's support for my efforts to help people in the inner city. Cleveland obviously had a lot of advantages, including the fact that Sara had family in the area.

After the eight years I had spent feeling embattled and underappreciated in the Eagles organization, it was an incredible feeling to have the Browns and many other teams rolling out the red carpet and saying, "We want you." I was amazed at how many teams understood what I was truly looking for—not just more money but a place to win a championship and a place to carry out my ministry. For example, when Redskins general manager Charley Casserly talked, he didn't start talking salary and benefits and bonuses. He talked about a winning tradition. I had played against that winning tradition, and I knew it wasn't just talk. And when I talked to Coach Jerry Glanville, he told me that the Atlanta Falcons would be very supportive of my ministry efforts. I told him to remind Deion Sanders (who was then with the Falcons) that he promised to buy me a church if I came to Atlanta!

It was the most difficult decision I ever made in my life. The deals that were offered to me by the various teams were complex and structured in different ways. Some offered me five years, some four, some three. Washington and Cleveland were both leading contenders for a while, but it soon became clear that, with the salary cap the league had adopted, Washington was going to low-price themselves out. I began to sense in a very clear, inner way, even apart from outward considerations such as a tradition of winning or money, that God was telling me I would be going to San Francisco.

The last place on my list was Green Bay, Wisconsin—no, I take that back. Green Bay didn't even make my list. The Packers' record ranked low. The place is cold. It's the smallest franchise in the league. I didn't even want to go visit there, but my agent, Jimmy Sexton, kept telling me I should at least talk to them. Finally, I decided to visit Green Bay as a quick stopover after my meeting with the Detroit Lions. I was surprised and impressed by what I saw.

I didn't know until I got there that the Packers are owned by the community—that is, by the *fans*—and that a sizable portion of the gate receipts goes to support the local post of the Veterans of Foreign Wars. Every home game plays to a sellout crowd. The Packers' small staff and low overhead allowed the club to amass a much larger war chest than many of the other teams, so the team was poised to buy winning talent at exactly the time free agency came to the NFL.

The difference in team atmosphere between Philadelphia and Green Bay was like night and day. The upbeat attitude, cheerfulness, and positive confidence at Green Bay were, I think, largely the results of fan ownership. Instead of feeling beholden to a single cigar-chomping owner with his eye on the bottom line, the Packers were owned by a community of 1,500 loyal, loving, dedicated fans who were on their side, win or lose. The fans didn't care about making money. They cared about *winning*—and that made a big difference in the mindset and the emotions of the entire organization.

Though fewer than 100,000 people live in Green Bay, it is unquestionably the biggest football city in the world. As I toured the Packers Hall of Fame building—a place that truly rivals the Football Hall of Fame in Canton, Ohio—I was awestruck by the tradition of the Packers organization. Of course, there was memorabilia belonging to the great names of Packer history—Bart Starr, Don Hutson, Paul Hornung, Curly Lambeau, and Vince Lombardi, names that gave Green Bay the nickname of "Titletown, U.S.A." There was even memorabilia dating back to an earlier era, when the Packers won three titles in a row—1929 through 1931. I saw that the traditions of Coach Lombardi were still strong in Green Bay, especially the tradition he expressed in the simple phrase, "God, family, and the Green Bay Packers." You *have* to concentrate on those three things—because in Green Bay, Wisconsin, there's nothing else to do!

In late March of '93, Packers coach Mike Holmgren and defensive coordinator Ray Rhodes surprised me by flying into Knoxville for a visit—totally unannounced. They checked around town and found out that I was speaking that day at a local Kiwanis Club meeting, so they came with me! It really touched me that they would go so far out of their way to find me. After the speech, we went back to my house, had coffee, and talked for a couple hours. Mike and Ray were very low pressure; they just wanted to get acquainted, and they seemed genuinely interested in me as a person, in my family, in my ministry, in my work with the community. I told them how impressed I had been with Brett Favre when he kept playing—and beat us—with an out-of-joint wing.

One reservation I expressed was that Green Bay is a college town, a football town—essentially one big suburb with a main street. How could I have an inner-city ministry in a town that has no inner city to speak of? They pointed out that Milwaukee is only a hundred miles away and has one of the highest teen pregnancy rates in the country. They promised they would support me in an effort to build an inner-city ministry there.

I instantly liked both of these men. Still, I was 99 percent sure that God was calling me to San Francisco. Besides that strong inner sense of God's leading, all the outward signs seemed to point to San Francisco as well. The 'Niners were offering a lot of money and a five-year contract. The team appeared to be headed for the Super Bowl (in fact, if I had gone with the 49ers, I'd have gotten a ring with them).

Soon afterward, my agent called and said, "You know that deal San Francisco is offering you? It's not a guaranteed five years, like we thought. In fact, the contract gives them the right to cut you after three."

That jolted me. I called 49ers president, Carmen Policy, and asked him if that was true. He said, "Well, we want to sign you to a five-year deal, but we can only make a three-year commitment to you."

After I got off the phone with Mr. Policy, I said to Sara, "I don't feel good about this. I don't want to go out there always looking over my shoulder, wondering if I'm gonna get cut. I want to play for a team that's gonna make a commitment to me."

Sara agreed. We had nothing against the 49ers, either the team or the organization. Sara and I truly liked Mr. Policy and 49ers owner Eddie DeBartolo. I understood their position. But I couldn't go to San Francisco under those conditions. I was baffled too, because I was so sure that God had told me I would go to San Francisco. I wondered how I could have been so mistaken about God's leading.

I was back to square one, completely undecided. And I had to make a decision soon.

"WHAT DO YOU THINK OF GREEN BAY?"

Whenever reporters asked me what team I had chosen, I replied, "I just want to go where God wants me to go." One weekend, Sara and I returned from a trip and checked the messages on our answering machine. One of the messages said simply, "Reggie, this is God. Go to Green Bay." It's amazing how much God sounds like Mike Holmgren!

A short time later, Green Bay came back with an offer. A *big* offer. To top it off, the offer was heavily front-loaded. They said, in effect, "Reggie, we want you here for four years, minimum. And to prove it, we'll give you almost half of your money right up front." It was an iron-clad guarantee—not just that they would *pay* me, but also that they would *play* me. No other team in the league had been willing to make that kind of commitment. The other teams were hedging, which was another way of saying, "Reggie White's probably slowing down. Just in case, we better only commit to him for a couple years or so." Green Bay wasn't saying that; they thought I could help the team win games for four years—and it wasn't a fall-back negotiating position, it was what they offered me right from the get-go.

I really wanted that four-year commitment because it was going to take some time to build the Packers into a championship team. They had made a big start by hiring Mike Holmgren as head coach and making Brett Favre their starting quarterback. They had acquired other free-agent talent, such as guard Harry Galbreath from the Dolphins, tackle Tunch Ilkin from the Steelers, and defensive end Bill Maas from the Chiefs. The Packers had finished the '92 season as a winning team but still had a long road ahead before they got themselves to a Super Bowl. Still, I really began to believe that together we could go all the way.

But was that really where the Lord was telling me to go? I didn't know. So I began to pray.

I prayed half the night. I prayed and I cried because I wanted to make the right decision. I wanted God to tell me, loud and clear, where He wanted me to go. I wanted to be smack-dab in the center of His will, but I just wasn't hearing anything. I knew God had clearly told me to go to San Francisco—and then He had closed that door and opened another door to Green Bay. I was confused and I was in anguish, yet I knew it wasn't God who was confusing me, because God is not the author of confusion. Throughout that long night of praying and crying, I couldn't hear Him telling me what I should do.

By the time I finally fell asleep in the early hours of the morning, I still didn't have an answer.

I got up the next morning and immediately began praying again—not just talking to God, but listening, waiting to hear what He wanted to say deep inside me. As I listened for the Lord's voice, I heard a question in my thoughts: *Reggie, where did the head coach, the defensive coordinator, and the offensive coordinator of the Packers come from before they went to Green Bay?* Instantly, I remembered: All three of them had come from San Francisco, from the 49ers. In my mind, I heard the Lord say, *And what do the reporters call Green Bay? And what do they call Green Bay's offense?* And it came to me: They kept calling Green Bay "the San Francisco of the East," and they called Green Bay's offense "the West Coast Offense."

Then aloud I said, "Huh! So that's the 'San Francisco' that You have been talking about!" And again, in my thoughts, I heard, *That's right. Reggie, I want you to go to Green Bay. That's the "San Francisco" I was talking about.*

My next reaction was, "Well, Lord, why didn't You just tell me?" And God spoke to me and said, *Because then you wouldn't have prayed like you prayed. You wouldn't have cried like you cried. You wouldn't have even sought Me. You would have made a rash decision on your own—and you would have regretted that decision. I wanted you to seek Me.*

As painful as the process was, it was ultimately a blessing to me that God allowed me to go through that time of indecision, prayer, and crying so I would know that I was really in the center of His will. Once I had gone through that process, once I clearly heard the Lord telling me He wanted me to go to Green Bay, I felt peace—and I also felt excited. The question of my future had finally been settled, and now a whole new adventure lay ahead of me.

I found Sara and asked her, "What do you think of Green Bay?"

She said, "I'll support any decision you make. I know you'll make the right decision."

"Well, the decision's been made. We're going to Green Bay."

She smiled. "Then that's the right decision."

Next, I called my agents, Jimmy and Kyle, and said, "We're going to Green Bay."

They said, "Are you sure?"

"I'm positive."

"Well, bundle up, brother," they said, "because it gets mighty cold up there."

Next, I called Mike Holmgren. "Mike, I'm gonna sign the deal." Well, *he* sure thought I had made the right decision!

I knew it was right. So did Sara. She had never even visited Green Bay before I made the decision, but when she flew up there for the first time, she fell in love with the city and the people.

Green Bay instantly became our home.

Chapter 9

THE RAMBOS
OF LAMBEAU

In April of '93, Mike Reinfeldt, the chief financial officer of the Packers, flew to Chattanooga, and we had a contract-signing ceremony in the auditorium of Howard High School, where I played high school football, where Coach Pulliam had first recognized my abilities as a defensive player—and where he had jabbed an elbow into my solar plexus to toughen me up. There were a lot of people and a lot of cameras there that day as I stood and was welcomed as an official wearer of Packers green and gold.

"Green Bay is a team that started off the championship tradition," I told the crowd and the reporters. "Back in the days of Vince Lombardi, the Packers won six NFL championships, including the first two Super Bowls that were ever played. I believe the Packers will be a championship team again—and when they are, they will capture the heart of America." I was so certain that God had clearly, specifically led me to Green Bay that I added, "I know in my heart that I made the right decision. I will never regret it. Even if Green Bay goes 0 and 16 every year for the next four years, I will never regret it."

There was a lot of sniping from the sidelines when I signed that deal. The press called me "The $17 Million Man" because of the size of my four-year contract. Some said that the only "green and gold" I cared about was money. None of the critics knew the inner agonizing I had gone through to come to that decision.

Mr. Braman, who never even tried to keep me in Philadelphia, fired a parting shot at me, saying my decision had nothing to do with being led by God or wanting to build a ministry. "He's just going for the money," he said. "Reggie White did a super job of marketing himself, and the press fell for all that [stuff] about God."

I didn't let that bother me. There were important things I wanted to do for God and for people, and I needed money to do them. Making an impact on lives was even more important to me than winning a championship, and since nobody was stepping up to put money into these ministries, I knew I would need to do it myself. Not only had Green Bay made the best commitment to me, but when I compared the tax climate in Wisconsin to that in California, it was clear that Green Bay would be a better place to conserve capital for ministry building. Why should I shortchange myself or the Lord? Mr. Braman had this peculiar idea that Christians aren't supposed to care about money, and he never understood me or what I was trying to do with the money I earned playing football.

Rich Kotite also made some public statements to the effect that there had been a "lack of leadership" on the team in recent seasons—comments I believe were aimed at me. I had worked my tail off for the Philadelphia Eagles, I had done everything my coaches had asked, I had helped Rich keep discipline on the team when he couldn't do it himself—and when I left, I left without appreciation or respect. It stung a little for the moment, but it was nothing more or less than I had received in the past. I put it out of my mind and focused on the exciting new things that lay ahead.

I believed Green Bay could win and win soon. I also believed God had a plan in store for me out there on the frozen tundra. Now I see that He had a plan that went far beyond football, far beyond a ministry in Milwaukee, far beyond a ministry in Knoxville, Tennessee. God could see to the future, to the destruction and the hatred and the church burnings that would begin sweeping the South a couple years later. And He saw how the Green Bay community would be used in a big way to bring help and healing in that time of trouble and sorrow. I truly believe that God is bringing a spiritual revival to America, and that Wisconsin is going to play a major part in that revival.

I didn't talk to the press very much during the '93 season, mostly because the press tends to be so negative. I've never liked dealing with them because reporters are often so rude, bothering you with questions while you're trying to take a shower or while you are hurting after a loss. It's amazing how a bunch of people armed with tape recorders can get things wrong so much of the time, even to the point of making up quotes and putting words in your mouth! To this day, I try to hold the press to a certain level of dignity and decorum in their dealings with me, and I refuse to give interviews until I am showered and dressed.

During my first year with the Packers, it seemed there were only three things reporters wanted to talk to me about: (1) how much money I was making; (2) how I disliked my old Eagles teammates; or (3) how unhappy I was that I had come to Green Bay. I refused to get drawn into that because: (1) my money was nobody else's business; (2) I love the guys I used to play with, each and every one of them; and (3) I was deliriously happy with my decision to come to Green Bay. I don't know how these rumors get started in the press, but I do know this: Every time a newspaper reported some false rumor about me, it was written by somebody who didn't have the decency to call me and talk to me about it person-to-person.

THE BEST FANS IN THE WORLD

While I love and appreciate the fans in Philly, a lot of Eagles fans will toss you out the back window the minute you lose two in a row. Man, they'll boo you and worse. Lose three games in a row, and many of them stop coming to the games. Not all of them are like that, not even a majority, but some of them are. As a whole, I know the fans in Philadelphia love me and I love them.

But I have to tell you, man, the fans in Green Bay are incredible. They will support their Pack no matter what. Throughout all the losing seasons they had in Green Bay, those loyal Cheeseheads sold out every home game and cheered their team as proudly as if they were Super Bowl champs. They are the best fans in the world: dedicated, caring, committed, knowledgeable. Nobody knows the team, the players, the stats, the team history, and the workings of the game like a Packer-backer. They know the difference between when you played well and lost to a better team and when you just plain blew it. Packers fans have an incredible grasp of the intricacies and dynamics of the game. They are also the friendliest, politest fans in the world. Not only do they not cuss you when you lose, they don't even cuss the other team—at least, not very much. They deserve the best, and I always want to give them something to celebrate.

You want to know just how dedicated a Packers fan is? Would you believe that some have been on a waiting list for as long as a quarter of a century to buy season tickets? That's no exaggeration. There are currently about thirteen thousand people on the waiting list, and the only way they can move up on the list is if current ticket-holders give up their tickets—or die. The right to buy a season ticket expires with the owner of the ticket—you can't will it or convey it in any other way to any other person, not even your kids. Most years, there are at least a hundred or so season ticket-holders who die or move to Tahiti or whatever, but some years there are as few as ten season passes that become available. The other 12,990 fans just have to wait in line another year.

There are a lot of traditions that go with being a Packers fan or a Packers player. During a team practice, fans line the fence to watch and cheer. When we hold preseason scrimmages, thirty or forty thousand people show up to demonstrate their support. There's one tradition in which kids from all around Green Bay come to the locker room before practice and offer their bicycles to the players. The players hop onto these kids' bicycles and ride from the locker room over to the practice fields. I pity the poor kid who gets his bike back after letting it be used by a 300-plus-pound offensive lineman!

GETTING IN SYNC

The moment I joined the team, I discovered that the chemistry on the Packers team, throughout the organization, and across the community is something special, something I had never experienced before. I quickly became aware that I was part of one of the most close-knit, least ego-fractured teams in the NFL. It was really refreshing to be on a team that wasn't constantly rocked by jealousies and rivalries. Sure, there were a few guys who didn't get along, who weren't on the same page with the rest of the team. There were some issues that needed to be worked through between some of our defensive and offensive players. But those were minor problems compared to the intense internal competition I had seen in Philly.

I knew—and I think everybody on that team knew—that if we were going to win, it had to be with Brett. Though he was only in his twenties, I could see that Brett had the confidence and the leadership abilities to take us far as a team. In fact, he had that rare kind of confidence that is able to lead without being arrogant, egotistical, or cocky. Brett is able to lead and inspire while respecting everyone else on the team as an equal, while being laid-back and getting along with everybody and never putting anybody down.

We all understood our roles. As a minister and a football player, I'm a leader—but I'm not the field general of the Green Bay Packers. That's Brett's job. He's the man. He'll always be the man. The rest of us have to fill our roles and do our best to get in sync and stay in sync with Brett. We have to let him know that we support him all the way, and we'll do whatever we need to do to get the job done. When you've got a first-class quarterback like Brett Favre, you've got to give him his props, because it's guys like Brett who will take you to the championship.

It didn't happen right away, of course. That first year I spent with the Packers, the two words that were most often used in the media to describe Brett Favre were "amazing" and "erratic." He was amazing because during the 1993 season he threw for over 3,000 yards, including 19 touchdown passes. He was erratic because he also threw 24 interceptions that year. Nobody was harder on Brett about that last statistic than Brett himself. He knew he couldn't keep throwing more picks than TDs. He finished eighth in passing in the NFC that year, and he knew he was capable of more than that. We all knew he had better seasons ahead of him—and we were right.

Two years later, Brett Favre was named the NFL's most valuable player, throwing for 4,413 yards, including 38 touchdown passes—more TD passes in a season than Steve Young or Joe Montana, and second only to Dan Marino. I would say there are two reasons for Brett's emergence as one of the best quarterbacks ever to play the game. One is work. Brett pushes himself and disciplines himself, in-season and off-season, to be the best. He likes his fun, but he also has a work ethic that just won't quit. The other reason is patience. Brett began to curb his impulse to go for the big play, and he began selecting his passing opportunities with greater care. He contented himself with shorter yardage and stopped clocks on individual plays to protect the ball and maintain the drive. Patience may not yield as much spectacle and glory, but it can go a long way toward winning football games.

Brett Favre is definitely a character. Just as Jerome Brown personified the style and attitude of the Philadelphia Eagles under Buddy Ryan, Brett personifies the style and attitude of the Green Bay Packers. He's an unpretentious working-class guy playing football in an unpretentious working-class town. He cares about his teammates, he cares about his family, he cares about his friends, he cares about winning. He's hardworking and very smart. He's generous; he spreads credit around to the entire team, and he never spreads blame. Brett has a great sense of humor, and it's a pleasure to practice with him because he keeps us laughing and enjoying ourselves all day long.

People have sometimes said things about his drinking. He enjoys going to bars and drinking, but it doesn't affect his play. I never have and never will condemn Brett about the things he likes to do. That's just something he enjoys. He makes sure he doesn't get hurt and that he doesn't hurt anybody else.

Brett is a bayou farm boy, so he likes to eat some strange stuff— big bowls of crawdads, red beans and rice, shrimp po-boys (that's a shrimp sandwich on split French bread with lettuce, tomatoes, and tabasco sauce). He's part French, part Choctaw Indian, and his family name should actually be pronounced *fahv-ray*, but somewhere along the line, many years ago, somebody began pronouncing it *farv*, and that's the way it's been ever since. The way Brett tells it, he started out as a wide receiver in high school. On the very first play of his very first practice, the quarterback fired a pass at him that hit him right in the numbers. The impact of it knocked him down, and he fell right on top of the ball with the wind knocked out of him. It hurt so bad, he got up crying and told the coach he didn't want to be a receiver anymore. So the

coach tried him at quarterback, and he's been quarterbacking ever
since.

In '93, when I joined the team, the offensive strategy of the
Packers was pretty simple: Get the ball to Sharpe. All-Pro receiver
Sterling Sharpe was one of the best ball-catchers ever to play the
game. He caught 108 passes in '93, breaking the previous NFL
record established by Washington's Art Monk (106 receptions in
1984). Then, the next year, Sterling broke his own record by catching 112 in a season. In just three seasons, '92 through '94, Brett
and Sterling established themselves as the latest in a succession
of great Packers pass-catch combos like Arnie Herber to Don Hutson in the '30s or Bart Starr to Boyd Dowler in the '60s.

Sterling was a great player with great hands and a lot of speed
after the catch. He had a large repertoire of moves and was a genius
at eluding coverage. He's a big dude, built like a linebacker, and
he was the most physical receiver I've ever seen. He'd get the ball
and instead of trying to juke you or jink you, he'd run right over
the top of you. He'd find a way to get open, and he'd just make
things happen. He worked hard to be ready, and he played with
some major injuries. When you see a fighting, winning spirit like
that, you can't help but admire the guy.

Sterling Sharpe was way underrated. There's no question in my
mind, he was as great as any of the great receivers. But because
he was playing in Green Bay before Green Bay came back into
prominence, he didn't get the plugs and the attention that Jerry
Rice or Michael Irvin got. If he was a Packer today, with the team
on the rise as it is, I think he would be clearly seen for what he
is: one of the best wide receivers to play the game.

I'll tell you something else about Sterling Sharpe: He was selfish. He would tell you that himself: "I'm selfish. I want the ball."
At times, that presented a problem. But when he got the ball, he
made stuff happen. He just made it happen. If a neck injury hadn't
forced him to retire, there's no telling what else he might have
accomplished.

Brett and Sterling had a great rhythm going. Usually, Brett
would fire a few short slants to Sterling, then stun everybody with
a long pass. There's a danger, of course, in putting too many eggs
in one basket, even if that basket is Sterling Sharpe. So Coach
Mike Holmgren began moving our offense in the direction of

spreading the workload to other receivers, especially Robert
Brooks. Coach Holmgren's foresight paid off. In '95, our first season after Sterling retired, Robert Brooks really stepped up, catching
102 passes for 1,497 yards and 13 touchdowns.

MIKE HOLMGREN, COMMANDER-IN-CHIEF

If Brett Favre was our field general, Mike Holmgren was our
commander-in-chief, and Ray Rhodes was his secretary of defense.
Ray is a very intense guy (I've actually seen Ray smile before—
most people haven't) and a great coach. With Ray as our defensive
coordinator, our Packers defense finished second in the league in
'93. In '94, he moved back to San Francisco and won his fifth
Super Bowl ring as defensive coordinator of the 49ers and the
following year became only the third black head coach in the
history of the NFL when he was hired by the Eagles' new owner,
Jeff Lurie. I really enjoyed playing for Ray, and his successor, Fritz
Shurmur (former defensive coordinator for the Cardinals and the
Rams) has done an outstanding job as well.

Mike Holmgren became the Packers' head coach the year before
I arrived. As offensive coordinator of the 49ers in the 1980s, Mike
was schooled in Bill Walsh's West Coast passing game, and he's
been a tremendous strategist for Brett Favre's offense. Mike is a
calm, cool, collected kind of guy—but if things aren't going his
way, he gets rowdy. He can holler if he has to. He's straight-up. He
has a problem with you, he'll tell you right away. You have a
problem with him, he wants you to tell him.

One of Mike's innovations was to establish a six-player committee, all leaders on the team, to help him maintain team discipline
and structure. If he has a problem with someone on the field, he
goes to the committee and asks, "How should I handle it?" You
have to respect that, because he wants to be fair. He wants the team
to be disciplined, but he doesn't want to make rash judgments and
act in a dictatorial fashion. If he says, "Should I fine this guy for
this action?" we often say, "Yeah, you should." We on the committee know it cuts both ways, and we want to be judged by the
same fair standards. If Mike has the support of the players, then if
something really serious comes along and he has to discipline or
even fire a player, there's no team-versus-coach split. We know that

the decision has been made fairly, by the team, for the good of the team.

Mike is learning to be a good delegator. When I first arrived in Green Bay, he was trying to do everything as head coach, and he couldn't do it all. My third year with the Packers, Sean Jones and I sat Mike down and asked him to allow us to take some of the load off his back. For example, we asked Mike to let us keep the team accountable, so that if anybody got in trouble off the field, that person would have to face the team.

For example, there's a custom in the South that at midnight on New Year's Eve, people fire guns into the air. You just don't do that in Green Bay, Wisconsin! Well, a couple of our guys did it, and they got in trouble with the law. So Mike came in and he was ticked. He just blasted everybody.

A week or two later, when the season was over, Sean and I went to Mike and said, "Mike, let us handle this sometimes. You shouldn't have to do this all the time. It's going to make you pull your hair out. When you come in and get mad at us all, the guys who didn't participate in it are wondering why you're getting on all of us. When stuff like this happens, let us take that role so we can take some of the pressure off of you." He was wide open to that.

I remember one occasion when a guy left practice early. Sean and I went in and talked with Mike about it, and he said, "He shouldn't have done it, but I don't want to get on the guy because he's doing well right now. I don't want to hurt his game. I just wish he had come in and asked me. I would have let him off early."

So Sean and I went and talked to the guy. When we told him he shouldn't have left early, he got a little defensive and said, "I just wanted to go out. I had some things I needed to do." We said, "Well, why didn't you ask Coach Mike? He would have let you go. What you did, just ducking out like that, was wrong. We think you owe Mike an apology, and you owe the team an apology."

The guy thought about it—and then he nodded. "Yeah, you're right." At the next team meeting, he stood before the team and said he was sorry.

Mike is a very reasonable guy. If something makes sense to him, he's gonna go with it. There've been times when I had some ministry or community work to attend to, and I would say, "Hey, Mike, I've got something going on. Can I miss this meeting?"

He'd say, "Sure." There was none of this I'll-show-you-who's-boss stuff that we had to put up with on a daily basis in Philly. The players and coaches respect and trust each other in Green Bay, which makes for a very reasonable relationship on both sides. It makes you feel good to be in an organization where you are working with reasonable people.

OVER THE HILL?

At the beginning of the '93 season, someone put up a green and gold sign in the locker room: "This is the year of the Packers!" The season opener looked like that promise was on-track as we demolished the L.A. Rams 36 to 6. Our next game would be against the Eagles on our home turf at Lambeau Field in Green Bay. I wanted to win that one bad.

The night before the Packers-Eagles game, I went out to eat with a bunch of my former teammates—Eric Allen, Ben Smith, Seth Joyner, Clyde Simmons, and Mike Flores. I picked them up at the hotel in my truck, and as they were piling in, Ben Smith said, "I hope you kick tail, Big Dog!"

"What do you mean?" I asked.

"We're all mad at the Eagles organization, the way they dissed you, man," said Ben. "You're real special, Reggie, and we know how much you gave the team. And for Richie Kotite to say what he said—"

"Well, what did he say?"

"At practice," Ben explained, "before we came out here, he said, '@#! Reggie White!' He said, 'The Eagles are a better team without him! @#! Reggie White!' For him to stand up and say that about you . . . Well, I just hope you kick their behind on that side of the ball!"

That disturbed me big-time. Even though we represented different teams, there should still be a measure of respect between coaches and players who once went to war for each other. I couldn't believe Rich Kotite would say that. But the other guys in the truck all agreed with Ben. "Yeah," they added, "that's what he said, all right."

On the one hand, I wondered, *What did I ever do to Rich Kotite to make him say something like that?* But I was also touched that my old buddies appreciated and loved me like they did. Even though they were going to take the field the next day and do everything they could to beat the Green Bay Packers, even though they wanted their entire team, offense and defense, to win, part of each of these guys was pulling for Reggie White.

Sometime later, I talked to Rich directly and asked him if he had said that about me. He said he never said anything like that. But I know these guys well enough to know they wouldn't lie to me.

The next day, when I came out of that tunnel and took the field, I wanted to win that game bad. I couldn't have been more determined or focused if it had been a Super Bowl game. The adrenaline was really pumping as that game got under way.

It was a strange feeling at first, chasing down Randall Cunning- ham and throwing him on the ground. For eight years, I had been conditioned to recognize the green uniform and the winged helmet as belonging to our side. But very quickly I adjusted to the fact that Randall was just another quarterback, and this was just another football game.

The first half of that game, I was pretty much able to have my way with the Eagles offensive line. I ripped 'em and bull-rushed 'em and sent 'em flying from sideline to sideline, no problem. I made four solo tackles, assisted three others, and nailed down the 125th and 126th sacks of my career. I forced two fumbles, which we recovered and turned into a touchdown and a field goal. The Eagles had four turnovers in the first half, and by the second half, they were down 17–7. The game sure looked to be going our way.

But sometime in the third quarter, the Eagles began to get better coverage on Sterling Sharpe by inserting cornerback Ben Smith and strong safety Wes Hopkins. That slowed down our passing game big-time, leaving Brett without anyone to shoot at. My old buddies on the Eagles defense, Clyde Simmons and Seth Joyner, were also making a lot of trouble for us. Offensively, the Eagles began running Vaughn Hebron and Herschel Walker away from my side, and they really began pushing into our territory.

Finally, late in the fourth quarter, the Eagles were third and ten as Randall dropped back. I battled Antone Davis until I finally slipped between him and center David Alexander. That face-off with Antone in the trenches cost me a second or two. I saw Randall roll right—he's most dangerous when he's rolling out—and I had to make a decision whether to rush him high or dive at his feet. I decided to dive.

At the same time, out of my line of vision, rookie receiver Victor Bailey took off down the sideline. Randall released just as I came flying at him—too late. Bailey scored a touchdown catch. Roger Ruzek kicked the extra point, tying the score. I was mad, getting beat like that. We had one ineffectual drive after that, ending in a punt, which Randall answered with eight strong plays, deep into Green Bay real estate. On our 13-yard line, he ran down the clock to five seconds, called in Ruzek again . . .

And Roger Ruzek booted the ball dead-center between the uprights. We had lost it by a field goal, 20–17—and that loss hurt so bad, I felt I'd had a vital organ ripped out of me.

It's always a bit of a surprise to open the papers the next day and read the sports reporters' dissection of a game and see how their impressions differ from my own experience. Some guys in the media got on our defensive line coach, Greg Blache, for taking me out of a couple of plays in the last half. But Greg didn't take me out. I took myself out for a couple plays because I wanted to be fresh down the stretch.

One reporter wrote, "In the second half, Reggie White looked and played old and tired and slow. . . . Maybe there is truth to the whispers and the speculation that the strongest, most dominant defensive player of our time has begun to lose it."[1] The truth is, I didn't feel "old and tired." I mean, you play a whole game and you get tired; everybody on *both* sides gets tired. But I still had plenty of energy and mental focus to play a full game. The fact that I didn't get as many sacks and tackles and forced fumbles in the second half doesn't mean I was old, tired, or slow. It just means I couldn't get to the passer as often. I had such a big first half that Rich Kotite had to make some emergency adjustments at midgame. They didn't run the ball on my side as much in the second half, and the adjustments they made didn't allow me to do what I did in the first.

That loss set off a disappointing, frustrating three-game losing streak, capped off by a miserable game against the Cowboys in Texas Stadium, October 3, 1993. We fought hard, twice having to beat the Cowboys back from the 1-yard line. Brett got sacked once—for 22 yards. It was awful.

After that game, the press took a look at our 1 and 3 record and began crowing about the Packers' "bad investment" in Reggie White. Some of the same reporters who were saying "The Pack is back!" a few weeks earlier now said that Reggie White was an "overpriced disappointment" and "over the hill." Fact is, I knew I was playing well. I was having one of my best years in terms of personal performance. But the Packers weren't winning games. And I had only gotten two sacks in four games, and that's how the media judges performance. It was discouraging because I had guys evaluating my game who had never played my game. There were dozens of times when I was just a fraction of a second short of making the plays. I knew that if I could just start making those plays, I could fire up the entire line and we could start winning football games.

Our defensive line coach, Greg Blache, saw how down I was, so he called me into his office. "Reggie," he said, "I know there's been a lot of talk in the papers saying you're not playing like you used to. I just want you to know that I see the work you've been doing out there, and I can see that your play is as solid as it ever was. The other coaches see it, and so do the players. Don't let those people bother you. Just hang in there, and it'll start to click."

That was good for me to hear. I began to think, *Greg's right. I'm allowing my feelings to be influenced by a bunch of guys who have never lined up. Hey, even if I ended up having a bad season, they could never take away my stats. They could never take my greatness from me, because God gave me that greatness.* From that point on, my game began to settle into a groove. That was important to me, because I really wanted to justify Green Bay's faith in me.

And I wanted a championship.

Mike Holmgren and Ray Rhodes gave me the same kind of affirmation. Ray even went to the reporters and said, "People talk about Reggie having been in the league too long, but they're wrong. Reggie's getting better. He's at the top of his game. He takes care of himself. He works hard. He enjoys practice. He's living up to everything we knew he would."

Mike often tells me not to take too much onto myself. He sees that I have a tendency to shoulder the burden of a loss. I always try to figure out, *What could I have done to help us win?* Truth is, it takes twenty-one other guys to make it happen. If I have a bad game, I know it and I can admit I had a bad game, so I should be able to admit it when the team has a bad game too. I'm grateful that Greg, Ray, and Mike understood something that a lot of coaches miss: Sometimes great players need to be told when they're playing great. Coaches will often take you for granted. When those three coaches reassured me after our first four games, it helped for the rest of that year.

I've come to the conclusion that you should never believe what you read in the papers—good or bad. Reporters hardly ever see what I see. I've read reporters praising my performance when I knew I was having one of the worst days of my career. And I've read reporters ripping my performance when I knew I was at my peak. Ever since I turned thirty, people have been saying I was slowing down. Tell you what: If you think I'm slowing down, come on out to the facility and I'm sure my equipment manager can find some equipment and suit you up. After you sign the medical release form, we'll go out on the field and I'll show you— bone by bone—exactly how much I've slowed down.

Any takers?

A GRUDGE AGAINST LOSING

I was very disappointed with the 1 and 3 showing we made at the start of the season. I knew we could have and should have done better. One of the things I noted after the first couple games was that a lot of the guys on the team had never been on a winning team before. They were used to losing, so there was a mentality of losing that I could feel in the team. I had to do *something* to help break that losing atmosphere, and I figured the best way was just to be honest with them.

I went to Coach Holmgren and the Packers general manager, Ron Wolf, about what I was sensing in the team, and we agreed to call a meeting. Then I got up and said, "We've played a few games, and I've seen that there's a problem on this team. I've noticed that there are a few guys on this team who make an excuse for every mistake they made. There are guys who are just happy to be here. Some of you guys walk in here when we lose and it don't even bother you. Some of you guys are too comfortable. I assure you, if I keep seeing that, I will help them get you out of here, because I want to win, and the only way we gonna win is we get everybody on the same page.

"Let me tell you something. It bothers me to lose. It bothers me big-time. I didn't come to Green Bay to lose, and I hope none of you guys did either. From this day on, I hope every man on this team has a grudge against losing. I hope losing puts a knot in your throat and makes you cry and makes you want to put your fist through a wall. Because if losing makes you mad and makes you cry, then you're going to go out there and bust your gut to keep from losing. If we're not here to win games, we shouldn't be here at all.

"There are plenty of guys on this team who can play, so let's play. If you make mistakes, 'fess up to 'em and do better next time. If a coach says you messed up, don't argue with him. Listen to him and try to do what he asks you to do. Let's figure out ways to be tougher, better, faster than we've ever been before. Let's do whatever it takes to start winning football games."

I'm not saying my tough talk turned things around. There were a lot of changes that we, as coaches and teammates, began making to turn that 1 and 3 record around. But I think it was one factor. At that point, we began to win. Today we have an atmosphere of winning because we've started building a tradition of winning. When guys start winning, they want to keep on winning. So we don't have many guys on the team walking around with a lackadaisical attitude anymore. We still have to get after guys now and then, but there is a much more pervasive attitude today that we are here to win. That's our purpose, that's our mission, and we're not going to be satisfied with anything less than a championship season.

THE BIRTH OF THE LAMBEAU LEAP

One problem that our first few games pointed up was that we had a bad habit of blowing games in the fourth quarter. Maybe it was because our opponents would get their offense and defense dialed into us at halftime. Or maybe it was because we would mentally and physically let down in the second half. I didn't know why it was happening, but I sure wanted to put a stop to it.

The week after the Dallas game, we hosted the Denver Broncos at Lambeau Field—and once again, we almost lost it in the fourth quarter after having it comfortably in the bag. By halftime, we had a comfortable 30–7 lead—but then the Broncos staged a comeback. They picked off three of Brett's passes, including one that Mike Croel ran back for a touchdown. Bronco kicker Jason Elam kicked a 47-yard field goal that brought them to 30–27—way too close for comfort. I got three sacks in that game, including two on consecutive plays in the final minutes of the game to stop John Elway's drive and preserve the win.

On Halloween Sunday 1993, we beat the Bears, 17–3. I sacked Bears quarterback Jim Harbaugh twice in that game, which moved me ahead of Lawrence Taylor for the all-time sack record (I had 130½ versus L. T.'s 129½).

My coaches, Mike Holmgren and Ray Rhodes, found creative ways to use me, shifting me all around the defensive line to keep the enemy offense from keying in on me and my linemates. I often played over the right guard as well as the right tackle so that I was playing not only defensive end but also defensive tackle. They didn't know what we were doing from one play to the next.

Our entire defense was making more hits, more tackles for big losses—and that, coupled with what Brett & Co. were accomplishing on offense, quickly translated into wins. I soon noticed that all that talk about Reggie White being "over the hill" or "overpriced" began to get mighty quiet. I think my value to the Packers was demonstrated in my first three months, as the Packer defense went from number 22 to number 5 in the league in sacks, from number 23 to number 6 in total defense, and from number 26 to number 10 in rushing defense. Over that same period, the Philadelphia Eagles plunged from the top of the league to the bottom in defense statistics!

One of our biggest games in 1993 was the game against the L.A. Raiders at Lambeau Field, the day after Christmas. That game not only clinched us a place in the playoffs, it also started a new Packers tradition: the Lambeau Leap. The temperature was 0 degrees (with windchill -22). The Pack controlled that game from start to finish, but early in the third quarter, the Raiders were knocked out cold—or at least their quarterback was. That's when Raiders QB Jeff Hostetler dropped back to pass on a first and ten from his own 37. Packers linebacker Tony Bennett charged right past Raiders tackle Bruce Wilkerson and plowed into Hostetler— a devastating blindside hit that slammed the quarterback into the ground. The tundra was *really* frozen that day, and Hostetler hit it mighty hard—so hard that he was unconscious for a short time and didn't get up for five minutes.

Sterling Sharpe made seven catches in that game, giving him 106 catches for the season. With that game, he became the first receiver in NFL history to have two 100-yard seasons back to back.

The craziest and most memorable moment came in the first few plays of the fourth quarter. Taking the snap at his own 47, Raiders quarterback Vince Evans (Hostetler's replacement) tossed the ball to halfback Randy Jordan. Instantly, our safety, LeRoy Butler, piled into Jordan, forcing a fumble. I caught the ball on the first bounce and began running. I got no more than 10 yards with the ball when Raider lineman Steve Wisniewski grabbed onto me and tried to bring me down. I looked around for someone to pitch it to and there was LeRoy. I flipped a lateral to him, and he ran it the rest of the way—25 yards—for a touchdown.

When LeRoy got into the end zone, he didn't stop. He just kept right on going! He skidded across the icy ground right up to the stands, then took a big vertical leap up the wall and tumbled onto the fans. They were hugging him and slapping him and they wouldn't let him go! They just held him there, cheering and celebrating, for about a half a minute. I had never seen anything like it.

Later, our wide receiver, Robert Brooks, went up to LeRoy and said, "That was cool, man! I'm gonna steal that from you, because I figure I'm gonna be going into the end zone a lot more than you will!" Fact is, a lot of our guys now do it—except Brett. He says he's afraid he'll fall and make a fool of himself. Anyway, that's how the Lambeau Leap got its start.

Coach Holmgren doesn't mind it. "It beats the heck out of those crazy end zone dances Deion Sanders does," he says. "It's okay with me if they jump into the stands—as long as they don't hurt themselves, and as long as the crowd throws 'em back. Our fans just love it." I've never done it myself, cause I've never had a touchdown in Lambeau Field. Someday, maybe. A lot of our guys are waiting to see Gilbert Brown try it. He's a 325-pound nose-tackle, and if he could get up there—like, if we all hoisted him on our shoulders and threw him up there—he'd probably send about thirty or forty Cheeseheads sloshing out onto the end zone.

We finished the season 10 and 7—not bad, considering that shaky 1 and 3 start. Mike Holmgren had coached the Packers to their first back-to-back winning seasons since Vince Lombardi in '66–'67. I tied that season with the Saints' Renaldo Turnbull for the NFC lead in sacks—13. It was certainly not the most sacks I ever collected in a season (my record was 21 in the strike-shortened '87 season), but it was a respectable record. Of course, there's a lot more to being an effective defensive lineman than sacking the quarterback. By occupying the attention of two or three offensive players, I was opening up additional opportunities for Tony Bennett, John Jurkovic, Bryce Paup, and the rest of our defense—and together, we were really getting the job done.

The day after Christmas 1993, we played our next-to-last regular season game, shutting out the L.A. Raiders, 28 to zip. It was, without a doubt, the *coldest* game I have ever played in. The kickoff temperature was 0, with a windchill factor of -22 degrees. I didn't envy Sterling having to catch a frozen football in that kind of weather; I was glad all I had to do was hit guys. They tell me it was the coldest game played in Lambeau Field since the "Ice Bowl," the '67 championship game in which the Packers beat the Cowboys in a game that was -13 at kickoff, with a windchill factor of 46 below.

On Saturday, January 8, 1994, the Packers beat the Detroit Lions 28–24 in the first round of the playoffs (the win was especially sweet because, just a week before, we had lost our final regular season game to the same team, 30–20). It was the Packers first nonstrike playoff game in 11 years—since the strike-shortened '82 season (though most fans don't count that season). The last playoff game in a nonstrike year was 1972, when the Packers last won the division. The Detroit game featured an incredible 101-yard interception return by our safety, George Teague—the longest touchdown in NFL history. The game concluded with a winning 40-yard touchdown pass from Brett to Sterling with less than a minute left to play.

From there we went to Texas Stadium in Dallas. We had a sour taste in our mouths from that 36–14 drubbing the 'Boys had given us back in October—and when the second-round playoff game was over, it didn't taste any better. It was a raggedy, sloppy game on both sides—Dallas had two interceptions, a lost fumble, and a whole passel of penalties, while Brett was picked off twice and lost a fumble. Several times, we had great offensive field position— and then we squandered it. I spent most of that game bumping up against big ol' Erik Williams, and ended up with only one tackle, one assist, and no sacks. It was a frustrating day, to say the least. In the end, we lost it pretty bad, 27–17. The Cowboys would go on to defeat San Francisco for the NFC championship, then beat Buffalo in the Super Bowl.

Earlier that season, I had told my team that losing makes me mad and it makes me cry. That's exactly how I felt when that game was over. We had come a long way just to have the dream trampled into the artificial turf at Texas Stadium. *Please, just one Super Bowl before I retire,* I prayed as I trudged off the field. *Not two or three, I ain't greedy. Just give me one.*

A few months later, I got the chance to meet David "Deacon" Jones, one of the legendary defensive linemen of the game. (That's right, "The Rev" meets "The Deacon"!) He played defensive end with the Rams throughout the 1960s, and with the Chargers and Redskins in the '70s. Since the NFL did not record sacks as an official statistic until 1982, there's no certain count of his sacks, but football historians believe it to be around 172. So I said to him, "I heard you had 172 sacks. I'd like to get that many before I retire." In reply, he said something I'll never forget, and something I fully understand. He held out his hand and said, "Reggie, you don't see a ring on my finger, do you? Winning a championship means more than all the individual accomplishments combined."

Amen, Deacon.

RETURN TO THE VET

In April '94, Norm Braman sold the Philadelphia Eagles (8 and 8 in 1993) to Hollywood producer Jeffrey Lurie for $185 million. One of the first things Mr. Lurie did was to publicly thank me for all I had done for the Eagles organization (something his predecessor never did), and announce that he would not assign my number 92 jersey to any other player. When I heard about it, I called Mr. Lurie and told him that it meant a lot to me and was an act of extraordinary kindness coming from an owner I never even played for. I believe it signaled the start of a new attitude of respect and cooperation between management and players in the Eagles organization. I even started wearing my Eagles T-shirts after that—and I wasn't even an Eagle anymore!

In August 1994, I was one of forty-eight players named to the NFL 75th Anniversary All-Time Team, selected by a fifteen-person panel of NFL and Hall of Fame officials, former players, and sports reporters. Only five active players were chosen—Joe Montana, Jerry Rice, Rod Woodson, and Ronnie Lott, and me. I was in awe of the names of past and retired players included—names like Walter Payton, Jim Brown, Bronko Nagurski, Ray Nitschke, Steve Van Buren, Johnny Unitas, Mean Joe Greene, Dick Butkus, Lawrence Taylor, and the great David "Deacon" Jones.

That same year, Green Bay recruited a lot of talent to boost our offense and keep us on an upswing. We drafted LeShon Johnson, the nation's leading college rusher, from Northern Illinois, and Aaron Taylor of Notre Dame, winner of the Lombardi Award for the top college offensive lineman in the country. We signed Reggie Cobb, a free agent running back from Tampa Bay, to rev up our ground threat. We signed a bunch of guys.

Our 3–4 defense in 1993 had ranked number 2 in the NFL behind Minnesota. For 1994, we added Sean Jones, giving us a strong 4–3 scheme. The previous season, Sean had collected 13 sacks as a defensive end with the Houston Oilers. We counted on Sean to dilute the effectiveness of some of the double- and triple-teaming the opposition had been putting on me. With a front four consisting of Sean, Steve McMichael, John Jurkovic, and me, we were ready to take on anything they could throw at us.

We won our 1994 season opener against the Vikings, 16–10, then lost our next game against the Miami Dolphins, 24–14, at Milwaukee County Stadium. We played the Miami game pretty flat. In terms of my own performance, it was one of the worst games I've ever played. The only upside to that game was that I got to see some of my old Eagles teammates, transplanted via free agency to Miami—Keith Jackson, Keith Byars, and Ron Heller. I especially remember one incident from that game. I was lined up against Ron Heller, who had been doing a good job against me. Ron's a little like Jerome Brown, in that he usually keeps a lot of chatter going during the game. This game, however, he was real quiet. Maybe it was because he was concentrating so hard on keeping me in check. He only said one thing to me during the whole game. After I threw him down hard on the ground one time, he looked up at me kind of shaken and said, "Who made you so mad?" That made me laugh.

Our third game of the season was against the Philadelphia Eagles—my first return to Veterans Stadium since I signed with the Packers in April of '93. Like us, the Eagles were 1 and 1. I was excited about going back to Philly and playing before all my friends at the Vet. I had returned to the city numerous times— always to a warm reception—to continue the community and ministry efforts I had begun there during my eight years as an Eagle. For example, it was on one of my return visits to Philly that I announced the formation of the National Society of Nehemiah, a unity movement designed to address the spiritual and social problems of America's inner cities. Though I certainly had my public differences with Eagles management, I felt my ties with the community and the fans were still very strong.

The Philadelphia game was held during the NFL's "Throwbacks Weekend," featuring a masquerade ball. I wore a 1937 Green Bay Packers uniform—and I've gotta tell you, the uniforms guys wore in those days were ugly beyond belief! The jersey and pants were a strange combination of yellow, tan, and off-blue, and the helmet was a gaudy, tawdry metallic gold. I looked like something from a low-budget 1950s science-fiction movie.

It was kind of strange going back to the Vet—not just because I would take the field from the visitor's tunnel instead of the Eagles' tunnel. It was strange because a lot had changed in a year. Many of my old Eagles teammates were gone—Clyde and Seth, Keith Byars, Andre Waters, Ron Heller, Mike Golic, Mike Pitts, and Wes Hopkins. Still I was looking forward to seeing and playing against my good friends who still wore Eagle green—including guys like Byron Evans, Freddie Barnett, Eric Allen, Antone Davis, and Randall Cunningham.

There were a lot of cheers—and just a few boos—as I loped out onto the turf for the pregame warm-up. A few boos ain't bad; I was, after all, wearing a Packers uniform, and this was the Eagles' house. In the lower deck, above the 50-yard line, a couple of fans held up a big sign that read, "WE LOVE YOU, REGGIE—BUT NOT TODAY!" That was a good one. Jeff Lurie, the Eagles' new owner, came over and shook my hand. "Have a good game, Reggie," he said, grinning, "but not *too* good!" I wish I'd had a chance to play football for that man. At the start of the game, the teams were introduced, and a loud, long cheer went up when my name was called. I knew they weren't cheering for me to win—they were just cheering for me. That felt real good. Thanks, Philly. I love you too.

Early in the game, Brett fired a pass to Reggie Cobb, who was all alone in the left flat. That 37-yard touchdown pass and point-after gave us a quick 7-point lead. Brett also unloaded a lot of firepower in Sterling's direction—Sharpe caught six passes for 108 yards that day, despite double coverage. The Eagles defense, anchored by William Perry and William Fuller, gave our young offensive linemen a lot to handle, and before the game was over, Brett had been sacked six times.

About a minute before the end of the half, the Eagles intercepted a pass in the end zone, ending our push for another touchdown. Pressed by the clock, Randall managed to drive his way upfield pretty quickly. On one down, I broke past Eagles lineman Broderick Thompson and practically had my arms around Randall when he unleashed the ball for a 34-yard completion. That pass set up a 26-yard field goal by Eddie Murray with one second left in the half. When we went into the locker room, we were up a scant 7–3.

After halftime, the Eagles defense really came out kicking tail, holding our offense to only three first downs in the second half. We couldn't get our running game going—we only gained 37 yards on 14 carries.

The Eagles double- and triple-teamed me through most of the game, much of which I spent butting heads with the Eagles' Broderick Thompson. Broderick is a tough player—very experienced and real strong. I've been playing against him since 1985, when he was a guard with Portland and I was on the Memphis Showboats in the USFL. Whenever he and I get down in the trenches, it's a dogfight. I salute the refs in that game—they flagged Broderick three times for holding, more than they usually do when guys are holding me.

Randall didn't throw any TD passes, but he did pull off a 1-yard quarterback sneak in the third quarter. That was followed by a second Eddie Murray field goal, which gave the Eagles a 13–7 advantage in the fourth quarter.

Just before the two-minute warning, on second and eight from his own 33, Randall called a bootleg—a fakeout in which he pretends to hand the ball off, then hides it and tries to run around the end. After the snap, I was engaged in hand-to-hand combat with Broderick. To my right, I caught a fleeting glimpse of Sean Jones and Steve McMichael breaking through the line and streaking toward Randall. I batted Broderick away, but not in time to have any effect on the play. I thought, *Go, go, go!* And they went! Sean and Steve both got their hands on Randall, and one of them—I don't know which one—managed to pop the ball out of Randall's grasp. The ball took a couple bounces and Sean dove on top of it, smothering the ball at the Eagles' 11-yard line. It didn't look like there was any way the Eagles could stop us now.

The stadium had been loud and raucous for most of that game, but suddenly it was like the inside of a jet engine—and the afterburner was kicking in. Some 63,922 throats (give or take a few) were screaming, "Dee-Fense! Dee-Fense! Dee-Fense!" I thought my eardrums were gonna pop. The walls and columns of the stadium seemed to shudder. As I jaunted happily off the field, I thought, *Go ahead and holler, folks! This game is ours!*

As I removed my helmet and watched from the sidelines, I didn't envy my old Eagles buddy Byron Evans having to hold those 11 yards against an assault by Brett Favre. Both teams came together in the trenches. Brett called the numbers, but I don't know how anybody could hear him. I don't know how he could even hear himself. At the snap, he dropped back. He didn't have a lot of time, but he didn't need much. The ball didn't have that far to go. He found Sterling. He fired. He missed.

They lined up again. The ball was snapped. Brett dropped back into the pocket. He aimed a quick slant to tight end Jeff Wilner. No good.

Finally, on fourth and five, Brett gave the ball to halfback Edgar Bennett, who made a run for it—only to be brought down by Otis Smith. With 1:46 left in the game, we turned the ball over to the Eagles on their own 6-yard line. They preserved their 13–7 advantage over us until the final gun.

It was a painful loss, but I wasn't ashamed of the way we played—or the way I performed. Even though I only got three tackles and no sacks in that game, the Eagles had to game-plan around me big-time. Though they usually run a pretty balanced offense, side to side, on this game they ran and passed the entire game away from me. In the end, we got beaten in a close game by a good team. The Eagles put out an outstanding effort that day. So did the Eagles fans, who really pumped up the volume.

After the game, some of my Packers teammates and I went out to mid-field and knelt and prayed with a number of my former Eagles teammates, including William Fuller, Byron Evans, and Antone Davis. I embraced Randall and I told him I loved him, and he told me the same.

TO BE AN ELITE TEAM . . .

In October of '94, we had a game in New England against the Patriots that was memorable primarily because of bad officiating. I mean, it was so bad that Jerry Seeman, the NFL director of officiating, actually telephoned Coach Mike Holmgren and apologized for the erroneous penalties that were flagged on us. Seeman singled out five bad calls—an encroachment and an offsides on Sean, a crackback block called on Robert Brooks, holding on cornerback Lenny McGill, and an unnecessary roughness on me. We lost that game by an eyelash, 17–16.

The following month, in the third quarter of a game against the Buffalo Bills, I made a lunge for running back Thurman Thomas. My teammate, Fred Strickland, got to Thurman ahead of me. Somehow, I got my left arm wedged between Thurman Thomas's helmet

and the crushing bulk of Fred Strickland. The result: sprung ligaments in my left elbow. I was out of the game (which we lost, 29–
20), and my arm was set in a plaster cast. I truly thought it was
broken, but praise God it wasn't. After the doctor did an MRI, he
told me I would be out of action for two to four weeks—and our
next game was against the Cowboys (9–2) in Texas Stadium,
Thanksgiving Day. It would be the first missed game in my entire
NFL career—a 148-consecutive-game streak (not counting the '87
strike).

Thanksgiving Day came—and the one thing I was most thankful
for was that I could play against Dallas! I had prayed that God
would heal that sprung elbow, and He did. More on that in the
next chapter, but for now, it's enough to say that God let me play.

The main obstacle I had faced year after year in Texas Stadium,
both as an Eagle and as a Packer, was a 300-plus-pound offensive
tackle named Erik Williams. This year, however, Erik was sidelined
with a bum knee he picked up in a car crash a few weeks before.
In his place was a twenty-three-year-old, 327-pound rookie tackle
named Larry Allen. I heard later that when Allen saw me suited
up and going through my pregame warmups, his heart sank. He
thought I was out of action. All the news reports had said I
wouldn't play. "During the national anthem, I looked over at Reggie White," he later told a reporter, "and he was all pumped up
and jumping around. I thought, 'Oh no!'"

First time we lined up, I faked to the outside and Larry followed
the fake. When I cut back inside, he was off-balance, so, tucking
my left arm to protect it, I ripped under his arm with my right.
He was instantly and seriously airborne—and from the look on his
face, it was obvious he couldn't figure out how it happened. On
the next play, when he came back to line up again, I grinned at
him and asked him if he had accepted Jesus as his Savior. Larry
didn't answer; he just licked his lips kind of nervously, then hun-
kered down and waited for the snap. After a few plays, he seemed
to get his confidence back, and he played me plenty hard from
then on. I'll tell you this: Larry Allen is tough, he catches on fast,
and he doesn't quit. He later said he learned a lot that day—
including how it feels to be weightless.

We had the Cowboys down 14 points at the half, but they came
back with incredible intensity in the second half, scoring 36 points

in the last two quarters. And they managed all this without the services of Troy Aikman, who was out with a pulled knee ligament. Backup quarterback Jason Garrett played smart, going mostly to short, quick-release passes that moved the ball steadily toward the goal line. In the end, we lost 42–31. The next week we slid to 6 and 7 with a disappointing loss to Detroit, 34–31. The following Sunday, we kept our playoff hopes alive by beating the Chicago Bears 40–3. We played one of our best games of the season that day, gaining 257 yards on the ground and 259 in the air.

In two games in December, against the Atlanta Falcons and the Tampa Bay Buccaneers, our superstar receiver, Sterling Sharpe, suffered pinched nerves in his neck—what they call "stingers." They turned out to be caused by a loosening of the first and second cervical vertebrae, which produces a loss of sensation in his limbs. At age twenty-eight, right at the peak of his career, Sterling was out of football for good.

On the very last day of '94, we got our revenge on the Detroit Lions by knocking them out of the playoffs, holding my good friend Barry Sanders to an unheard-of -1 yard in 13 carries, beating the Lions 16–12.

A week later, we were back in Texas Stadium, where the Cowboys once again played like champs. They won the game and they won it big, 35–9. When it was over, man, I didn't want to talk to nobody—especially the press. I told the Packers p.r. man to keep the reporters away, then I showered, got dressed, and went to the team bus. I was tired of telling reporters, year after year, "We got beat by a good team this year, but next year . . . !" After ten years in the NFL, it was starting to sound a little hollow.

We had proved we could play a couple winning seasons, even a couple playoff seasons, back-to-back. We had gained a lot of respect. The press was calling us "the Rambos of Lambeau," and we were making our fans proud. But we were not yet one of the elite teams of the NFL. To become an elite team, you have to beat an elite team—a team like the 49ers or the Cowboys. And you have to do it in a playoff game. We hadn't done that yet.

As the bus took us back to the airport for the flight home, I thought back over my career in the NFL. My years with the Philadelphia Eagles were years of enduring the storms of change, conflict, and loss. My first year with the Packers was a year of transition and adjustment. My second year with the Packers was a year of building, of making gains—but of falling short of my ultimate goal.

I had no idea what lay ahead of me in 1995. I had no way of knowing the miracles I would see.

Chapter 10

MIRACLES IN THE TRENCHES

Let me take you back to that game against the Buffalo Bills, Sunday, November 20, 1994. Third quarter of that game, both Fred Strickland and I dive for ballcarrier Thurman Thomas. Coming down, my left arm gets trapped between Thurman's helmet and Fred Strickland's body. There's a popping sensation deep in my elbow, and pain shoots through my arm like a spear. Man, I'm sure it's broken.

As I went back to the sideline, I kept working my elbow, kept moving it. It really hurt, but I'd played hurt before, and I really wanted back in the game. Our team physician, Dr. Patrick McKenzie, kept checking me and prodding that elbow, and I got kind of indignant.

"Leave it alone," I said. "I'm gonna go back and play!"

I asked one of our guys on the bench to get up and let me hit him. So I launched from a three-point stance and hit him three times, and each time, my elbow exploded in pain. Worse, I couldn't move it. It was stiffening up on me. I said, "That's it, man," and I just sat out the rest of the game.

Doc McKenzie wrapped it up for me and said, "I'm sorry, Reggie. I think you tore the ligament and muscle in that elbow."

I left the game with my arm in a hard cast, and Doc McKenzie did an MRI on it the next day. Then he gave me one of those good news/bad news things: Good news, it wasn't broken. Bad news, it was badly sprained—that is, the ligaments and muscles were torn—and I would be sitting out the next two to four weeks, breaking my 148-consecutive-game streak, and ending my season.

"It looks like you're human, just like everybody else," the doc told me. "Your muscles and ligaments tear too."

When I got home with Sara, she told me, "You know, God's gonna heal you, Reggie. You're gonna play in that Dallas game."

My response to Sara was, "Maybe God wants me to rest right now, because I can't even move my arm." I didn't even ask God to heal me, because I was resigned to the fact that this was a season-ender, and there was no way I was gonna play any more football in 1994.

"I L-O-V-E YOU"

When I went back to the Packers facility on Tuesday, Coach Mike Holmgren saw I was hurt pretty bad. He and the other coaches had seen me play hurt before, and they knew this was different. Fred Strickland looked absolutely miserable. I said to him, "You're not bothered about it, are you?"

He said, "Yeah, man. We really need you for the Dallas game, and I'm the guy who put the hit on your arm."

"You didn't do that, Fred," I told him. "It just happened. You shouldn't be feeling bad about it." But he did.

Throughout that day I got calls and phone messages from friends across the country, saying, "We're praying for you, Reggie." Some even said, "We know God's going to heal you."

I went into the training room to get treatment for the arm at around 12:30. Pepper Burruss, our head trainer, is a Christian, and he said to me, "You just watch, Reggie. God is going to heal you as a testimony before the nation."

"That's exactly what Sara told me," I replied, "But look, Pepper, I can't even move my arm! I think maybe God just wants me to rest."

I got up on a table, and Pepper and an assistant trainer, Sam Ramsden, began treating my arm with ice and electric stim, stuff like that. I kept trying to move the elbow a little, but it was no good. After I had been there about an hour, I said to Sam, "Hey, put some Take 6 on the stereo, would you?" So Sam put the

Take 6 disk on the CD player. There was one song on that disk called "I L-O-V-E You," and I asked Sam to put that song on the repeat mode, so it played over and over. About the third time the song played, I fell asleep for about two minutes.

When I woke up, I cleared my eyes and straightened my left arm out—and then what I had done hit me. "Oh man!" I shouted. "Hey, baby, my arm's feeling good, man! Sam, God done healed me, man!"

"What do you mean?" asked Sam.

I flexed my arm back and forth in front of Sam's eyes, which were about as big as tennis balls. "Look, man! God done healed me!"

Looking back on it, I believe God inspired me to ask for that song, "I L-O-V-E You." He wanted that song to be playing over and over as He touched my arm and healed me because He wanted to reassure me of His love for me. As I straightened my arm, I said, "Sam, call Pepper, call Coach Mike! Tell 'em I'm playing on Thanksgiving Day!"

"Okay," said Sam, looking kind of dubious, "but I'd better call Dr. McKenzie too because he needs to check you out."

"Go ahead and call him too," I said, "because God done healed me!"

So the doc came in and did all the same tests he had done the day before. "It looks good," he said. "How does it feel?"

"It's sore," I said, "but I'm all right. I feel I can play. What do you think?"

Dr. McKenzie scratched his head. "Remember what I told you yesterday? That you're made just like everybody else? Well, I was wrong. You're *not* made like everybody else."

I laughed and said, "It's not me, man. It's God! He healed me."

He said, "Well, somebody did something to you."

"That's what I'm telling you," I said. "God did it."

About that time, Coach Mike came in. Doc said to him, "Reggie's all right. You probably ought to put a brace on this arm just to protect it, but he's all right."

Then Pepper came in, and he was grinning at me. I grinned back at him, because I knew what he was getting ready to say. I said, "You told me this would happen, didn't you?"

"Yeah," he said, "I told you God was going to heal you."

Mike was ecstatic, of course—but cautious too. "Let's do some tests." They put me through some tests—hitting the bags, stuff like that—and I passed the tests.

Later, our defensive coordinator, Fritz Shurmur, came in with his glasses on his nose. "I heard there was a divine healing."

"Yep," I replied, "there sure was."

"That's good," said Fritz, "I'm glad He did it for you." Fritz is really matter-of-fact about things.

On Wednesday, the team flew down to Dallas for the game. Mike was still not sure if he wanted to play me or not. Meanwhile, the media was all over me, asking, "Are you gonna play?"

I just kept saying, "Watch God. Just see what He does."

At the Dallas facility, Sean Jones came and told me that Howie Long, the great defensive end of the Raiders, had called for me while I was out. Howie had asked him, "Sean, I heard Reggie's playing in the Dallas game. What kind of treatment did they give him for his arm?" Sean said, "Howie, it wasn't a treatment. God healed him. People were praying for him, and God healed him." And Howie was like, "Come on, Sean! Tell me what really happened!" Sean said, "Look, you call Reggie and ask him."

Later, Howie got through to me and said, "Big Dog, what happened?"

"Look, I don't know what you believe, but I'm telling you the honest truth: God healed me. Sure, I got treatment—ice, electric stim, the usual—but the treatment didn't heal me. The muscle and ligaments in my elbow are still torn, but God has given me strength back in my elbow to where I can straighten it out and I can play football with it. Man, that's what happened."

He said, "Reggie, I've known you for a long time, and I believe anything you tell me."

Pat Summerall, the sportscaster, found out about it and talked about it the next day throughout the Dallas game—pregame, halftime, all through the game. I later got letters and reports back about people who were so awestruck by this healing that they reevaluated their lives and their beliefs, and they turned their lives over to God. It was a miracle, a healing from God—and it was having the effect on lives and hearts that God wanted it to have. But there was more—a lot more—to come.

"I'M NOT GETTING UP
UNTIL SEAN GETS UP"

On Monday, September 11, 1995, I witnessed another miracle as I stood on the sidelines at Soldier Field in Chicago: a 99-yard touchdown pass from Brett Favre to Robert Brooks. That touchdown gave us a 21 to zip lead in the game (near the end, the Bears gave us a serious scare by eating way into our lead, but we finished the night with a 27–24 win). The play came on a third and ten from our own 1-yard line in the second quarter. The ball was snapped and Brett dropped back into the end zone. He pump-faked, scanning the horizon. The fake move drew the Bears defense in short. Downfield, Robert Brooks maneuvered to escape the coverage of the Bears top defender, cornerback Donnell Woolford. He beat Woolford with an inside move just as Brett released the ball. As Robert crossed our 30-yard line, the ball whistled into his arms, and he sprinted down the right sideline for a touchdown with about ten minutes left in the first half.

(The reason a 99-yard pass is the longest pass play possible is that the closest the ball can be spotted to the end zone is the 1-yard line. I had seen such a miracle only once before, back on November 10, 1985, when my Eagles teammate Ron Jaworski completed a 99-yarder to the receiver we called "Quick Six," Mike Quick. Brett's 99-yarder was only the eighth such pass in NFL history. To be present and see that sight twice in a lifetime is truly a miraculous experience.)

During the second half of the game, the Bears made giant strides, and by the fourth quarter they were really breathing down our necks. Trailing 27–21, they rumbled all the way to our 2-yard line and had to settle for a field goal. On their next drive, with two minutes left, I hit Bears quarterback Erik Kramer behind the line of scrimmage, adding another sack to my stats and forcing a fumble. Our own Wayne Simmons recovered at the Bears' 22, and Chicago's fate was sealed as we ran out the clock.

On November 5, we played a tough, injury-ridden game against the Vikings at the Minneapolis Metrodome. Brett left the game late in the second quarter with an injury to his left ankle after a blocker rolled over his leg. While he was out, his backup, Ty Detmer, suffered torn ligaments in his right thumb—a season-ender for Ty.

After X-rays showed no fracture in Brett's ankle, he started the second half. Our wide receiver, Anthony Morgan was carried off the field with an ankle injury.

In the fourth quarter, Sean Jones and I were both going after Vikings quarterback Warren Moon. Sean was aiming to hit him low, I was coming at him high. As I came around the corner, I jumped. Some people would say it was instinct, but I know God told me to jump. In the next instant, Sean and I collided. His helmet hit me right in the thigh. I felt something tear the instant he hit me, and I thought, *Oh, no, I tore my knee up.* That was bad enough—a knee injury can easily end a player's career—but thank God, my foot wasn't on the ground! If I hadn't jumped, if my foot had been planted on the ground when Sean's helmet hit me, I know the impact would have shattered my leg.

I hit the ground and I didn't get up; I knew my leg was hurt bad. I was yelling about my leg, and then I looked over at Sean, and he wasn't getting up either—just holding his head and rolling from side to side. Then he seemed to relax and lie still.

It was a blessing to me that the first person who came over to me was Cris Carter, a Christian player on the Vikings and a good friend. I was holding my leg and writhing on the ground, and he bent down and grabbed my shoulders and he said, "C'mon, Big Dog, you're gonna be okay! You know how the Lord does for you!"

Mike Holmgren came out on the field and looked down at Sean and me, very worried. He doesn't come out on the field when a guy is hurt unless it's pretty serious. He said, "Reggie, are you all right?"

"I'm gonna be all right," I said. "How's Sean?"

"Pepper and Doc are with him," he said. "They're having trouble getting him to wake up."

"Well, you forget about me right now. You just work on Sean." I was really afraid for Sean, and I started crying for him.

Some of my teammates, including Keith Jackson and Mark Ingram, came off the bench and stayed with me while the doctor and Pepper worked on Sean. I propped myself up a little so I could see what they were doing, and someone asked me if I needed help getting off the field. I said, "I'm not getting up until Sean gets up." Finally, they got Sean to come to, and they got him on his feet. When he got up, I got up. I walked off the field with my leg hurting bad.

I sat on the bench with an ice wrap on my leg, but Sean went back in and played out the quarter. A lot of people question how a player can go back onto the field just minutes after being unconscious with a probable concussion. Fact is, it's probably not very smart. But when a tough player like Sean is pumped up for a game, it's hard to keep him down. His engine is racing. He's running on adrenaline. He could probably lift a car over his head in the middle of the game—and as soon as the final gun sounds, he's done for. That's pretty much what happened to Sean.

He played out the quarter (we lost by a field goal); then he went into the locker room and sat down by his stall and all the air seemed to go out of him.

Our general manager, Ron Wolf, was there, plus several trainers and me. "Are you okay, Sean?" Ron asked him. Sean said, "I'm fine." But he didn't look fine. He sat kind of slumped and dazed. We all kept talking to him to make sure he was still alert.

Dr. McKenzie came over to him and said, "Sean? Sean? Can you hear me?" He couldn't hear nobody. He had passed out again. "Okay, Sean, we're getting you to the hospital," said the doc. "Get a gurney in here. Let's get him outta here now."

The paramedics came in and took Sean to the hospital, where he was diagnosed with a concussion. He doesn't remember much of that day. It's like he played the rest of the game on autopilot.

The next day, I got an MRI, and the doctor told me I had a deep thigh bruise and torn medial collateral ligaments (MCL) in my knee. I said to Dr. McKenzie and Coach Holmgren, "Man, God's gonna heal me again. He healed me last year, He's gonna heal me again."

Tuesday morning, Cris Carter called me and said, "God told me to call and pray for your knee, because He is planning to heal you, man." Other people called and let me know they were praying for me, all across the country. Nothing spectacular happened—no sensation of warmth or power or anything like that. But sometime during the day, I noticed that I could move that knee. The doctor checked it, and, just like my elbow, he could see that the ligaments were still torn, yet I was regaining near-normal use of my knee. Obviously, God honored the prayers of the people who had been praying for me all around the country. He healed me the second time, because He knew I was going to give Him all the credit and the praise.

"YOU AND YOUR HEALED KNEE"

Sean seemed to recover pretty well from his concussion. Brett spent most of the next week on crutches, or in the ice tub, or with the electric stimulator on his ankle. His ankle looked bad, all black and purple. He didn't practice at all until Friday, and then all he did was take half a dozen snaps. When he was working his ankle, our trainers had it taped so tight he was practically in a cast. Coach Holmgren had serious doubts about playing him in the Bears game on Sunday.

He was equally dubious about playing me, even though I assured him I could work my knee, no problem. He officially listed both Brett and me as 50–50 for Sunday, which I'm sure made the fans in Chicago real happy. Word even got out that Coach Holmgren had talked by phone with his old friend from their 49er days, Joe Montana, and rumors started flying about Joe coming out of retirement to sub for Brett. There wasn't anything to the rumors, though. Not much, anyway.

Coach didn't make a decision whether to play me or not until the very morning of the game. He wanted me at least to wear a knee brace. "But I don't need a knee brace!" I protested. "My knee's been healed!"

"Well," said Mike, "you and your healed knee will have to sit the game out if you don't wear that brace."

So I wore the brace.

Mike decided not to start me. It was only the third missed start of my career. But he put me in for the second series, and I stayed in for the rest of the game. I got four tackles, a pass deflection, and a shared sack—plus the satisfaction of watching the Bears try to steer the game away from my side. The press, the team, and the coaching staff all thought I had a great game. I thought I had a decent game, but I've had better. The knee didn't bother me, though. The newspaper accounts called it a "stretched" ligament, because the reporters couldn't believe I could play with a torn knee ligament—but torn is exactly what it was.

Brett, meanwhile, had one of the best games of his career, including a career-best of five touchdown passes. Brett also extended
his league-leading streak to 55 consecutive starts. He completed
25 of 33 for 336 yards and no interceptions—not bad for a guy
with a gimpy leg. He was hurting out there, no doubt about it.
You could see the pain in his face. You could see it in the fact that
he didn't do as much scrambling as usual, less play-action, no
rollouts. You could see how he favored that ankle a bit when he
walked back to the huddle. The only place you couldn't see it is
in the way those passes kept hitting their targets and the way those
points kept racking up. The game was so intense and emotional,
you didn't even notice how Brett had cut back his game plan to
compensate for his bad ankle.

In the end, we won it for the fans at Lambeau Field, 35–28. That
win left us tied with the Bears for the lead in the NFC Central at
6 and 4. It was a cold and windy day, but 60,000 fans stayed and
yelled to the very end. I was the last player off the field, and before
I left, I led the stadium in a round of cheers, holding my helmet
up over my head. It was too loud in that stadium for anyone to
hear, but I was yelling, "Thank You, Jesus! Thank You!" at the top
of my lungs. "Thank You for letting me play today!"

And that was the second time God had healed me.

"I WAS HOPING FOR
ANOTHER MIRACLE, BUT . . ."

One month after Sean and I collided, tearing my knee, I had an
even scarier injury. On December 3, the Packers led the Cincinnati
Bengals, 17–10, with 6:43 left to play. The Bengals had possession
of the ball, and I was in the trenches. The ball was snapped. I beat
the tackle off the ball, and as I was coming around the corner, he
tried to dive at me and cut me, so I jumped. When my foot planted,
I heard my hamstring pop. It just tore—and I mean it just tore
right off. The hamstring is a tendon in the hollow behind the knee,
which anchors the muscles of the rear thigh. When that hamstring
popped loose, my muscle bunched up in a big knot in the rear of
my upper leg—and it is still bunched up like that today. You can
put your hand to the back of my thigh and feel my upper legs and
you'll immediately see the difference between those two legs.

The instant I heard and felt that pop, I knew I was hurt bad. The pain was not excruciating—not like when I sprained my elbow or my knee—but I knew I was hobbled and weak in that leg. I grabbed my injured left leg and hopped on my right until the play was over—Bengals quarterback Jeff Blake threw a pass which was intercepted by LeRoy Butler—then I hit the ground and stayed there. Pepper and Doc McKenzie came out on the field and looked me over, then LeRoy and Sean helped me off the field.

At the bench, guys swarmed around me and said, "Reggie, what did you do?"

"Man," I said, holding my leg, "I tore something in here." I stayed on the bench most of the rest of the game, about 35 minutes. When I finally stood up, a lot of people started cheering. I stayed on the sidelines and watched the Packers beat the Bengals 24–10. I thought about guys I knew who had suffered a torn hamstring and who saw the end not only of a game or a season but a career. I was hoping it was just a bruise or something—but I knew a bruise didn't make a popping sound.

The Green Bay Packers were having their best season ever—maybe even a championship season. If the Packers went all the way to the Super Bowl, would I be a part of it all? Or would I be sitting on the bench for the rest of the season and the postseason, watching from the sidelines?

After the game, Dr. McKenzie gave me an MRI and confirmed that the hamstring was torn off. He was awestruck. He couldn't believe I was able to walk around on it.

"Doc," I said, "I want to be able to play this week."

He shook his head. "I don't think you'll be playing any football on that leg any time soon."

"I'm walking on it."

"Yeah," he replied, "but you shouldn't be. Most guys would need crutches to get around after an injury like that. A lot of guys, that's a career-ender. The muscle that provides most of the power for that leg is not even attached. You need surgery to reattach the hamstring so you'll have strength in that leg."

"I'm not gonna have surgery. I'm gonna play."

Doc shrugged. "We'll see, Reggie."

I went through that week determined that I was going to play. I got a lot of rest, and the leg seemed to get a little better each day. I kept riding the Stairmaster and stuff, just to be ready if I played.

Saturday night, the night before the game against Tampa Bay, I went out to run, but I didn't get far. The doctor was right: I had no strength in that leg. So I resigned myself to the fact that I just couldn't do it. I didn't dress out for the game against Tampa Bay, and that finally broke the streak—166 games. That was hard. I knew in my heart that if I had been out there, we would have found a way to win. Just being on the field, I could have made something happen for us. Instead, the Buccaneers beat us in a close game, 13–10—and I watched it all from the sidelines, churning with frustration.

I came into the facility on Monday and worked out, and the leg actually felt pretty good. Tuesday came around, and I said to the coaches, "Look, I want to go out and test my leg."

So I went out with one of the guys from the practice squad and tried some moves and some hits. I didn't have the strength or speed to get past the guy. I felt like Superman in a pit full of kryptonite, like Samson with a buzz-cut. I told our strength and conditioning coach, Kent Johnston, I needed to talk to Doc.

Dr. McKenzie came in and I told him, "Man, I gotta get this hamstring restrung, 'cause it's hurting and I'm crippled. Looks like I need that surgery."

He said, "Okay, you tell me when, Reggie."

"Let's do it Sunday," I said, "because I'm sure Mike won't want me to travel to New Orleans."

A short time later, Coach Holmgren found me in a real emotional state, because we were getting ready to hit the playoffs, and all I wanted in the world was to play. I worried that my being sidelined would psychologically wound the Packers as we headed down the stretch. I was real emotional about it. I cried about it. It really got to me. "Mike," I said, seeing him in the doorway, "I'm sorry, man."

"I know you're hurting, Reggie, but you don't have a thing in the world to be sorry about. Let's just get you patched up and ready to play next year."

"I really wanted to be there this year."

"Reggie, you've always given me all you had. I was hoping for another miracle, but . . ."

"I was too."

"Don't say anything to the guys yet," Mike added. "I want you to tell the team all at once—and I don't want this to get out to the press just yet."

"Well, I want to talk to Sean Jones and Keith Jackson about it," I said. "They're special to me. I'll talk to the rest of the team tomorrow."

Later that day, I talked to Sean and Keith. Both of them told me, "You can't cry when you tell the team, man."

"I might get a little emotional," I said.

"You've gotta make the guys believe they can win without you," they said. "You get up before the team and cry, they're not gonna believe you. You can't be emotional, standing up there. You've gotta make this team believe that they are good enough to win without you."

The next morning I came into the facility and the media had somehow gotten wind of my news. I didn't know how they got it. I was really mad at the press, because one reporter called Brett and said, "Did you hear about Reggie White? We understand he won't be playing in New Orleans and he's probably out for the rest of the season." I couldn't believe the reporters had so little respect that they would call and give my teammates disturbing news like that before I got a chance to talk to them myself.

We called a team meeting, and I got up and told the team I wasn't going to play. Like Sean and Keith told me, I really tried to let them know they could win without me. I believed it, and I wanted them to believe it. I wanted them to win the game in their minds, so that they could go out and win it on the field. "You guys gotta do it. That's what it boils down to. With or without Reggie White, this is a great team, and we're building a great tradition. This is the year of the Green Bay Packers."

I could see in their eyes that some of them were distraught about me. I wanted to be with these guys and encourage them. I stayed around the facility all day, and at one point, Mark Ingram came to me and said that his mom had called the previous night. She's a very strong believer, and Mark asked her, "Why would God allow Reggie to get hurt like this? You look at Reggie's situation, he gives his life to others, to the community, he does things that are right. Why would God allow the devil to overcome a man like this?"

Mark's mother had said to him, "Boy, the devil hasn't overcome Reggie White. Just you hold on. Something powerful is getting ready to happen. Just trust God. I don't know what it is, but God is getting ready to do something that's going to amaze all of us." I don't know how Mark's mother knew that, but she was right.

"I'M GONNA PLAY"

That night, I was playing with my kids, running around in the house and up and down the hall. As I was chasing and laughing with the kids, it hit me: *Hey, my leg feels pretty good!* I kept running and playing and flexing that leg, and I thought, *Could it be? Nah, I'm fooling myself!* But the more I ran on that leg, the better it felt. I told Sara about it and said, "I want to test this out." So I called Kent Johnston, our weight coach, who is a Christian. I said, "Kent, I've been running around the house, and my leg feels pretty good. Would you mind running over to the facility with me?"

Kent's from Texas, and he said, "Yeah, man, Ah'll go over theah with yuh!"

I picked Kent up and we stopped by Barry Rubin's house—he's the assistant weight coach and he had the keys—and then we went to the workout facility at the Don Hutson Center. I started going through my paces, doing workouts and stuff. I was running 30- and 40-yard sprints. I was hitting the sled. I was not getting quite the same speed and power I had before the injury, but I was a lot faster than the day before. Kent was watching me and getting more and more excited. "Praise God! Ah cain't believe it! Ah cain't believe it! God's getting ready to get the glory out of this, man!"

I couldn't believe how good I felt. "Man, this is incredible!" I said. "We gotta go over to Mike's house!" So we got in the car and rushed over to Mike Holmgren's house. The way Mike tells it, it was midnight or 3:00 in the morning or something when we got there, but it was really about 9:30. I won't say Mike exaggerates, but he sure loves to make a good story even better.

We walked up Mike Holmgren's front walk. Just as I raised my hand to knock on his door, the door flung open and there he was. He jumped and so did I. I'm like, "Hey!" And Mike's like, "Ohmigosh! Where did you come from?" It was just a coincidence that at the same instant I was about to knock, he was coming out to cut his Christmas lights. "Man, you scared me, Reggie," he said. "I thought you were Santa Claus."

I grinned and said, "With what I'm about to tell you, man, you may think I *am* Santa Claus!" So Kent and I told him all about the workout I just had, and I finished by saying, "So Coach, I want you to play me in New Orleans."

Mike took a deep breath, thinking it over. "Reggie," he said at last, "you know I want you to play, but I don't want you to do anything to damage your career."

"Mike," I said, "you've always been able to trust me to be straight with you. When I hurt my elbow and my knee, I asked you to trust me. Again, I'm asking you to trust me and believe me on this."

He said, "Okay, you're right, I trust you. I'll put you in the game—but we'll monitor you real close."

"Fine. You can monitor me—but if I'm hurting, I promise you same as I did the last time, I'll pull myself out of the game. You have my word."

"Okay," Mike said. He shook his head and laughed. "Man, how are we gonna explain this to the media?"

"Leave that to me," I said.

The next day, I went to the morning team meeting and sat in my usual place next to Sean Jones. I was grinning. I couldn't hold it in. Sean looked over at me, caught me grinning, and he started grinning back at me. "What?" he said.

"What what?" I said.

"What are you so happy about?"

"I'm just happy because I'm playing this week."

Sean exploded. "What!? Oh man! I can't believe this! I had a dream last night that you told me this, that we were sitting here like this and you told me you were going to play! I can't believe this! This is weird, man, this is almost spooky! Are you kidding me, man?"

"I'm not kidding you, Sean. I'm gonna play."

Later, we had a meeting of the defensive team. Larry Brooks, our defensive line coach, was drawing up plays on the board in the front of the meeting room. I was sitting there with the guys from the defensive squad, and not too far away was Matt LaBounty, my backup. As Larry drew up one play, he said, "And Reggie, you're gonna be right here, and Matt, you're gonna come around here like this—" And Matt did a take and shouted, "Reggie! Are you playing!"

"Yeah, I sure am!"

Matt shook his head incredulously and said, "Man, I've gotta start reading the Bible more! That clean living must be doing it for you!"

A MIRACULOUS WEEK

The next few days were absolutely amazing. I held a press conference and told the reporters that God had healed me and I was going to play in the New Orleans game. The next thing I knew, TV and radio stations in Wisconsin interrupted daytime talk shows and soap operas, announcing that I was going to play and admitting that it was nothing less than miraculous. Reporters went out on the streets and interviewed people, asking, "What do you think of Reggie White's announcement that he has been healed?"

I didn't see all the interviews, but a lot of friends, like my teammate Keith Jackson, told me they heard people saying, "You know, I was an atheist, but after what happened to Reggie White—? Hey, I think I need to go home and get straight with God!"

They ran interviews with me on ESPN and the network newscasts. They ran two clips side by side, one where I told a reporter, "I'm not going to play no more this year, but I know this team can win without me," and another where I said, "I don't know what happened, I can't explain it, but I know that God healed me and I'm gonna play this week."

For the most part, the media ran with it without being sarcastic or cynical about it. There were a few times where media guys interviewed doctors who claimed it had to have been a misdiagnosis or gave some other skeptical explanation, but for the most part, the press reported the healing pretty much the way it was.

The suggestion that Dr. McKenzie—an experienced and extremely qualified specialist in sports medicine—could have made a misdiagnosis of something so obvious as a torn hamstring was ludicrous, and it made me mad. Dr. McKenzie's a professional, and I was insulted on his behalf that some doctor who had never seen my MRI or felt the bunched-up muscle in my leg, would second-guess his diagnosis. Doc was still so convinced of his diagnosis, he wanted me to take the rest of the season off and have the surgery. I was the one who demanded I play. There will always be people who will judge a situation, even without looking at the evidence, in order to avoid having to believe in the reality and power of God. So I told the press on no uncertain terms, "Some of you guys don't want to believe God healed me. Well, He really did heal me, and if you got a problem with that, don't ask me no more questions."

Day by day, that amazing week just got more and more incredible. I got reports of people who had turned their lives over to the Lord after hearing about my healing on TV. I had an opportunity to lead a lady to the Lord over the phone after she called and asked me to pray for her son who had cancer. A lady who owned a restaurant really blessed me by telling me that when she first heard of my injury, she questioned God and asked why He would allow me to be hurt like that, and there seemed to be no healing as there had been the first two times. She finally concluded, "Well, maybe Reggie's faith is not as strong as it should be." The very next day, she was watching TV when the announcement of my healing came on—and it blew her mind! "It was almost like that happened for me," she said, "and I had to get in touch with you because you're the only person I trust." And she made a decision on the phone to give her life to Jesus.

Some people asked me, "With all the problems in Bosnia, the Middle East, and Somalia, with all the crime and starvation and suffering that goes on, why would God decide to stop by and do what He did for you?" I said, "God didn't do this for Reggie White; He did this for His people. God knew that I would honor Him with my healing. I didn't ask Him to heal me so I could play great, so I could come back and the Packers could go to the Super Bowl. I asked Him to heal me so that His name would be honored and so that people's lives would be impacted."

Of course, those miracles also helped me and the rest of the Green Bay Packers to express something other than love to the New Orleans Saints. Fact is, we whupped 'em, 34–23. One of my favorite memories of that game and the games that followed were the signs Packers fans displayed from the stands: WE BELIEVE. I don't think they were only saying they believed in Reggie White or the Green Bay Packers. I think they were expressing their belief in the God who healed me.

DOES YOUR WALK MATCH YOUR TALK?

It bothered me when, the day I had announced I was out for the year, the press began to write off the Packers' playoff chances. I took it personally, because I knew that our guys could do it. Whether or not I was on the field, I knew our top gun, Brett Favre, could provide the leadership and inspiration it takes to win, as he later did in the game against the Steelers, Christmas Eve of '95. In that game, he was hurt so bad he left the field vomiting blood, then came back in to throw the winning touchdown pass. Brett would have kept the Packers fired up whether I was on the field or not.

Even so, after God healed me, I saw a different kind of emotional charge firing up our team, a charge that came directly from God. The healing really elevated the play of our team—not because of my physical abilities; I really didn't play that many snaps. The boost came from the emotional, psychological, and spiritual fact that I was there, that I had my pads on, that God was at work in my life and in our team. The excitement that the healing generated really inspired our guys to keep their momentum going and their game focused.

These guys didn't have any room for skepticism, because they know what a hamstring injury is all about, they could see the MRI and feel the muscle in the back of my thigh with their own hands. The coaches and the trainers could see it too. Coach Holmgren knew it was a miracle, and he knows exactly where miracles come from. He told the press again and again that there is no other explanation for what happened to me, and he doesn't disguise the fact that he really enjoys having a defensive lineman on his team who has miracle healings happening to him every now and again. I'm not saying all the guys on the Green Bay Packers are born-again followers of Jesus Christ, but they all respect my faith, and I believe they would all acknowledge that something has happened in my life that has no natural explanation.

I haven't always gotten that kind of respect for my faith. When I first joined the Philadelphia Eagles, I was really tested and hazed by my teammates precisely because I was an outspoken Christian and a minister. They'd prod me in the locker room, try to get me to react, try to get me to lose my cool. They'd tape pictures from *Playboy* and *Penthouse* in my locker and wait for me to find them. They did a lot of things to test, tempt, and goad me into sinning or going back on my faith—nothing malicious, but a lot of things that were real annoying and frustrating. They wanted to see if my Christianity was just a show or if it was real. They hassled me so bad during my first few months in Philly, I was getting mad and discouraged.

Finally, I went to the pastor of the church I was going to and told him what was going on. "I don't know how much more of this stuff I can take," I said. "I tell you, I'm about to jump on a few of them next time it happens."

"You should feel complimented," my pastor replied.

"What do you mean?"

"These guys are trying to make you fall," he said, "but they really don't want to see you fall. Deep inside, something is crying in them, saying, 'Reggie, please stand for your faith. We're throwing everything we can at you because we want to see if you're serious about the things you say. We're gonna give you all we can give you, just to see how you react, just to see if your walk matches your talk. But we don't want you to fall. We want you to stand.' I assure you, Reggie, when they have problems, you'll be the first guy they come to for advice."

Over the next few weeks, I saw that my pastor was right. Every time those guys prodded me, they were watching me closely. They marveled that a guy who could play as aggressively as I did and who hit as hard as I did never used profanity on the field or in the locker room—even when they tried their best to make me mad. Soon the guys who had been on me the most began coming to me with their problems. They had gained a lot of respect for the way I lived and the way I responded under pressure. I was real glad I didn't give in to my feelings and start jumping on a few of them. God has given me a sense of humor, and I often used it to defuse what could have been explosive situations.

In time, I saw guys turning their lives over to the Lord. Fred Barnett ended up getting saved after I left Philadelphia; he and his wife called me and Sara and let us know we had a part in their coming to the Lord, and that was a real blessing to me. Mike Flores and his wife also called us and told us we played a part in their coming to the Lord.

I remember the talks I used to have in the locker room with Andre Waters. I used to get on him because I cared about him and I wanted him to live right, and he didn't like that. He'd say, "You can't judge me, Reggie." And I'd say, "I'm not judging you, 'Dre. You're judging yourself by the things you say. The things that come out of your mouth tell me what's in your heart."

After I left the Eagles, Andre came up to me at Jerome Brown's camp (a lot of Jerome's friends kept the camp going annually after Jerome died). 'Dre grabbed me and said, "Big Dog, I want you to know I got saved!" And I knew it was true, I could see it in his eyes. I was so excited for him; it just blessed my heart. He's really been growing as a tough, committed Christian. Since 'Dre joined the Arizona Cardinals, he's real close friends with a Christian teammate, Aeneas Williams.

Over time, I acquired many good Christian friends on that team—guys like Randall Cunningham, Keith Jackson, Keith Byars, Mike Quick, Britt Hager, Eric Allen, the kind of guys I would be willing to go to war with any day. These guys are my brothers, we're tight, we talk about all the issues going on in our lives. I remember praying with Eric when his wife was having trouble getting pregnant, and many months later, celebrating with them when their little boy was born.

We began holding Bible studies on Thursday nights and the night before each home game. A lot of guys from the team came to those studies—some consistently, some off and on over the years. Keith Jackson, Keith Byars, Roynell Young, Antone Davis, Herschel Walker, Calvin Williams, Randall and Felicity Cunningham, Cedric Brown, Mike and Stephanie Flores, Cris Carter, Alan Reid, Eric Bailey, Byron Evans, Todd Bell, Alonzo Johnson, Rob Sterling, Ron Moten, and Eric Allen. A lot of guys came who were not yet Christians but who had questions about life or God or the Bible and wanted to be where they could work through those questions in an accepting atmosphere.

For most of us on the team, these home Bible studies were our church. Most Sundays, we were busy playing football, so we did our worshiping in homes, like the early Christians did in the book of Acts. We sometimes even baptized guys in the big bathtub on the second floor of our condo in South Jersey. It was all real laid-back, and folks would show up in warm-up suits, T-shirts, shorts, and jeans, and we'd sit in chairs, on the sofa, or on the floor. We'd open our Bibles and notebooks and study God's Word, applying it to the everyday situations in our lives, to our marriages and other relationships, to our struggles and our problems, on the field and off. We'd rotate leadership of the group from person to person, and we'd usually meet for about an hour or so. Afterwards, we'd often have something to eat—maybe a mess of buffalo wings or a couple pizzas—and we'd keep talking for a while.

I've been fortunate to have found that kind of fellowship again in Green Bay with guys like Sean Jones. Keith Jackson, my good friend from my Eagle days, is my teammate on the Packers today—and as close as a brother.

Bryce Paup has also been a real close friend. I remember one time in '95, he came to me discouraged over his performance on the field, feeling there was too much going on in his mind. I understood exactly where he was coming from, because I had been going through a period of frustration myself. What got me through it was thinking about how David went through a time of frustration and fear, when people sought to take his life, and the Bible says that David began to encourage himself by remembering all the victories God had given him in the past. I shared that with Bryce and said, "You have to focus on the good things you have done on the field, on your accomplishments and your victories. You've been focusing only on what you've done wrong, on your mistakes, and that is self-defeating." He thought that over, began encouraging himself by thinking on his accomplishments and victories, and soon he was playing great. He thanked me, and he really elevated his game from that point on. Bryce plays for Buffalo now, and I miss him.

HITTING HARD FOR THE GLORY OF GOD

There's one question people ask me and other Christians in the NFL again and again: "How do you reconcile the love of Jesus with the violence of football? How do you reconcile being a Christian and being a football player?" I've always thought that was a strange question. I've never seen any conflict between Christianity and football. I don't see football as a violent sport; I see it as aggressive. And I see Christianity as an aggressive faith.

To a lot of people, being a Christian means being a wimpy, mild-mannered, nonconfrontational person. They read Matthew 5:5, "Blessed are the meek, for they shall inherit the earth," and get the wrong idea of what Christian "meekness" really is. In the original Greek language of the Bible, the word that's translated "meekness" doesn't mean weakness, it means *controlled aggression.* In order to be a Christian, living after the example of Christ, you have to be aggressive, just as Jesus was aggressive. He wasn't timid or weak; He was tough and aggressive, more tough and aggressive than anyone who ever played the game of football. The controlled, purposeful, targeted aggression of Jesus got Him nailed to a cross—and that ended up changing human history.

A Christian has to be aggressive in order to tell other people about Jesus, in order to lead other people to Christ, in order to get up and confront evil and racism, in order to love and forgive people who revile him and hurt him. True Christian love is not a fuzzy feeling in your heart; it's a tough, aggressive act, a decision to ignore the pain when people hurt you and to do good to them, even when they spit on you and call you names. True Christian courage is the decision to confront and denounce evil even when you know that evil men will nail you to the cross. Jesus was aggressive when He preached, when He cleansed the Temple, when He took on the religious leaders and the Roman leaders of His time, and I want to be as aggressive and relentless as He was. It takes a real man to be a Christian man. It takes a real woman to be a Christian woman.

Football is a very aggressive game, and I enjoy playing it. I never try to hurt anyone. I try to have fun. If I get the opportunity to hit a guy, I really hit him. That's the way the game is designed to be played, so I go out and play the game the way it's supposed to be played. To be a champion, you have to play like a champion. I want people to be able to say of Reggie White, "He's the toughest, most aggressive, most fearsome, most awesome guy who ever played the position"—not because I want to be bragged about, but because God lives in me, His power flows through me, and I want Him to get the credit and the glory for my greatness on the field.

I'll give you an example of how my roles as Christian and foot-ball player blend together. I often talk to guys on the field. I may sack a quarterback, then say, "God bless you," once I've got him on the ground. There've been times guys would curse me to my face on the field, and in response I'd say, "Jesus is coming soon, and I hope you're ready!" Instead of cursing them back, I choose to bless.

One time, when I was playing for Buddy Ryan with the Eagles, an offensive lineman for the Detroit Lions was cursing me on every scrimmage, and I kept telling him that Jesus is coming soon and I didn't think he was ready. Finally, I lined up against him and just before the ball was snapped, I snarled, "Here comes Jesus!" I don't think he was ready for that, because I rushed him and sent him back five yards with a single shove. After that, whenever Buddy wanted a big play out of me, he'd say, "Get out there and tell 'em Jesus is coming!"

One time, in a Packers-49ers game, I was lined up against 49ers offensive tackle Harris Barton. As Harris and I came together and lined up in the trenches, I asked him, "Have you accepted Jesus as your Savior?"

He said, "Reggie, I'm Jewish!"

I said, "So is Jesus." Then the ball was snapped and we went to war against each other.

Reconcile football and Christianity? Man, there's nothing to rec-oncile. Football is my job. I don't go out with the intent to kill nobody, to end nobody's career. I go out to play football and to win. My life on the field represents my life off the field. What I do on the field is very aggressive, and it takes a lot of physical and mental toughness to do it. Off the field, it's no different. I have to take that same "meekness," that *controlled aggression,* and I have to apply it off the field just as I apply it on the field. I have to be—*aggressively*—the husband I need to be, the father I need to be, the minister I need to be, the spokesman for racial healing and social justice I need to be. There's absolutely no division or inconsistency between my life as a football player and my life as a man and a minister in the "real world." Those aspects of my life are intermin-gled, seamlessly joined, and totally integrated.

And I believe the same can be said for Keith Jackson, Bryce Paup, Herschel Walker, Aeneas Williams, and all the other guys who live for Jesus and play the game to win. These guys have nothing to apologize for. We are blessed with gifts that give us a platform, a vehicle, for spreading the Word of God. Our pulpit, our sanctuary, is a football stadium on Sunday mornings, or a microphone thrust in our faces by some network sportscaster. As my friend Cedric Brown once said, "God hasn't called us to be wimps. What you do in life, you do with all your power. On the field, that means hitting hard—not being cheap shotters, but hitting hard. When you hit 'em, you hit them for the glory of God."

BLITZING THE 'HOOD

Back in the mid-1980s, God began to deal with me about my preaching. In the process of listening to what God was saying to me, I came to evaluate the preaching ministry I had been in since I was seventeen. I realized there was nothing wrong with what I was doing, but something was missing. Football had given me an expanded ministry and I was invited to speak at churches and rallies around the country—yet I came to realize that the majority of the people I preached to were white. Nothing wrong with that, per se. But I began to hear God saying to me, "I want to take the message back to your people."

I thought about that, and I wasn't crazy about the idea. I wasn't eager to take my wife and kids into communities that were being devastated with violence and drugs to do ministry in the streets. But the Lord reminded me of the words of Revelation 12:11: "And they overcame [the devil] by the blood of the Lamb and by the word of their testimony, and they did not love their lives to the death." God was saying to me, "Reggie, if you were to die, would you rather die in My will or out of My will?" I also came across the quote by Dr. Martin Luther King, "If you can't find a cause to die for, you've got nothing to live for." It was a challenge to me.

So, beginning in 1989 when I was in Philadelphia, we began doing street ministry. I invited some of my teammates to go down in the streets with me. Funny thing is, the guys I asked to go with me reacted the same way I initially did: They were scared! "Hey, man," they said, "that's the 'hood! You know, they've got gangs and guns and stuff there! They've got crime there! Are we gonna have our limousines and a police escort?"

I said, "No, man. What's more, we're gonna just go in there with our trucks. No Benzes, no Jags. We're going in there to talk about Jesus, not to tie our Gospel to material wealth or give the kids in the neighborhood a lot of false hope about getting a lot of material stuff." The guys agreed with that.

We chose a playground in South Philly, and I went to a house next to the playground and knocked on the door. A lady came to the door and said, "I recognize you."

"Yes ma'am, I'm Reggie White."

She saw the guys I had with me and said, "What are y'all doing?"

"Ma'am," I replied, "we'd like to use your electricity. God's called us to preach the Gospel to your neighbors."

She was so happy and pleased. "I've been praying for something like this to happen in the community."

It's always exciting to discover that God is using you as an answer to another person's prayers. So we used that as our base and we went there every Friday through the football season. We'd go there with a couple of flatbed trucks, some microphones and speakers and music, and maybe some pizza to hand out to people. It always generated excitement in the neighborhood. People wanted to know what we were doing there, and some wanted our autographs. But they all stayed to listen to what we had to say.

The next season, we found a playground in North Philly, and again we went to a house near the park and knocked on the door. A couple of ladies lived there, Miss Alice and Miss Elaine, and they reacted the same way the lady in South Philly had—so happy we were there.

We started our ministry by blitzing the neighborhood—me, Sara, our kids, Bruce Colley, Keith Jackson, and some other guys from the Eagles. We bought a stack of brooms at the market and we took those brooms into the 'hood and started sweeping up trash in the courtyards of the projects. We saw people looking out their windows and standing in doorways, looking at us like we were crazy. We told them, "We all got some brooms. Why don't y'all come out here and help us?"

At first, nobody moved. But we just kept sweeping and cleaning the sidewalks and the doorsteps, and pretty soon people from the neighborhood joined us and started helping us clean up. After that we preached and played music from the flatbeds, and people were real responsive because we had shown them we cared about them and their community.

During that time, I felt I was doing the work God gave me to do, yet I often came home and felt a void, like we hadn't really gotten the whole job done. I didn't know why I felt that way until a few years later, after I had gone to Green Bay. I was sitting in the house, thinking back over our street ministry, wondering why I felt we hadn't accomplished anything. Then I felt God saying to me, "Because you only gave them a message, but your message didn't have any substance. You didn't give them an opportunity to change their situation. You didn't help meet their needs." I began to realize that, even before Jesus proclaimed Himself as Lord and Savior, He always met people's needs. He fed the hungry crowds. He healed the sick.

Sara and I could sit in our big house with all our luxuries, thinking, *Man, sure glad we have it made in the shade.* But you know what? We couldn't enjoy the blessings that God had given us if we were not blessing other people. All around us, people are dying because their needs are not being met, and what do we offer them? A bunch of words. A bunch of promises. They want jobs, a decent living, a safe place to live; we give them words. They want hope, opportunity, security; we give them words.

Some years ago, I got together with Roosevelt Grier in San Diego. And Rosie said to me, "Reggie, you and I get up in front of people, and we tell people they need Jesus. But that's not enough. I had an opportunity to lead a kid to Jesus; he was about sixteen years old. After I led him to the Lord, this kid asked me a question. He said, 'Rosie, will you get me a job?' And you know, I had to get the kid a job. I couldn't lead him to the Lord and then say, 'Okay, kid, now you're on your own.'"

And that made me think: *Golly, we have missed it big-time! We have not met the needs of the people!* Jerry Upton, my minister in Knoxville, Tennessee, and I talked about it a whole lot, and God began to reveal things to me through Rosie, through Jerry, through other Christian athletes like Meadowlark Lemon who are involved in meeting people's needs.

I began to realize that if I wanted to be heard, I needed to invest in people's lives—not by handing out money but by setting their feet on the first rung of the ladder and showing them how to climb the rest of the way themselves. Of course, it would take resources to get folks on that first rung. Most smaller, black churches don't have the resources to do that.

It was also during this time that I took a couple years off from preaching in churches. I realized that while I had been *gifted* to preach, I had not been adequately *prepared* to preach. I saw in the Scriptures that the disciples walked with Jesus for three years. He taught them and equipped them so that when He left them, they were able to invest in others what He had invested in them. They were able to preach with the power that comes from the Holy Spirit. So I began to sit under the teaching and authority of men who were spiritually more mature and who could mentor me in the Christian faith—men like Brett Fuller, a Washington, D.C., pastor who mentored me in Philly, and my pastor in Knoxville, Jerry Upton. God pulled me out of preaching for a while so I could work in church programs at the grassroots level.

It was during the time that I pulled back from preaching that I began to have a vision for black churches and white churches working together to reach the people of the inner city. If churches, black and white, could come together, start investing in people, creating opportunities for people, fighting for people, then people would feel the church cared, and they would respond and find complete healing—spiritual healing, economic healing, racial and relational healing—of their entire lives, body, soul, and spirit.

THE MOST OVERRATED PEOPLE IN AMERICA

I believe God has blessed me with physical ability so that I would have a larger platform to preach the gospel, impact the lives of people, and promote healing and reconciliation between the races. I believe it took the burning of an NFL star's church to bring the entire problem of church burnings out into the open. And it took the church burnings to focus the issue of racism in America— an issue that rises to the surface after a Rodney King or O. J. Simpson verdict but that we as a society try to push back down, bury, and deny. God has given me the gift of greatness on the football field in order to extend the reach of my voice when I speak prophetically to the nation.

A lot of people look at athletes as role models. I try to live in constant awareness of that responsibility. I try to live a certain way, in the hope that my life might have some effect on other lives. But I also try to keep it all in perspective. Football has made me a celebrity, and I accept that—but I don't glory in that for my own ego-enlargement. I understand and continually remind myself of something that I think a lot of celebrities forget: Celebrities don't deserve to be celebrities. Celebrities have not acquired godhood simply because they are idolized by the public. The fact is, celebrities—athletes, actors, authors, entertainers—are the most overrated people in America. People make heroes out of us and say that we are great. Most of us in the entertainment business (and let's face it, professional sports is nothing more or less than entertainment) do not use our celebrity status wisely or well. We do not use it for the benefit of others. In fact, many of us end up being killed by our celebrity status—by the money, power, sex, and drugs it can bring our way.

As celebrities, we have achieved a status we don't deserve—but since God has allowed me to achieve it, I will use that platform to tell people that God isn't going to let Reggie White into heaven because of who he is but because of the change in Reggie White's heart; to tell people that God has a plan for lifting up people and for healing the division between the races. Every person in the world, every homeless derelict on every sewer grate and park bench in America, every criminal on death row, every person working to feed a family on minimum wage, is as important in God's eyes as the football stars and talk show hosts and movie stars that the public praises and follows. When I face the final judgment, God isn't going to ask me how many Pro Bowls I played in or ask me to recite my stats. He's going to ask me if I knew Jesus, and if I helped to bind up the wounds of people.

I take my position in the public eye very seriously. I have lost money, given up honors and awards, and refused to endorse products because I felt that linking my name to a certain product might hinder the message that God wants to send through me. For example, I took myself out of consideration for the honor of NFL Lineman of the Year because it was sponsored by a brewing company.

Even though I could have directed the $25,000 award to a charity of my choosing, I felt I would be sending the wrong signal to young people about drinking. In taking such a stand, I am not passing judgment on those who sell or drink beer. I just happen to know that alcohol kills more people every year than cocaine or any other drug. I happen to know that while beer companies say they want people to "drink responsibly," a guy who's had a few brews in him doesn't have a clue what he's doing when he gets behind the wheel of a car. It is the very nature of alcohol to take away your ability to act responsibly, so that the phrase "drink responsibly" becomes a contradiction in terms. I simply cannot link my name with that.

Our nation cries out for role models, yet we keep making role models out of the rebels, the self-centered, the self-destructive, the outrageous, the promiscuous. I've heard some athletes say, "I don't want to be a role model. I just want to be myself."

Celebrity status does not allow us to choose whether or not we will be role models. A celebrity, simply by being a celebrity, is automatically a role model. Like it or not, you can't escape it. All you can choose is whether to use it wisely, for the benefit of people, or selfishly, to the detriment of people. Unfortunately, all too many role models are teaching young Americans the "glories" and the "glamour" of living on the edge, ending up dead or in drug rehab, being convicted of rape, being stopped for drunk driving, or contracting AIDS because of a promiscuous lifestyle.

The media has a lot of responsibility for the creation of the "heroes" of our times. The media has a lot to do with shaping the values and ideals of our culture and our young people. The media glorifies the vulgarities and obscenities and outrageousness of some sports celebrities, while ignoring the contributions that are being made by a David Robinson, a Boomer Esiason, or an A. C. Green. This fact was made powerfully clear to me early in my career.

It was 1986, and the Eagles had just played a big game at Soldier Field in Chicago, a 13–10 overtime loss. That game was especially important because it represented the return of Buddy Ryan—former Bears defensive coordinator—to Chicago as the head coach of an opposing team. After that game, the locker room was absolutely crawling with reporters. They interviewed everybody in the locker room, including me. A dozen sportswriters crowded around me, shoving those little tape recorders in my face. I began to give Jesus the credit for my play—and instantly, as if on a signal, as if it had been planned in advance, I heard a dozen tape recorders click off, and the reporters all turned to walk away.

"Looks like I scared y'all off," I growled at them. That made me mad. I didn't care about them walking away from Reggie White, but God had given me a platform from which to speak, and they were yanking the props right out from under that platform. I wasn't the star in those days that I later became—but very soon, it became clear that the sportswriters needed me a lot more than I needed them. I let it be known that if a reporter left out the things I had to say about Jesus, I wouldn't talk to him any more. If they could write all day long about other players cursing, drinking, gambling, getting women pregnant, getting arrested, getting suspended from games and all, they could save at least a few column inches in their paper for the name of Jesus and for positive values and role models.

The NFL itself has also had a lot to do with presenting the wrong kind of role models. I believe the league thinks it serves the economic interests of football to have the game presented as a mean, violent contest in which there is no place for Christian conduct and Christian values. I think there are people running the league who are embarrassed by the fact that Christian football players pray together. In the locker room before the game, we huddle together and ask God *not* for victory on the field but for a good game, a clean game, for God's protection over the players of both sides. We finish by saying the Lord's Prayer together. After the game, a lot of us from both sides will meet together at mid-field, embrace each other, and pray together.

For some reason in 1991, the NFL tried to keep us from coming together in prayer after the games. The league issued a rule prohibiting players from lingering on the field after games; since there had never been fights or other problems after the games, the only thing a lot of us could figure out was that the league thought that having football players being open about their faith and their love for God and one another was not good for the image of the game. Whatever the league's reasons for that rule, Keith Byars, Keith Jackson, and a lot of us players openly chose to defy it because it was wrong, it was stupid, it was discriminatory, and we couldn't abide by it. The league eventually had to back down.

I'm not saying Christian athletes should be put on a pedestal or idolized. I would much rather see myself and other Christian role models presented as we truly are, with our flaws and problems and temptations. I would much rather have people understand that celebrities are nothing more or less than normal human beings who have gained an abnormal measure of public exposure. I would much rather see Christian athletes presented as people who sometimes fall but who pick themselves up. When people are given illusions to believe in about Christian celebrities, those illusions can lead to disillusionment.

I remember one time when a Christian friend of mine, a great football player, came out and took a public stand along with a number of other Christian athletes for sexual purity. Some time later, this athlete made a tragic moral error and got a young lady pregnant. I truly believe that this guy was sincere when he took that public stand and fully intended to keep himself morally pure. In the heat of the moment, he did something that, as a Christian, he soon came to regret. When his sin became a public scandal, he was condemned by a lot of Christians. I don't believe he should have been condemned. He should have been given a chance to be forgiven and restored. The condemnation he received hurt him greatly, both emotionally and spiritually.

I have talked to this athlete, and though he does not plan to marry the young lady, he is behaving responsibly toward her and the baby. He is providing for them like a man. I believe he has repented and is trying to live right, the way God wants him to. People need to understand that putting on a football uniform doesn't make anybody a Superman. Even celebrities need love, acceptance, and forgiveness from time to time.

HOW TO HAVE A MIRACLE

I have seen miracle after miracle in the trenches—not just the miracle of being able to play with an injured elbow, knee, or hamstring. I have seen far greater miracles than these. The greatest miracle of all is the miracle of a changed life, the miracle of guys who used to curse with every other word, who used to abuse alcohol and drugs, who used to treat women as if they were only toys for their own pleasure, suddenly having their lives completely transformed and cleansed. I believe a miracle always begins with prayer. I learned this fact at an early age, even before I became a Christian. Not surprisingly, I learned this lesson while I was involved in competitive sports.

I was ten years old. Though I had played football in the Dixie Youth League, I was afraid of being hurt, of being hit too hard by the older guys who were bigger and tougher than I was. So I joined a baseball league, figuring I was a lot less likely to get tackled and hurt on a baseball diamond than on a football field. One time, we played against a team with a real good pitcher. I mean, that kid had a fastball that wouldn't quit, and I could never get a hit off him. I came up to bat late in the game with two, maybe three guys on base. I remember the pitcher intentionally walking the batter ahead of me, saying that I was going to be an "easy out."

Understand, I didn't believe God answers the prayers of children. No one had ever taught me that God answers only grown-up prayers; it was just a mindset I had. Even so, I figured there was no way I was going to hit the next pitch without some sort of outside help—so I prayed: *God, if You answer the prayers of children, help me hit a home run—please.* I stepped into the batter's box and raised my bat. First two balls hummed right over the plate—strike one, strike two. I thought, *Well, I guess God answers only the prayers of grown-ups.*

The pitcher zipped the third pitch and I connected. I opened my eyes and, man, that ball was gone! I mean, I hit it far. I was so shocked, I sprinted around the bases because I didn't know if it was a home run or not! Then I heard the coach holler, "Slow down, White! You hit a home run!" Some of the guys who went to get the ball came back and told me, dead serious, that the ball dug a hole in the ground where it hit. I knew that a ten-year-old kid couldn't hit a ball like that by himself. That's when I knew that it must have been God. Three years later, at age thirteen, I turned my life over to Jesus Christ.

Now, why would God give ten-year-old Reggie White a home run? Did He like me more than the kid who threw the pitch? No way. God doesn't play favorites. Prayer precedes miracles.

I'm not saying God is a genie in the bottle who exists to do our bidding and perform miracles at our command. God is God, and He will demonstrate or withhold His power according to His plan and His timetable, not ours. He doesn't exist to do our will; we exist to do His.

But there is a very simple, obvious principle involved in the realm of miracles: You don't get if you don't ask. There have been miracles that happened to me that I didn't ask for—but somebody did. When God healed my sprained elbow, it wasn't because of my prayers, because I didn't think God was going to heal me. Other people prayed, and God responded to their prayers in a mighty way.

God doesn't always answer prayer in the way we want or expect. He doesn't always answer according to our schedule. Sometimes we think His watch is slow, when ours is actually running way fast. There have been times I've prayed for selfish things, and God has said "No" to those prayers—and ultimately, I was always glad that He did. There have been times I've prayed, and I just got so frustrated because I thought, *Man, I must be doing something wrong, because God isn't paying any attention to me.* I later found out He was listening, He was active, He was answering my prayer—but first He wanted to teach me something through the waiting time. Sometimes prayer is just a matter of persistence; God wants to know that we are dedicated to seeking Him over the long haul.

I think sometimes we misunderstand prayer. We treat prayer as a ritual. Or we treat it as a chore. Or we think prayer is only about talking to God—"Lord, you need to listen to what I say, now!"—and we forget to listen to God. Some of my best times alone with God in prayer have been times spent not on my knees, but in an easy chair or flat on my back, with no agenda, no list of "gimmes" or "I-wants." Sometimes I fall asleep just basking in the presence of God, absorbing His love, saying nothing, asking for nothing. I think God wants us to relax in His presence and enjoy fellowshipping with Him. I think God sometimes wants us just to sit down, shut up, and listen—not just with our minds but with our feelings.

Oh, there are times when we need to get on our knees before God—but the Bible talks a lot about the men and women of faith who just prostrated themselves before Him. Why shouldn't we do the same? Why shouldn't we sit down, lie down in the grass, take a walk by the lake in the presence of God? When we talk to God and listen to Him and meditate on Him, why shouldn't we relax? What's to stop us from praying in our cars or at a football game or while we're hugging our children?

Prayer should be two-way communication. We shouldn't only broadcast, we should receive as well. When we read the Bible, when we meditate and pray, when we examine our circumstances, we should keep our minds tuned to hear God's voice, and keep listening for what He is saying to us. There have been times when God has spoken to me when I was just sitting, watching TV. I would be disturbed by what I saw on the screen, and I would realize this was God's Spirit in me, reacting to these events, speaking to me, revealing His will to me. For example, when I say that God spoke to me about how to heal the division between the races, I'm not saying He spoke to me at a single moment in time; rather, He spoke to me over a period of months or years, often through newspapers and television news broadcasts, making clear to me His perspective on the events that are going on around us, and focusing those events through the lens of His Word, the Bible.

One of the things God has opened my eyes to through the healings He has given me is that He is calling me to a ministry of healing. I have recently become involved in healing services where we have seen people healed of bad backs, cataracts, cancer, drug addiction, and emotional affliction. I personally know of one man we prayed for who was scheduled for cancer surgery, and even with the surgery was given only six months to live. The doctors put him on the table, opened him up, and found the cancer had dried up to a little spot. The doctors couldn't believe it. They said, "This guy's going to live," and he's alive and healthy today.

One lady we prayed for had cataracts. When we prayed for her eyes, she believed God had healed her. She wanted to get proof to show to others, so a few days later she went to the doctor to get her eyes checked. The doctor had already scheduled her for surgery a few days later, and wanted to know why she came to the office for an unscheduled visit. She said, "I want to get my eyes checked." He replied, "You already had your eyes checked. You have cataracts, and that's why we are doing surgery on you in a few days." She insisted, "Doctor, please just take one more look at my eyes." He did—and he was astonished. "I don't know what happened," he said, "but you don't have cataracts anymore." She replied, "I know exactly what happened. God healed me."

There is a story in the Bible about a man who was taken to Jesus for healing. You can read the story for yourself in Luke 5:17–26, but the gist of it is this: The man, who was paralyzed, was taken to Jesus by some friends of his. The crowd around Jesus was so great, the man's friends couldn't get close to Him. Finally, they took up some tiles and cut a hole in the roof of the house Jesus was in, and they lowered the paralyzed man down to Jesus. After the man was let down before Him, the first thing Jesus said was, "Man, your sins are forgiven you." The Pharisees, a group of religious enemies of Jesus, got mad at Him. They said, "Who does this guy Jesus think He is? Nobody can forgive sins except God!" Jesus asked them a question: "Which is easier, to say, 'Your sins are forgiven,' or, 'Be healed, get up and walk'? But just to show you that I have the power to heal this man's spiritual condition, I will deal with his physical condition as well." And the man got up and walked away.

It was a miracle of healing—of double healing in fact. The man's body was healed—but more important, his spirit was healed. His sins were forgiven—and that was by far the greater miracle. Physical healings don't last; people eventually die. My elbow and my knee and my hamstrings feel very good right now, but someday, according to the natural course of things, I'm going to die. But a spiritual healing is forever and ever. It lasts for an eternity. God wants to deal with our pain and our diseases. He wants to heal our spiritual ailments. He wants to work a great miracle in every human life.

When you look at the life of Jesus, you see that the reason Jesus healed people is that He had compassion for them. "He was moved with compassion for them, and healed their sick."[1] "So Jesus had compassion and touched their eyes. And immediately their eyes received sight."[2] When Jesus demonstrated compassion for people, that's when the physical and spiritual deliverance started.

God has been showing me that if you're going to pray for people, if you want to see lives changed and people healed, you must have compassion for them, you have to care truly, authentically for them.

That's the only way they're going to be healed, physically and spiritually.

When we pray, when we trust God, when we care about people, miracles happen. God's power intervenes on our behalf in a way that could never happen in a purely natural realm.

The time from the fall of 1994 through the end of 1995 was a time of miracles in my life—a time of a vivid and emotional demonstration of God's incredible power in my life and the lives of others. The year 1996 began with a different kind of demonstration of God's power—the power of God to bring about His will, to accomplish His purpose, even as we undergo a trial by fire.

Chapter 11

FIGHTING FIRE

A little after midnight, in the wee hours of the morning of a '96
NFC playoff game between the Packers and the 49ers, the phone
rang at the front desk of the San Francisco hotel where our team
was staying. A woman at the desk picked up the phone. The voice
on the phone spoke rapidly—so rapidly that the woman was not
sure what she heard. "Wait a minute," she said, "did you say—?"
The phone clicked in her ear.

The other night clerk at the counter asked, "What was that
about?"

"I'm not sure," said the woman. "It may have been some kind
of threat." She called hotel security, and the hotel security chief
called the room of our team's head of security, waking him up.
"I'm sorry to disturb you," the hotel employee said, "but we just
got a strange call here, and I thought you ought to know. Our
night clerk thinks the caller either said, 'Reggie White's church is
burning down,' or, 'Reggie White's church is going to be burned
down.' She tried to get the caller to repeat the message, but he
hung up."

Our security man thought for a few moments, then said, "Thank
you, but I'm sure it's just another prank call." A San Francisco
radio station had encouraged the 49ers fans to call our hotel and
bug us, and crazy calls had been coming in all day. This call
seemed to be just another of many, so our security man dismissed
it and went back to sleep.

Hours later, I awoke with nothing on my mind but football. That
day—Saturday, January 6, 1996—my fellow Packers and I beat the

defending Super Bowl champions in their own backyard, 27 to 17. It was one of the greatest, most thrilling days of my life. No one told me that day that a call had come in, threatening my church. Nor was I aware that a threatening letter had been circulated in the Knoxville area by a group called "Skinheads for White Justice."

Early Monday morning, January 8th, the threat was carried out. The brick-walled sanctuary was gutted by fire; additional fuel and a large number of Molotov cocktails were found in an unburned adjoining building. Racist graffiti was spray-painted on the walls and doors of the church. I first learned of it when I got back to Green Bay and picked up my phone messages. Skip Lackey of the *Knoxville News-Sentinel* had called, telling me that the church had been firebombed. I didn't call Skip back right away, because I wanted to make sure that the media in Knoxville and around the country would not just treat this as a sensational story. I wanted to know that the people who reported this story really cared about our church and about the division in this country. I had seen so many tragedies in our nation simply exploited in order to sell newspapers or to boost ratings. I didn't want to see the burning of our church exploited in the same way.

Until our church burned down, I had no idea that there had already been four churches torched in western Tennessee during the previous year, plus many other churches across the South. With a 400-member congregation and new, recently constructed facilities such as a radio station and a child-care center, our church was the largest black church to feel the fire and fury of the arsonist's torch. All of the previous church fires had either been buried in the back of the local papers or not covered at all. Because the Inner City Community Church was the church of an NFL star, and because the fire occurred immediately after our big playoff win in San Francisco and just days before the climactic game against the Cowboys, the event was magnified in the media far beyond what it would have been at practically any other time of the year.

Though I hurt for the people of our church, especially my friends Jerry and David Upton, I just knew that something good was going to come out of this horrible loss. The devil had tripped himself up by coming against our church like that. All the good things our church was doing had finally gotten the devil's attention—and he had decided to come mess with us. All things, even the burning of a church, work together for good to those who love and trust the Lord Jesus, and who are carrying out His purpose in the world.

A FIRESTORM OF HATE

Just a few days after our church burned, the night of January 11, 1996, two more black churches were torched in a single night— the Little Zion Baptist Church in Tishabee, Alabama, and the Mount Zoar Baptist Church in Boligee, Alabama. The wood-walled Little Zion Church, which had stood on a secluded hilltop since the days of slavery, was lit up around 9:30 P.M., and it burned so hot, it wilted the flowers among the headstones in the graveyard. The Mount Zoar Church, just eight miles away, was found burned to the ground the next morning.

Another black church in the area—the Mount Zion Baptist Church in Boligee, had burned to the ground just a few days before Christmas. Yet another, the Rising Star Baptist Church of Greensboro, later burned to the ground in June of '96—the day before an emotionally charged, racially divided election. The circumstances of all four church burnings are remarkably similar. The county where these four churches were located is 80 percent black. Just a week before the two churches burned down in January (just days before Martin Luther King, Jr., Day), two white men were sentenced to jail for severely vandalizing three other black churches in 1995. In February 1996, the black judge in the case was awakened when shotgun blasts were fired into his house; when he tried to phone the police, he found his phone lines had been cut.

Federal investigators are looking into similarities between the Alabama fires and a 1995 cluster of church burnings in western Tennessee. On the night of January 13, 1995—again, just before Dr. King's birthday—the Johnson Grove Baptist Church of Denmark, Tennessee and the Macedonia Missionary Baptist Church of Fruitvale, were burned to the ground. On December 30, the Salem Baptist Church of Fruitland also went up in flames in the middle of the night, just a few days before a planned celebration in Dr. King's memory. All were torched by fuel-fed fires and all were located within 12 miles of each other, in a rural area outside of Jackson, Tennessee.

Over Super Bowl weekend 1995, a man and his two buddies soaked their brains in beer, then went on a rampage, damaging two black churches with Molotov cocktails. All three men were white and the leader of the group blamed blacks for a number of personal and family problems. The two churches—Friendship Baptist Church in Columbia, Tennessee, and the Canaan African Methodist Episcopal (A.M.E.) Church in Mount Pleasant, Tennessee, were repaired by neighbors of the churches—mostly whites— who gave money and time in an act of caring and love to black church members.

Other churches in the western Tennessee cluster that may be related to observances of Dr. King's birthday or to racial motives include the January 31, 1995 fire at Mount Calvary Baptist Church in Bolivar and the May 15, 1996 fire at Mount Pleasant Baptist Church of Tigrett. The Tigrett church burned down at mid-day, and was so hot, it melted the vinyl siding on a house across the street. A few months earlier, when the church was observing Black History Month, someone spray-painted KKK RULES on the sidewalk near the church.

Investigators have noticed that the western Tennessee and northern Alabama fires all occur within a 200-mile region, which also includes two churches burned the same night in Kossuth, northern Mississippi, near the western Tennessee border, on June 17, 1996. In all, at least 15 black churches were burned in that cluster during in 1995 and '96, and most of these burnings were marked by similarities and circumstances that suggest racist motives.

Another arson cluster has emerged around I-95, the major north-south route along the eastern seaboard of the United States. In June 1995, two black South Carolina churches—the Mount Zion A.M.E. Church in Greeleyville and the Macedonia Baptist Church in Bloomville—were firebombed by men with clear ties to the Ku Klux Klan. Other churches along that route have also been torched, apparently by people with racial motives.

The Bloomville church has endured years of harassment from the KKK, which even held rallies in the field next to the church.

After the Greeleyville church was rebuilt, President Bill Clinton spoke at the dedication, and the church's pastor, Rev. Terrance Mackey, declared that those who set the fire "didn't burn down the church. They burned down the building. The church is in our hearts."

When I say that the devil himself has come against my church and these other churches, I don't mean that in any symbolic way. I mean that literally. Many churches that have been burned—including many white churches as well as black—have been targeted by satanists. The St. John Baptist Church in Dixiana, South Carolina—established in 1857 and one of the oldest African-American churches in America—has been repeatedly vandalized and desecrated in recent years. Satanic rituals, including grave-robbing, have been carried out in and around the church. Finally, on August 15, 1995, it was burned to the ground by white teenagers. The gates of hell will not prevail against St. John's, however. White and black neighbors have joined to raise money to rebuild the historic church.

These are just a few among many black churches that have disappeared along the I-95 corridor in North and South Carolina and Virginia.

In Louisiana, four churches were damaged by fire in one night, February 1, 1996, the first day of Black History Month. Those churches—Cypress Grove Baptist of Zachary, Sweet Home Baptist of East Baton Rouge Parish, St. Paul's Free Baptist of Baker, and Thomas Chapel Benevolent Society of Baker—all were burned within a single five-hour period, beginning at 1:30 A.M. Many other Louisiana churches have been hit, some in the middle of the night, some in broad daylight.

Many churches, which have never been torched, never even had a window broken, are paying the price by having their insurance rates raised. Pastors and church members pick up their telephones and hear ugly name-calling and threats. In some cases, homes of pastors and church members have been torched or vandalized. Black children attend Sunday school classes in fear, and can't sleep in their beds at night. A firestorm of hate has been unleashed in our land.

But hate doesn't have the last word.

THE WRONG-WAY INVESTIGATION

The news media has been quick to point out that church build-
ings have long been a favorite target of arsonists, and that more
white churches have burned than black (due to the fact that there
are many more white churches in America). And, of course, some
churches have burned down because of faulty wiring or because
a tall steeple is a great attractor of lightning. But the fact remains
that, in percentage terms, more black churches are being torched,
and a large number of those torchings were sparked by racial motives. Many other churches, both black and white, have been
burned by devil worshipers. Whether the motive is anti-black or
anti-Christian, it is the devil, inspiring hate and division, who has
lit the match. The devil is our enemy, and we as black Christians
and as white Christians must stand together. If anything ever happens to a white church, then I as a Christian black man want to
stand with my white brothers and sisters against the devil, just as
so many white brothers and sisters have stood with me.

I am not happy with the way these investigations have been
conducted. In the case of our own church, federal and local agents
have turned the investigation against our own congregation and
our own ministers, and they have stopped looking for suspects
outside the church. They have subpoenaed financial records of
our members, our pastors, our church, the Knoxville Community
Investment Corporation (the bank operated by our church), and
even people who have taken out loans from the bank. Though they
deny it, I know the government has investigated me, including
pulling my financial reports. They have strapped 11 of our pastors
and church members to lie-detectors. They have questioned more
than half our 400 members.

One of the worst things about this government investigation is
the way government agents have lied to our people and deprived
them of their rights. They "invite" people in for questioning, and
when our people ask, "Am I a suspect?" the government says,
"Oh, no, of course not! It's just a formality." Once the agents get
them in there, they proceed to grill our people, trying to trip them
up, asking questions that make it clear our people are being treated
as suspects. The whole purpose of these lies is to keep our people
from coming in with attorneys who will protect their rights. After

I saw what was going on, I asked an ATF agent why our people were being treated this way if they were not suspects. His reply: "Everybody we talk to is a suspect."

I understand that when you investigate a crime, you must check out all possibilities. You've got to question everyone and everything as you try to acquire clues and leads. If I was in authority, I would certainly try to see if anyone in the church had a motive to burn it down. But these investigators have taken it way too far, and I am personally offended by the fact that this investigation has proceeded that way.

Shortly after the fire occurred, I received a call from Vice President (and fellow Tennessean) Al Gore. He offered his condolences over the destruction of our church and pledged any help he could give me. I thanked him and thought that would be the end of it. But after the FBI and the Bureau of Alcohol, Tobacco, and Firearms began subjecting our people to such intense investigation, and refused to return my calls, I called the Vice President and voiced my concerns. Then I left for Hawaii to play in the Pro Bowl. When I returned from the Pro Bowl, I found three messages from investigators—apparently the V.P. has some pull with those guys!

Still, the arson investigators have not changed their approach to the case. Why have investigators spent so much time looking inside the church for suspects and hardly any time looking outside? Investigators point to a few signs that they say suggest an "inside job." For example, the burned building seemed to be locked, without signs of forced entry. Gas lines were found open inside the building, and investigators claim someone had to know exactly where to find them. True? Hardly.

Our church was not just black, it was interracial, with some white as well as black members, so one or more white arsonists could have brazenly entered our church during worship services and no one in the church would have thought the presence of white people unusual in any way. The fire took place during a late Sunday night to early Monday morning period, so the arsonist clearly could have hidden inside the church building after Sunday services, and would have had free run of the entire building after the church was empty and locked—plenty of time to locate gas

lines and open locked doors from the inside. So the government
theory just doesn't hold water.

The question these federal arson investigators have never adequately answered is this: What would be the church's motive for
burning down its own building? Investigators say a $500,000 in-
surance policy. Yet the church was vastly underinsured. We had
just invested large sums of money into a new daycare center, a
radio station, a new balcony, and other improvements. Why would
anyone in the church burn the building down immediately after
these improvements had been made? It doesn't make sense.

There is no way anyone could have possibly foreseen the incredible generosity of so many people in Wisconsin and across the
country to help us rebuild. Simple common sense tells you that if
a person is going to burn a building to turn a profit, he's not going
to do so on the wild speculation that hundreds of thousands of
dollars will miraculously roll in. He will leave nothing to chance,
and will make sure the structure is abundantly insured. Government agents cannot deny the simple fact that our church was ex-
posed to enormous uninsured losses, which completely discredits
their crazy theory of an inside job.

I don't know why the government is trying to pin this crime on
our people. I suspect that it may be part of an effort to do what
was done with the other church burnings at first—sweep it under
the rug and forget it. I have since learned that the ATF and the FBI
has begun treating the pastors and members of other churches the
same way. But I think ours was the first church to be so treated. I
feel it has come down to the point where it is personal between
us and them. If it hadn't been for the burning of our church, this
rash of fires would never have become public. I think the fact of
so many of these unsolved burnings makes these agencies look
bad—and when I have come out publicly and criticized these agencies for their mismanagement of the investigation, it makes them
look even worse. I know from things they have said to me that the
government agents are mad at us.

I can't say for sure that investigators have a racist motive for
investigating our people. But I do know that a couple of investigators were removed from our case for past participation in the infa-

mous "Good Old Boy Roundup," an unofficial gathering of federal agents with racist overtones. So we've clearly had guys (and may still have guys) on the investigation who may not have their hearts in the right place.

AN OUTPOURING OF LOVE

In June 1996, I was in Washington, D.C., with a number of black pastors. We met with Attorney General Janet Reno, Assistant Attorney General Deval Patrick, Treasury Secretary Robert Rubin, and others, sharing our concerns about the way these arsons were being investigated. All were somewhat responsive, but I left without confidence that much would ever be accomplished, because federal investigators were looking in completely the wrong direction. The one bright spot of that trip was that the Congress passed a law doubling the penalty for church arson to 20 years, and backing $10 million in loans to help the churches rebuild.

It was exciting, in the days and weeks following the burning of our church, to see the response of the people of Wisconsin and all around the country. I got calls from attorneys, businesspeople, and Packers fans who wanted to help raise money to rebuild the church. Businesses donated everything from money to lumber to greenery for landscaping. Churches sent youth groups and other volunteers to help us rebuild. Children from all over donated pennies, dimes, and quarters—and all those coins added up to a significant amount of money. People stopped us on the street or in restaurants, writing checks or pressing cash into our hands.

My fellow pastors, David and Jerry, and my wife, Sara, and I were continually, daily moved to tears by the incredible outpouring of love and help we received—most of it from white brothers and sisters in Wisconsin. These people were saying to us, "We want to walk with you, Reggie. We will not tolerate these church burnings. We want to stand with you and fight the spirit of racism alongside you." The most incredible experience of my life has been to see what God is doing through His people in Wisconsin.

One of the big questions that is always asked and which does not yet have an answer: Are these church burnings part of an organized conspiracy—or are they just a bunch of unrelated copycat crimes? There are indications that at least some of these fires are linked. It is interesting that a number of the arsonists who have been caught are young and not well educated, yet many of them have carried out very sophisticated, efficient fires. Some of them seem to know how to place flammable liquids for maximum effect, and how to make the fire spread quickly. It is hard to believe they have not somehow been "schooled" in how to set a fire—and that suggests the possibility of higher-ups and conspiracies.

But what if there is no conspiracy? What if these fires are actually a rash of unrelated hate crimes, the result of a pervasive climate of hatred? It's hard to say which is the scarier possibility.

GETTING OUR ATTENTION

Why does God allow His churches to burn? Why does He allow such suffering and loss? I believe it is because God is getting ready to do something great. All of these churches must have been doing something right for the devil to show up on their doorsteps. When the devil aimed his artillery at the Inner City Community Church in Knoxville, Tennessee, God could have said, "You can't touch that church. I will send My angels to Knoxville to fireproof that church." But God didn't do that. Instead, what happened was a lot like what happened to Job in the Old Testament. Just as God allowed the devil to afflict Job but not to kill him, just as God knew that Job would never curse God for his troubles, God said to Satan, "Go ahead, burn down the Inner City Church. Inner City ain't gonna curse Me, these other churches ain't gonna curse Me, so do your worst."

God had a plan in mind. God said to Himself, "I've got Reggie there in that church, and he's going to be all over the nation's TV sets when the devil lights that fire. I'm even gonna use football and Reggie White and a burning church to shine a light on what is wrong in the world. I'm gonna use these fires to bring about revival and restoration and healing among the people." And that's exactly what happened, and what is continuing to happen today.

Fire grabs our attention. I believe God has allowed these fires to burn in order to focus America's attention on the suffering and hatred that is ripping this country at the seams. The problem has been going on through slavery, through segregation, through the civil rights marches, through the riots and beatings, and now through these church burnings. God has been trying to get America's attention for a long time. Are we paying attention to God? Are our eyes and ears finally opened?

I believe there's a small percentage of people in America who want whites and blacks to fight against each other. They benefit financially and politically from the fighting. The devil is using a small minority of hate-filled people to keep this race war going on. We see it openly in the form of "race-baiting," where a white politician runs a commercial about affirmative action in which a white man is filling out a job application—and a black hand reaches out and snatches the white man's hand away. We see it in the news programs and tabloid talk shows which turn up the heat on issues of racial tension, trying to get blacks and whites to argue with each other and blame each other in order to generate excitement and pump up the ratings.

Some politicians and people in the media have painted a black face on many of America's problems, and this has made a lot of white people mad at us blacks. Take, for example, the welfare problem—and let's face it, welfare is a problem. It destroys initiative, it tears families apart, it is a drag on the economy, it causes people to become addicted to government programs, it hinders the advancement of the very people it was intended to help. But having said all that, I have to point out that welfare is not a black problem. Some opinion leaders in America have painted a black face on welfare, but by far the majority of people on welfare are white.

People have put a black face on the unemployment problem, even though the majority of unemployed people in America are white. When companies downsize, those who are most affected are usually white. Affirmative action wears a black face, even though the people who benefit most from affirmative action are not blacks, but white women. The fact is, white families benefit as much or more from affirmative action, because these policies have stabilized employment and economic opportunity for the working women in those families. But you'll never hear that from politicians or from the media.

Blacks in America are hurt and angry because the laws of America seem to be rigged against us. Most people don't realize the U.S. Constitution was not written for black people or with all people in mind. Check it out: In Article I, Section 2, it says that representation is apportioned to each state by adding up "the whole Number of free Persons, including those bound to Service for a Term of Years [that's whites] and excluding Indians not taxed [that's Native Americans], three fifths of all other Persons [that's blacks]." As originally written and ratified, the U.S. Constitution deems me to be three-fifths of a human being.

And what about the Declaration of Independence? It wasn't written for black people. In that document, Thomas Jefferson wrote, "We hold these truths to be self-evident, that all men are created equal, that they are endowed by their Creator with certain inalienable Rights, that among these are Life, Liberty, and the pursuit of Happiness." Jefferson was a slave owner, and the irony is that he probably had a black bond-servant bring him the ink and quill pen on a silver tray so that he could write those words.

We look at those documents today, and we think, "How blind could they be? How could the founding fathers of this country say that a black man is only three-fifths of a man, a black woman only three-fifths of a woman? How could they say 'all men are created equal,' yet ignore the servants in their very own households?" Yet similar inequalities are built into our laws today. Our Constitution and our laws continue to be interpreted in ways that bring division between black and white Americans, for the profit and benefit of the powerful few.

We live in a country where 1 percent of the population controls 25 percent of the wealth—and a lot of that wealth is generated from the conflict between the races and from the inequalities in our laws, which benefit the few. It costs an average of $30,000 to keep one inmate in prison for one year. Multiply that times all the men and women in prison cells across America and you can see that there is a lot of money to be made from putting people in prison. When you get caught buying 5 grams of *crack* cocaine you can get twenty years in prison; but when you get caught with 500 grams of *powder* cocaine, you can get five years probation. Why? Because crack cocaine is a "black" drug, an inner city drug. Powder cocaine is a "white" drug, the drug of the suburbs and the young professional class. That's one of the reasons 55 percent of the people in jail are black males—the laws are designed to put more black men in prison than any other class. And I believe that a lot of black men are in prison for no reason.

What if we took the $30,000 we now spend keeping a guy in prison for a year and spent it instead on education and on providing opportunities. But we don't do that. Why? Because there are rich people and rich corporations getting even richer off of crime. I'm talking about those who make their living writing laws, prosecuting and convicting lawbreakers, defending lawbreakers and handling appeals, and imprisoning lawbreakers. Ultimately, young inner city men are really nothing more than a commodity to be bought and sold. They'll sell your drugs for you, buy liquor and pornography from you, and not only that, they'll break your laws and go to jail for you so that somebody can make the $30,000 a year it takes to keep an inmate in prison.

NOT LIBERAL, NOT CONSERVATIVE

The spirit of racism is doing its best to keep God out of America, because if everybody starts getting right with Him, it will affect the economy. People will stop buying and smoking cigarettes, stop using drugs, stop drinking alcohol, stop having promiscuous sex—and all of those activities are big money-makers for a powerful few in this country. You don't believe there's a profit to be made from sexual activity in this country? Well, let me tell you something: When Magic Johnson came out and announced he had the AIDS virus, condom sales went up 400 percent the next day. The people who make money off of condom sales call it "safe sex"— but they don't tell the kids that condoms fail about 15 to 25 percent of the time.

Nobody's preaching abstinence today because nobody's figured out how to get rich off of other people's abstinence—but there's plenty of money to be made from other people's sexual activity. There's pornography, a $10 billion a year industry. There's money to be made off of preventing sexually transmitted diseases (condoms), from treating sexually transmitted diseases, from aborting unwanted babies, from exploiting the aborted babies for fetal tissue research, from brokering and adopting out the few babies that are not aborted, and on and on. Much of the money spent on various aspects of people's sexual behavior is *tax* money—money you and I shell out to the government, money that is spent without our say-so!

Many of the destructive industries in America are actually targeted on certain groups of people. The illegal drug industry, the
tobacco industry, the alcohol industry all have ways of targeting
their products in such a way as to ensnare certain groups of people.
What's more, racism does not want us to be educated, because if
we get educated, we're going to find out how to defeat it. That's
why one of the major efforts of racism during slavery and segregation was to keep black people from learning to read. And the
institutional church was complicit in the effort to keep blacks
deprived and uneducated. That is what the spirit of racism has
been doing in America.

I want to make it clear that this is *not* a liberal/conservative,
Democrat/Republican thing. To be candid with you, I really don't
understand all this liberal/conservative, Democrat/Republican
stuff. To me, that's all just another division amongst us that
shouldn't be. People sometimes tell me, "Reggie, you talk like a
conservative," or, "Reggie, you talk like a liberal." If that's what
you want to call me, that's up to you. But I don't line up on
one political wing or another. Jesus wasn't conservative or liberal,
Republican or Democrat. He was the Son of God. Many Christians
would like to put Him on the right wing or the left wing, but He
won't stay put on one wing or the other.

Political divisions have driven us so far from the compassionate
heart of Jesus, it's ridiculous. The same spirit that has divided
white and black has also divided liberal and conservative, Democrat and Republican. It has divided the church of Jesus Christ into
denominations and factions. The liberal agenda, the conservative
agenda, these don't make no sense to me. What makes sense to
me is: What are people feeling, thinking, talking about? Where
are they hurting? What do they need? How can we make their
lives better? Now, that makes sense. That I can understand.

YOU CAN'T DESTROY THIS TEMPLE

When churches burn, it's time to get mad. "Reggie," you say,
"you don't mean that! Christians shouldn't get mad, should they?"
Well, shouldn't we? You better believe we should!

Jesus got mad one day, plaited up a whip, sat there and took his
time—then He went into the temple and whupped everybody's

behind! I tell you, He was mad! He was mad that they defiled His Father's house! I'm a Christian, I'm a preacher, and I get mad sometimes. All of us should get mad sometimes. To see the things going on around us and *not* get mad, well, that would be wrong! To see churches burning and not get mad would be stupid! To see people distraught and desperate and deprived of opportunity and not get mad would be uncaring and unChristian!

We *should* get mad—but when we get mad, we should act in character. We should get mad the way Jesus got mad. We should use our anger not to hurt and destroy people, but to liberate people and generate change. We should get mad at the things that anger God—injustice, division, hypocrisy, oppression, exploitation, and racism.

Racism inspired the slave trade of the Middle Passage, when Africans were brought in chains to the New World. Racism inspired the murder of 6 million Jews during the holocaust. Racism inspired the ethnic cleansing in Bosnia. Racism inspires the killing and raping and drug trafficking that goes on every day in our cities. Racism has enslaved us all—black people, white people, Asian people, Hispanics, Russians, Jews, Native Americans, all of us.

Racism is threatened by decent people who take a stand against it. The spirit of racism only acts bold around its own. Once, when I was a teenager, a friend and I were walking on the sidewalk of an all-black neighborhood in Chattanooga. Just then, a carload of white guys pulled up. They cranked down their window and yelled, "Hey, you niggers!" I turned around and looked those boys right in the eye. Instantly, they rolled their windows up, tromped on the gas, and beat it outta there. Racism is a coward. Racism will burn your church in the middle of the night, but then it runs and hides. It's time we treat racism like the coward it is. It's time we kick racism's tail.

Did you know that Jesus battled racism in His day? When Jesus opposed the Pharisees and the Saducees, they called Him the worst thing they could think of: "You are a Samaritan and have a demon."[1] That's like calling me a "nigger." Those people had a big problem with Samaritans, a race of people who had mingled with their own people, and they considered Samaritans the lowest of the low, the vilest of the vile, people who had demons in them instead of human souls. Perhaps Jesus looked like He was of mixed race, so in their racist hearts, they accused Him of being one of those despised Samaritans.

If Jesus had come along dressed like they were, cheating people and grasping money and acting superior like they did, they would have welcomed Him. But Jesus was from the ghetto, He was a poor man, and when He came to town, He came to fulfill the Scriptures which said,

> "The Spirit of the LORD is upon Me,
> Because He has anointed Me to preach the
>   gospel to the poor,
> He has sent Me to heal the brokenhearted,
> To proclaim liberty to the captives
> And recovery of sight to the blind,
> To set at liberty those who are oppressed;
> To proclaim the acceptable year of the LORD."[2]

Those are the words Jesus read at the synagogue in His own hometown—and when the guys with all the power and money heard it, they didn't like it one bit. They made their living by keeping people poor, brokenhearted, captive, blind, and oppressed. The last thing they wanted was for Jesus to come along and set the people free. The spirit of racism is a spirit of murder, and the Bible tells us the people became so mad they jumped up, laid hands on Him, and would have thrown Him off a cliff to His death—but it wasn't His time to die. (The story's in Luke 4—check it out.)

Why was the spirit of racism so mad at Jesus? Because racism is watching the money, y'all! Jesus met people's needs—and that messed with the economy! He fixed fish sandwiches for thousands of people—and that cut into the restaurant business. He healed people—and that made the doctors mad! Luke 8:43 tells about a woman who had been hemorrhaging for twelve years and had spent every cent she had on doctors—so you can bet they were not too happy when Jesus healed her condition. And when He started raising people from the dead? Oh, man! The funeral home people went ballistic! "Raising the dead, y'all!" they said. "How are we gonna plant 'em if Jesus don't let 'em stay dead? We gotta do something about this guy!"

So the people who had the power and the money in that society went to the Roman government, and they took care of Jesus, all right. They put Him on a cross and they figured they had pretty well solved their problem. But they had left something out of their calculations: Jesus is the Son of God, and what belongs to God cannot be destroyed.

Standing before the temple in Jerusalem, Jesus once said, "Destroy this temple, and in three days I will raise it up."[3] The people who heard this couldn't understand what He meant, since it had taken forty-six years to build the temple. "But," concludes John, "He was speaking of the temple of His body."[4] The evil, racist system of Jesus' day destroyed the temple of His body on a cross— and three days later, the temple of His body rose again. The evil, racist system of our own day is destroying our temples with Molotov cocktails and torches—but our temples will rise again too. The spirit of racism can't destroy our churches with fire any more than the spirit of racism could destroy Jesus with a cross and some nails. Racism can wound us, pierce us, burn us, and make us mad, but racism can't destroy us because we belong to God.

NOT A BLACK PROBLEM

A man once said to me, "So many black athletes strike it rich in professional sports, yet so few go back to help their people. Why is that?" There's a reason. When you have been stripped of your heritage, as black people have been, you can't fully appreciate all that has been done for you, and the responsibility you have toward others. When you have not been taught about your people who sacrificed for you, who fought for you, who walked the streets of Selma for you, who were lynched for you, who were assassinated for you, you can't even appreciate yourself. And if you can't appreciate yourself, you can't appreciate your people.

The system gives us one month out of the year—and it's the shortest month of the year. Black history should not be black history, it should be American history. Slavery and segregation are not situations that just happened to black people. White people had a part in enslaving black people, and they need to understand their history just as we need to understand ours. It is also important for us as Christians to see the role the church played, both its tragic participation in justifying slavery and its positive role in the abolition movement. If our white brothers are going to understand the way we feel, if they're going to look back and see what their people did to our people—and how to keep such a thing from ever happening again—then our white brothers deserve to learn about their history too.

Racism affects everybody, not just one group of people. It is not a black problem. It is an American problem.

If you ever go to Los Angeles, California, you should visit the Museum of Tolerance. It's a fascinating place, run by rabbis, and it's filled with exhibits showing hate crimes from the beginning of history right through to the present day. As you enter the museum, there are two doors. One is marked "Prejudiced," the other is marked "Not Prejudiced." If you stand and watch, you'll notice that practically everyone who goes into the Museum of Tolerance tries to enter through the "Not Prejudiced" door. Surprise! It's locked. You can't go through that door, because everybody has some kind of prejudice. I have mine, so do you.

God wants us to admit what we are. He wants us to go through the door marked "Prejudiced." Only by admitting the truth about ourselves can we begin to be free.

WHEN BROTHERS COME TOGETHER

How do we defeat this enemy called racism? God has given us two powerful weapons: *Unity* and *love*. If we say we love Jesus, then let's push aside our religious differences and our political differences. Let's start working together and standing up for one another.

Does that mean we're always going to get along? That we'll never get irritated and annoyed with one another? Hey, get real! We're gonna have conflicts, we're gonna disagree with each other—but despite all our various disagreements, we must agree on one thing: We are committed to each other, and we will love each other no matter what. The Bible says where two or more are gathered together, the Lord is in the midst of them. There's power in agreement. If we can't agree on the issue of spiritual gifts or on which version of the Bible to read or what color carpet to lay down in the sanctuary, that's okay. We can disagree on those things and still agree to stand together against racism. We can still remain totally committed to each other.

I believe the reason the church today has so little power is because we are not in agreement. The Bible says that, by God's power, one man can send a thousand enemies fleeing and two can send ten thousand fleeing.[5] So just imagine what hundreds and hundreds of believers could do, linked arm in arm, agreeing together. Man, that's power!

The world system can't stop racism, because the world system is infected with it. I don't believe in the world system. I believe in God's system. If we as believers come under God's rule, we can get this stuff corrected. Outside the kingdom of God, I have no answers. Within the kingdom of God, we can solve the problem. Here are some steps that we can take as Christians, both black and white, to move our nation toward racial healing:

1. Understand Each Other's Feelings

Black Americans and white Americans have very different feelings and perspectives on the history of slavery and segregation in America. They have gone through very different experiences, and it is hard for them to understand each other's feelings.

For years, many black Americans have been asking for *reparation*, which means making amends for an injury or an injustice. Blacks see that reparations have been made to Native Americans for the loss of their land and Japanese-Americans have been compensated for being placed in internment camps in World War II—but what have black Americans received to compensate them for slavery and segregation? Some whites would say that freed slaves already received reparation after the Civil War—forty acres and a mule. Other whites would say, "We're already paying billions in reparation right now. It's called welfare."

Fact is, while Congress established the Freedman's Bureau in 1865 to provide 40-acre plots to freed slaves and Gen. William T. Sherman issued Special Field Order 15, authorizing the Army to lend each freed slave a mule to work the farm, blacks never received these reparations. Abraham Lincoln was assassinated soon after signing this measure into law, and his successor, Andrew Johnson, rescinded the law. Black people have never forgotten that.

And what about welfare? That is not reparation. The welfare system has destroyed the integrity of poor families, black and white. Welfare does not make amends for past injustices; it perpetuates injustice by keeping poor people in economic bondage to a government bureaucracy.

Many white Americans become annoyed or angered at the suggestion that reparation is owed to black Americans. Some would say, "I didn't have anything to do with slavery or segregation. Why should I have to pay reparation for something I didn't do?" My white brother, my white sister, I'm not blaming you for something that happened before you were born. I don't want to fault you or make you feel guilty because you are white. I just ask you to understand our feelings—the feelings of a segment of America which has been owned, exploited, despised, and pushed aside.

When President Lincoln signed the Emancipation Proclamation and freed the slaves, we received our freedom—but we did not receive the opportunity to compete economically. The legacy of slavery continues to exert a powerful grip over the lives of all Americans today, white as well as black. My people were taken from their homeland against our will. Once here, we built this land through our free labor. We created an economy that another group of people benefited from. White America has inherited the riches of that economy; black America has inherited only devastation. Our dignity and heritage was stripped from us through slavery, and it is still being stripped from us today.

Claud Anderson, author of *Black Labor, White Wealth*, offers a startling analysis of the state of black America, 130 years after the end of slavery. Today, African-Americans control only 1 percent of the wealth in America; white America controls the other 99 percent. And the economic status of black Americans is getting worse, not better. About 35 percent of all blacks live below the poverty line. Black unemployment in 1964 was 10.8 percent; today, 14.6 percent. The percentage of blacks in prison in 1964 was 33.0 percent; today, 45.3 percent. What have we done about this growing problem of too many blacks in prison? Well, in 1996 we passed a bill to set aside $29 million more dollars to build more federal prisons.

Today, a large number of black Americans are still living in the same squalid conditions in the inner cities that we once endured on the plantations. So nothing has really changed. If you don't deal with history as it truly is, history will repeat itself sooner or later. It may take a different form the next time around, but it will repeat itself. In fact, it is already happening.

Jesus prophesied that a time would come when "nation shall rise against nation."[6] When you look up that word "nation" in the original Greek New Testament, it's the word *ethnos,* from which we get our word "ethnic." Jesus is talking about ethnic conflict: ethnos shall rise against ethnos. The spirit of racism will rule over a time of racial warfare. All the riots we see, the racial wars, the ethnic cleansing, and yes, the church burnings—all of this was foreseen by Jesus when He said that ethnos shall rise against ethnos.

So what is the solution? I believe in my heart that healing between the races must start with the church. The church should be an example to the nation and to the world. And we begin that process when black brothers and sisters come together with white brothers and sisters, and they begin to talk to each other, listen to each other, and understand each other. As we build bridges of understanding between the races, we move to the next step:

2. Invest in the Inner City

I'm not advocating that white people simply hand money over to black people and call it "reparations." Instead, I pray to see grassroots programs started that would create opportunities for people. I pray to see a great movement of people investing in the inner city, so that we can begin to reap a harvest of spiritual renewal and economic revitalization in the inner city. Investing in the inner city is not an *obligation;* it's an *opportunity.*

I recently heard about a 3,000-member mostly-white church in Florida that was entered in *The Guinness Book of World Records* because it raised $1.6 million in offerings on a Sunday morning. This church has a big, beautiful facility that looks like a college campus. Yet only three miles down the street from this church is a neighborhood that is beset by poverty, crime, and drug trafficking. I've heard many white ministers say, "Why don't black people come to my church?" Answer: You have to give them a reason to come to your church. If black people find out that your church cares about the community and wants to create opportunities for people, they will come.

A lot of whites and Jewish brethren truly care and truly want to help our community. They just don't know what to do because we haven't told them. Instead, we have pointed fingers of blame and accusation at them, saying, "You white folk just don't care about nobody." We argue with them and make them feel guilty, but we have never had a plan to offer them. Many of them are business-people with businesslike minds. You give them something that looks good, and they'll run with it.

One of the keys to black economic empowerment lies in blacks starting their own businesses, so that black money stays in the black community. While the overall unemployment rate in America is around 5 percent, black unemployment tops 34 percent nationwide, and in some cities it soars to over 43 percent. Where do college-educated blacks usually go after getting their degree? Almost 70 percent of them end up working at some level of govern-ment. Most of the rest end up working for white-owned corpora-tions. Only 2 percent end up owning their own businesses in their own communities. As an economic bloc, black America spends about $400 billion a year—yet only 5 percent of that money is spent in black businesses. Fully 95 percent leaves the black com-munity and goes into white-owned businesses. If we, as black people, would put our own money back into our own community, black America would be the equivalent of the seventh most power-ful nation in the world.

We need to build businesses in our community so that we can put more of our people to work. And to do that, we have to create lending institutions that will lend to black businesspeople who can't get funding from the traditional sources. We're not talking about giving anything away. We're talking about giving people an opportunity to achieve their goals. We're talking about holding people financially responsible and accountable.

That's what we are doing with the Knoxville Community Devel-opment Bank (or Knoxville Community Investment Corporation).

The bank has been up and running since 1994, it has made almost a million dollars in loans, and has not experienced a single default. It is a nondepository bank, meaning it does not offer checking and savings accounts, nor does it issue credit cards. In the first three months of operation, we made more loans to minority individuals than all the banks in Knoxville put together. These are mostly character loans rather than collateralized loans.

These loans are not handouts. Handouts teach dependence and laziness, not responsibility. Handouts are the product of racism and they rob you of your dignity. When someone gives you a handout, he is saying, "Here, take this. I'm gonna give you everything you need, just so you stay in your place. Don't bother getting educated. Don't try to better yourself. Just shut up and take the money." The welfare state has conditioned people to look for handouts. In fact, when our bank started up, some people came to the bank thinking we were giving money away. But that's not the way it works. The bank isn't here to hand out welfare checks. It's here to invest in people.

At the Knoxville Community Development Bank, applicants are monitored carefully. Hard work and a good idea are more important than a track record. Those who want startup capital for a business must submit a business plan—and that business plan has got to look good. If it doesn't look good, we don't just reject their application. Instead, applicants go to the bank's entrepreneur school, where they learn principles of running an effective business. Local business and civic leaders offer advice and instruction to our entrepreneur school students. After several weeks in entrepreneur school, applicants rewrite and resubmit their business plan, and are usually accepted on the next try.

We also have a micro-loan section which uses a new concept called "peer lending." This concept was pioneered by the Bank of Bangladesh which has given out over a billion dollars in loans in amounts ranging from a few hundred to a few thousand dollars—and with a repayment rate of almost 100 percent. People are placed in peer lending groups, much like small groups or cell groups, consisting of three or four families. The groups receive instruction in budgeting, business planning, and money management, and they review each other's business plan together. They vote on which plan is most viable, and the person with the best plan gets the first loan. He must meet his obligation to the bank before the next person in the group can get a loan. This concept uses principles of accountability and peer pressure to make sure loans get repaid.

We have also made a number of housing loans, which we expect conventional banks to purchase after they see how these inner-city mortgages perform. The Knoxville Community Development Bank has enabled a number of people to buy brand-new beautiful houses. We've helped get single mothers off welfare by helping them start businesses with modest startup costs—housecleaning, seamstress, computer transcribing, or home daycares. We have helped a number of inner-city businesses to survive temporary cash flow problems, and we helped save over 140 inner-city jobs in the first year.

But there is a problem: The bank is severely undercapitalized. We raised $1 million, but that's a drop in the bucket compared with the need. We want to expand this concept beyond Knoxville and create at least twenty community development banks in cities across the country. Though we are seeking grants from other government and private sources, we really need to see individuals and corporations putting major resources behind this concept. I can't think of a better way to invest in lives than through a community development bank, which teaches responsibility while generating hope. Our ultimate goal is for these banks to become self-sustaining.

I've had a lot of people pat me on the back and tell me what a great job I'm doing to help fund this bank out of my own pocket. I don't need that pat on the back. I need help. God has given me a powerful vision for changing lives, and He's given me a platform in the game of football to express this vision, but I don't have the resources to do it all myself. We hope to involve a number of athletes and entertainers in giving money and lending their reputations to this effort, but we also need the involvement of churches, businesses, and individuals. So I challenge you to become involved. Help us fund this and other community development banks. If you're serious about investing in people in the inner city, contact me at

> Urban Hope
> Community Development Bank
> P.O. Box 11475
> Green Bay, WI 54313

Let's talk about it.

In the Old Testament, God told Moses to take His people out of Egypt and send them to Canaan, to the promised land. The promised land was a good land, a rich land, a land of limitless possibilities. Let me tell you something: God is pointing us toward the promised land today. But we have allowed the spirit of racism to divide us, and in our conflict with one another, we have allowed the land to be torn up. Even so, it is a land with limitless possibilities. What is the promised land I see before us today? The inner cities. God has given us the promised land of the inner cities to possess, redeem, and restore. The question is, does God have some Joshuas and some Calebs who are willing to go into the inner cities and take that land?

3. Create Wholesome Entertainment

I'm very concerned about the mess that is available to our children on TV, in the movies, and in the music industry. My wife, Sara, and I have already begun to address the problem by launching a recording company, Big Doggie Records, which produces positive R&B and rap for predominantly (but not exclusively) young audiences.

In May 1996, Sara, the kids, and I completed shooting of a motion picture with a positive message for the entire family. The film, *Reggie's Prayer*, is directed by Paul Makellips, and though it is not based on my life, the title character is strongly based on my own personality. I portray a football player (no stretch there) who reaches the end of his career and is challenged to find ways to encourage other people to be champions in some aspect of their lives. My character moves to Oregon to become a teacher, and becomes attached to a troubled, rebellious boy. In the process of trying to reach this boy and turn his life around, my character confronts drug dealers and other dangers. That's all I'm going to tell you about it, except to say that it is not a religious movie, but it does have Christian principles embedded in the story—and it's a great movie, don't miss it.

Reggie's Prayer is the kind of venture there should be much more of in the Christian community—especially the black Christian community. Why not create our own movies, sitcoms, and dramas with positive messages? Why not create our own network or cable channel to provide counter-programming to the entertainment swamp that currently prevails in our culture? And what about computer software and video games? And theme parks? For several years now, I have been researching and developing a Christian theme park concept called Zoeland. My goal was to create an entertainment complex that is wholesome, which teaches Christian truth as it entertains, and which would generate income to support Christian ministries. After examining sites in various parts of the country, I have been rethinking this concept. We are now looking at the possibility of opening a number of smaller entertainment centers in malls around the country.

I believe the entertainment industry provides the next frontier for challenging this generation with a message of hope and unity, and for generating financial resources which can be re-invested in the inner city.

4. Create Safe Havens for People in Need

I'm deeply concerned about the abortion issue. From 1973, when abortion was legalized, to 1995, over 10 million black babies have been aborted. I believe abortion is a form of racism and geno-cide, and that pro-abortion forces view this procedure as a way of limiting the "breeding" of black people. There have been docu-mented instances where white women entering a clinic have been counseled about various options, including adoption, while black women have simply had an abortion consent form and a pen shoved into their hands. Abortion is also an enormously lucrative business, and it exploits our people for profit.

If we want this activity to stop, we have to pay to stop it. If we want our young women to stop getting abortions, we have to start our own clinics. Sara and I tried to do this several years ago when we founded Hope Palace, a crisis pregnancy facility, on the grounds of our Knoxville home. We could not get other Christian individuals and organizations to stand with us and support this home, and it folded after two years. Yet I continue to believe that this is a concept that we, as Christians who value the life of both the mother and the child, must get behind. I believe it is much more effective to create alternative, caring clinics than to block the entrances to abortion clinics. We need to stand by women who are going through a crisis pregnancy. We need to support them through childbirth, and as they raise their children. If we practice more compassion and less confrontation, I believe we will see a lot fewer abortions taking place in America.

I also have a lot of concern for gang members and people who are oppressed by a culture of drugs and violence in the inner city. I believe the church can have an incredible impact on our cities by providing safe havens—places where young people can go to escape the pressures and dangers of street life. Many gang members want to escape the gangs but they can't because they would get killed. If you can help young people find a way of escape and a place of security, you can reach them with the love of Jesus Christ. This is a wide-open door of opportunity for the church.

5. Dialogue Together

I believe God has allowed the churches to burn in order to drive us together so we can talk to each other, listen to each other, and learn about each other's ways. I would like to form a group of twelve people of different backgrounds, and sit down with them every two weeks and talk to them for an evening. In this group I might have a minister, some businesspeople, an athlete, a homeless person, a gang member, a pregnant teenager. I would like to hear from people of various ethnic backgrounds. I would like to include my friend Steve, who lives near our family and helps us out—a man who just delights in being a servant to other people. I would like to hear him explain what drives him to be such a humble servant.

I recently heard of a church group in northern California that wanted to establish a healing dialogue with a Native American tribe on a reservation in the foothills. They wanted to say, "We love you, and we are sorry that our forefathers took your land and your heritage from you." And they wanted their words to ring with authenticity. So what did they do? They *walked*. It was a three-day walk from the town to the Indian reservation, and it was a three-day walk back. A group of men took a week out of their schedules and made this trek on foot for the sake of reconciliation. They were warmly received by the Indians, and a dialogue of understanding has begun between these Christian men and these Native Americans.

This Christian men's group is now making plans to open similar healing dialogues with other racial communities, including the black inner city community in that area. These white Christian men are investing themselves, giving themselves, humbling themselves so that healing can come to their community.

6. Bring White and Black Churches Together

The most segregated hour in America is from 11 to noon on Sunday mornings. This has to end. We have to come together. If blacks and whites can't heal the racial division among their own churches, how can we ever hope to heal the divisions in our society? For the most part, black people never wanted to be separated from whites. Blacks have said, "We want to be equal to you. We want to be amongst you. We want you to be amongst us." That's why we fought segregation. It's been the same story in the church. When black Christians have said, "We want to be with you, we want to be your brothers," we heard many in the white church say, "We don't want you to be our brothers." That cuts us deeply.

But the Bible has given us a model of how the church is supposed to love—even across racial and ethnic lines. In Acts 2, three thousand people got saved and were added to the church in one day. Because of the unique placement of Jerusalem on the main highway connecting the Middle East with Greece, Rome, Asia Minor, Africa, and Arabia, we know that there were people of different ethnic backgrounds in the early church. It was a diverse group—yet they were of one accord, one mind, and they agreed on their love for each other. The rich went and sold their possessions to make sure that the needs of the poor people were met. They fellowshipped and prayed every day. They met in the temple and they went to one another's homes, meeting in small groups—what we call cell groups today. They cared for each other and got to know each other in a deep, committed way.

I believe that is the example we should follow today as black and white churches in America. In addition to our regular Sunday worship services, we could meet together in homes during the week, studying the Bible together, sharing needs and praying together, encouraging each other, getting to know each other. Once we have learned to know each other in cell groups within our own church, we could establish a relationship with a sister church from a different racial background, and we would merge black and white Christians from both churches together into new groups of caring fellowship.

Imagine! Black and white Christians getting together, sharing meals together, praying with one another, learning each other's hurts, feelings, and needs, learning to care for one another and love one another. Then imagine what that might lead to! The Baptist church might invite a Pentecostal pastor to speak from its pulpit—and vice versa! Black inner-city pastors might be invited to speak in suburban white churches—and vice versa! We might have so much fun, celebration, excitement, and joy together that we'd wonder how our churches ever got divided among different races and denominations in the first place!

A couple of months after our church was burned down, I had the privilege of speaking to a large group of white men and black men from a number of churches in Charlotte, North Carolina. In that city, there is a growing fellowship of believers building bridges of understanding, cooperation, and community investment between white Christians and black Christians. The story begins a number of years ago when a black woman named Barbara Brewton lost her husband to a shooting in a crime-ridden Charlotte 'hood known as Double Oaks—an area which the *New York Times* once listed as one of the five most violent 'hoods in America. Devastated and embittered by her loss, she moved her family away—but over the next few years, God began to work on her heart. As she grew closer to Jesus Christ, she felt God calling her to return to Double Oaks.

Barbara Brewton returned to Double Oaks and started a Friday night ministry for neighborhood children, completely on her own. She not only taught the neighborhood kids about Jesus, but she helped them learn reading and writing, and she pulled them off playgrounds and streetcorners whenever gunfire erupted—which

was fairly often. Soon, she was ministering not only to kids, but
to their parents, too. As a result, the Community Outreach Mission
Church was started—and Barbara Brewton was its pastor. They
met in a house, placing speakers in the windows so the music and
preaching could be heard out on the street. Drug dealers, gang
members, and addicts began showing up and getting saved.

The church was soon moved to a brick building which previ-
ously served many other functions—including a community center
and a house of ill repute. The building housed Sunday school
rooms, offices, and a sanctuary. The church grew so fast that worshipers would spill out onto the stairs and out onto the sidewalk.
The reason the church was attracting so many people was because
people could see it was a church that truly cared. The church was
improving the lives of children and adults in Double Oaks, plus
increasing the safety and security of the 'hood by getting the city
to barricade traffic on certain streets (which led to less drug traffic
and fewer drive-bys) and increase policing.

Meanwhile, way across town in the wealthy south end of Charlotte, another woman, Mary Lance Sisk, began to feel that God
was calling her to become involved with the pain of the inner city.
Mary Lance has an international ministry which has taken her all
over the world, teaching people how to pray. She is also very
involved in the affluent, mostly white, 1,700-member Forest Hill
Evangelical Presbyterian Church. She contacted Pastor Brewton-
Cameron (who had remarried by this time) and met her for lunch.
That meeting began a partnership that has grown into a beautiful
example of what God can do to bring ethnos and ethnos together.
Mary Lance and Pastor Brewton-Cameron, two women from different worlds, white and black, suburban and inner city, came together—and in the process, they brought their churches together
in an incredible sister church relationship.

One of the first projects they decided to do was to clean up the
Double Oaks area. A partnership was formed between the church,
the city, and civic groups. This partnership went into Double Oaks,
bought up run-down or burned-out houses from the slumlords,
renovated them, and sold them to responsible, carefully screened
low-income applicants on low-interest loans. The renovated section was renamed Genesis Park ("genesis," of course, means begin-

ning, and this place represented a new beginning for the old
'hood). Even many of the streets, which had become synonymous
with murder, drugs, and prostitution, got beautiful new names—
names like Brewton Drive, Rush Wind Drive, and Peaceful Way
Drive. Streets so mean that even police cars and ambulances refused to drive them suddenly became zones of hope and pride.

Seeing that the Community Outreach Church was fast out-
growing its facilities, Mary Lance Sisk of the Forest Hill Church
sparked the drive to help the bold church in the tough part of town
begin building a larger worship center. A committee was formed
that took the proposal to the church board of Forest Hill Church,
and the church board did an amazing thing. Even though the
church leadership had been wanting for some time to build a new
and expanded ministry facility for itself, these leaders responded
to God's call and made a decision to spearhead a drive to raise
$150,000 to give to this black sister church. Forest Hill was so
serious about this proposal that the church leaders called for a
special time called "40 Days of Fasting and Prayer," during which
members could sign up for a given day to fast and pray for God's
leading and blessing.

In March of 1996, I spoke at a men's rally at Forest Hill. As I
looked out at a sea of faces, white men, black men, from Forest
Hill, from Community Outreach, from many other area churches,
both white and black, my heart just soared. This is what it's all
about: people coming together in a bond of unity, erasing the
differences between them, embracing each other, praying together,
worshiping the same Lord. That night I talked a lot about football
(you better believe it), and I also talked about city ministry, racial
harmony, and churches in partnership together. The audience was
right there with me, blessing my message with so many shouts of
"Amen!" and "Uh-huh!" and "Say it, Reggie!" that I knew these
men were already living everything I had to say!

In May 1996, a banquet was held to kick off the fund-raising
drive, but they were too late! The $150,000 goal had already been
reached! The people responded and met the goal by word of mouth
alone. So the "kick-off" banquet became a *celebration* banquet.

Barbara Brewton-Cameron spoke at the banquet and the Lord
must have anointed her words, because by the end of that banquet,

the amount of pledges toward the goal had more than doubled, to about $320,000! Even more important than the money, however, was the fact that members of the two churches were visiting back and forth, getting involved in each other's ministries and worship services, sharing communion together, praying together, asking forgiveness for past prejudice, and building unity and understanding. A powerful two-way partnership was emerging as Forest Hill members began to learn more and more about community ministry in the inner city.

Hope has come to the city of Charlotte, North Carolina. Lives are being changed. Church ministries are being given new life, new energy, new excitement. The spirit of racism is being tarred and feathered and run out of town on a rail. It can happen in your church, your community as well. All it takes is one person—say, someone like you—who is willing to make himself or herself available to God.

FIGHTING FIRE WITH LOVE

On May 24, 1996—in fact, while this book was being written—the Pleasant Hill Baptist Church of East Howellsville, North Carolina, was seriously damaged by fire. A few days later, police arrested the arsonist—a 17-year-old white firefighter named Billy. He confessed to setting the fire in order to play the role of hero and gain publicity. A month later, the church's pastor, Rev. Vinston Rozier, invited Billy to the church, where he made a tearful public apology before the congregation. As Billy sat down and wept, the members of the church expressed their love and forgiveness toward him, and prayed for him. The boy's white Baptist pastor, Rev. Baxter Leigh, went with him to the service. Afterwards, he told the church, "I have been Billy's pastor his whole life, and you folks have done more for him tonight than I've ever done."

That is not the way things are done in this world. Most people would say, "Fight fire with fire." But this church chose God's way: "Fight fire with love." That is how we are choosing to fight fire at the Inner City Church in Knoxville. This is how we must fight fire in churches all across America. We must stand up for one another, agreeing with one another, getting to know one another, and erasing the divisions between brothers and sisters in Christ.

The devil has come against us—but he has already lost the war. We are fighting fire with love—and when love is our weapon, there ain't no way we can lose.

Chapter 12

HOW TO BE
A HERO

I want to be a hero.

Uh-huh, that's right. A *hero*.

Now, you may be thinking that this game has finally gone to my head. You may be saying, "Reggie White has really gone and lost it now. He is completely full of himself. His hat size is now bigger than the number on his jersey!"

No, sir. I don't mean that in any kind of arrogant way. Fact is, a hero is nothing more or less than a positive role model. Face it: There are a lot of role models around today, but not all of them are heroes. Fact is, an athlete who competes at the level I compete at, and who receives the media attention I receive, is going to be a role model and a celebrity. That is unavoidable. Question is, what am I going to do with the celebrity status and media attention that comes my way? Will I put it to positive use—or will I squander it? Whether or not I turn out to be a hero is a choice I have to make.

I'm very concerned about the lack of heroes and the glut of negative role models today—in sports, in entertainment, in politics. People today—and especially kids—don't seem to know the difference between a celebrity and a true hero. The old values and virtues that once defined a true hero in the public eye are no longer prized.

The media makes "heroes" out of those who become stars by their outrageousness, their wild lifestyles, their spectacular hedonism, their drug use, their womanizing, the fights they get into (on the field and off), their arrests for wife-beating and drunk driving, their foul mouths and obscene gestures, the cheapshotting and abuse they get away with. It's good to be bad, and the badder, the better! A whole generation of kids have their eyes glued to these "heroes," and they imitate their walk, their talk, the way they throw a football or slam-dunk a basketball, the way they strut their stuff, they way they flip off the camera and head-butt the referee. Ultimately, these kids end up imitating the way their "heroes" end up in jail or in rehab or infected with the AIDS virus.

A lot of people assume that sports builds character. From everything I've seen, especially in the realm of professional sports, I would have to say that sometimes sports builds character, sometimes it destroys character. It all depends on whether you are prepared enough and mature enough to handle the money, power, and adulation it brings. When you become successful in professional sports, you suddenly have a lot of people telling you how great you are—and your ego can swell to about a hundred times its natural size. You suddenly have a lot of money—and with that money comes more temptation and opportunity for self-destruction than you can imagine. You suddenly have a lot of power, and few people in their early twenties are mature enough to handle that power well.

MY HEROES

As I said earlier in this book, O. J. Simpson was a role model to me—big-time. When I was a boy, he inspired me with the love of the game I play today. Man, I admired all the amazing things O. J. used to do on the football field. Remember 1972, "the Year of the Running Back"? And the best running back who ever played the game was Buffalo's number 32, O. J. Simpson. He gained an NFL-leading 1,251 yards in 1972—and the very next year he bettered that to 2,003 yards, beating the ten-year-old record of Jim Brown.

But it wasn't just the way O. J. carried the ball that was inspirational to so many people, it was where he came from. He grew up in one of the worst slums in the country, and he was diagnosed with rickets and malnutrition when he was a year old. His folks couldn't afford proper braces for his legs, so they made braces for him out of wooden slats. His legs were so thin and bowed as a child, the other kids called him Pencil Pins. He grew up in the streets, led a gang, and saw a lot of friends die from drugs and street fights. And he overcame it all, becoming a football star at USC and in the NFL.

Today, a lot of people who grew up hero-worshiping the man are disillusioned and even embittered. Personally, I don't know if O. J. killed his wife or not. The jury said no, and the rest of us have to abide by that. It wounds me to think of the thousands of fans, young and old, who were hurt when this hero's image was tarnished by the charge of double murder. I know, because he was my hero too.

Of course, basketball was always a big part of my life, so one of my great heroes of the sport was Dr. J, Julius Erving. He did everything to perfection on the court, and I copied all his moves. O. J. and Dr. J were my heroes on the field and on the court. But I never really had an off-court hero—a sports hero who was an example outside the game, in terms of his character and his faith—until I met Bobby Jones.

I encountered this great NBA star (former '76er, later with the Denver Nuggets) at a Fellowship of Christian Athletes camp in North Carolina. Bobby showed me how important it is to be not only athletically great, but also to seek to be a great man of God. Bobby talked about the danger of allowing sports to become a religion all its own, with success as the only creed—and he admitted that he himself had once gotten sucked into that false religion. "Basketball," he said, "became my god." He had grown up with the idea that Christians had to be meek "doormats" for other people to walk on. For a long time he couldn't reconcile this view of Christianity with the tough demands of professional athletic competition. It was only when he realized the toughness and aggressiveness it takes to be a follower of Jesus Christ that he began to see that his faith and his life in the NBA really didn't conflict— they complemented each other. He saw how God could use him in a powerful way because of his greatness on the hardwood court.

That was a powerful inspiration to a young aspiring athlete named Reggie White.

The problem with being a role model—especially a Christian role model—is that people expect you to be perfect. People idolize you, and can't picture you as being the flawed, fallible person you are. If you get caught in a mistake, people don't say, "He blew that one, but we'll just cut him some slack, he's still okay with me." No, they condemn you. They go right from thinking you're perfect, you're their idol, to thinking, "Oh, man, this guy's a phony, a hypocrite, a fake. I knew he was too good to be true. All that talk about Jesus was just a put-on." There's no room for you to be just what you are—a real person who tries to follow Jesus, but who is still human and who still makes mistakes. Fact is, I think people can learn a lot more from a role model who falls down and picks himself up again than from a guy who tries to project an image of saintly perfection.

Most important of all, a Christian role model has to take people's eyes off himself and point toward the only true perfection there is, Jesus Christ. You have to say, "Don't idolize me. Don't worship me. I don't deserve it and I can't live up to it. I may disappoint you from time to time, but Jesus will never disappoint you." My daily prayer to God is that when people watch my performance on the field or my life off the field, they won't see Reggie White; my prayer is that they see my Jesus.

THE MAKING OF A HERO

Being a celebrity or being rich doesn't make you a hero. Being talented or attractive or famous doesn't make you a hero.

We can all be heroes. We can all be positive role models. I can. You can. Anybody can.

A hero to me is the pastor who labors in obscurity for thirty or forty years in a rural or inner-city church—only to see his church burned to the ground. He rallies his congregation, dries their tears, holds them together, and leads them in spreading forgiveness and love over the ashes of racism and hate. No one's going to put up a statue to him or put his picture in a Preachers' Hall of Fame, but he's a hero to me.

A hero to me is a doctor or nurse who works in an AIDS ward

or a children's cancer ward or a hospice home. Nobody sees what they do. Nobody cheers them or gives them awards or writes about their performance in the sports pages—but they are heroes to me, they are making a difference in people's lives.

A hero to me is a teacher who not only teaches kids about reading, writing, and 'rithmetic, but is also a counselor, conflict-resolver, social worker, mentor, and even a substitute parent for kids whose parents are out of the picture. Teachers get a lot of criticism from a lot of quarters these days, but there are some very good, dedicated, caring teachers who are making a lasting difference in the lives of kids, and those people are heroes to me.

A hero to me is a hard-working, loving parent. It's not easy being a parent today, whether married or single. It means taking a lot of time out to help kids with their homework, to go to parent-teacher meetings, to drive kids to music lessons and basketball camp and Little League. It means making financial sacrifices and teaching values and praying every day for your kids. Parents like that are heroes to me.

Everybody can be a hero. We all are surrounded by people, and we can be an influence, a positive role model, a hero to the people we come in contact with every day. What does it take to be a hero? Let me suggest a few ingredients:

1. Have a Mission in Life

If you don't have a cause, you'll never have an effect. You have to be a part of something bigger than yourself. I sincerely hope and pray that your cause, your mission, would be the cause of Jesus Christ, because there is no greater purpose in life than the purpose of serving Him. But if that's not where you are right now, then at least get involved in the cause of making life better for people. That will give your life a sense of purpose, a sense of direction, a focus, a goal. Instead of drifting through life, your life will count for something that will be bigger than you—and something that will outlive you. Instead of being part of the problem, you'll be part of the solution.

2. Dream Big Dreams

Don't limit your possibilities. Open your mind to the amazing, incredible things you could do with your life: Adopt a needy child or become a foster parent. Think of something you could do to contribute to the community—being a coach or a tutor to inner-city kids or running for school board or Congress or starting a program to provide jobs, counseling, training, recreation, or other opportunities for people. Dream up something you can do, some way you can contribute to making this world a better place.

3. Study Greatness, Seek Out Great Role Models, Surround Yourself with Great People Who Want to Be Heroes

Frankly, I don't like hanging around mediocrity. I don't want my mind to be affected by a "just good enough" attitude. When you are on a team with great people, or meeting in a study group or accountability group with people who want to be great, or in a company or a family unit that believes in seeking excellence, you soon find that everyone in the group is motivating and inspiring one another to work their hardest and be the best. Don't be around negative people.

I remember a game I played as an Eagle in November of 1991. We were in the fourth quarter of a game against the Bengals in the Vet, and Mike Golic batted a pass up into the air. I went for it and so did Eagles linebacker William Thomas. An instant after I snatched the ball out of the air for an interception, William crashed into me. Wasn't his fault. This is football and guys crash into each other. But the impact, as my leg was stretched out in full stride, sent me to the turf with a hyper-extended right knee. I hugged that ball, preserving the interception—but for a while there, I was in no condition to get back on my feet. Man, that knee hurt!

Trainers came out on the field and began checking me out, and the whole ballyard got strangely quiet. William stood over me, looking scared, saying, "Hey, Big Dog, I'm sorry, man!" Finally, I got up and walked off the field and the crowd cheered. I stayed out for a few snaps, and when I went back in, the knee hurt so bad I couldn't push off with that leg. But I had to play—not only because I wanted it so bad myself, but because I was motivated by the greatness and the intensity all around me. During that difficult year for the Eagles, I had seen so many guys play through so much pain that I was truly inspired by their example. Jimmy Mac had demonstrated incredible courage, playing hurt that year. And Jerome Brown had been almost superhuman.

I remember during one game that year, Jerome went down with his leg hurting real bad, and he wasn't getting up. So I went over to him and said, "Jerome, you better get up," and I put out my hand. He said, "Okay, Reggie," and he grabbed my hand and hauled himself up and kept playing. We did that for each other as a team. We inspired each other and kept each other going. It's tough to be a hero all by yourself. It helps to have a bunch of other heroes, prodding you, leading you, and inspiring you to go all the way. Whenever I look at my shelf and see the game ball they gave me after that Bengals game, I think of my fellow Eagles and how they inspired me.

4. Work Hard

There's no substitute for hard work. Very few people ever become successful working 9 to 5. Most people who excel at what they do, who become heroes in their professions, work ten, twelve, fourteen hours a day. Sara can vouch for that. I had to work hard to reach this level of play, and the older I get, the harder I have to work to stay at this level. If you want to be great, you have to do a great deal of work. God wants us to be heroes, to get the big job done, and that's why He says, "And whatever you do, do it heartily"— that is, with all your heart—"as to the Lord and not to men."[1] Whatever you do, do it as if your life depends on it. Look at every day and every year, identify the things you do well, and concentrate on doing those things better. A hero always does what he needs to do in order to be great year after year.

I believe in being the absolute best you can be at whatever you do. "Good enough" is never good enough. Constantly strive to improve. Don't just show up; be a champion. Whatever "game" you are playing—teaching, coaching, parenting, running a business, entertaining, preaching, whatever—make it a Super Bowl performance!

In my profession, working hard means spending several hours a day in the weight room and on the Stairmaster, not only during the season but in the off-season. In your chosen field, it may mean taking extra classes, putting in extra hours, going the extra mile, doing more reading, watching less TV. If your goal is to be a good parent, it means setting aside special times to be a hero to your kids.

It's all a matter of emotional intensity and mental resolve. In order to stay motivated to get something done, you've really gotta *want* it. Some people say they want to lose ten pounds or quit smoking or write that novel or get that promotion, but they never seem to get it done. Problem is, they want it but they don't want it bad enough. They don't have the emotional intensity and mental drive to motivate the hard work it takes to get there.

If you really want it—whatever "it" is—you'll get it done. If you don't get it done, then you don't really *want* it, you just *wish* you had it. And there's a big difference between wanting and wishing.

5. Take Personal Responsibility

Don't make excuses. Don't blame other people for your failures, your problems, your dumb mistakes. Say, "That was me, man," accept the blame, say you're sorry to anyone you hurt, and get on with it. Don't worry about how unfair things are. There's bad officiating in life, same as in football, and you have to accept the bad calls with the good, treat it as just another playing condition, and get on with the business of winning.

6. Stay Focused

The 1992 season was a tough one for me. We lost Jerome that year, and just before Christmas '92, my stepfather, Leonard Collier, was murdered. I was going into those games with a lot on my mind—but I had to handle the distractions, I had to stay focused on what I was there to do: win football games. I remember the game we played against the Giants just after Christmas, a little over a week after my stepdad's murder. I knew it was also probably the last game I would play in Veterans Stadium as a Philadelphia Eagle. We had won every one of our home games that season, but we knew that this season-clincher would be tough.

As I was in the locker room, preparing myself mentally and physically to go out and play that game, I was determined to stay loose and to block out everything but the game in front of me. As the trainers were taping my wrists, I got a black marker and wrote in big letters across the tape, STEPDAD. That became my focus: Winning that game as a tribute to his memory. My teammates and

I went out there and won that game, 20 to 10. I sacked Jeff Hostetler for my 14th of the year, got 3 solo tackles (making 53 for the season), and forced a fumble. Our defense held them to 40 net yards and no first downs in the entire first half.

You've gotta stay focused. If you're running a business, a program, a ministry, a church, you've got to stay focused on your objectives. You have to block out distractions and make sure you're achieving your purpose. If you're writing a book or preparing to run a marathon or trying to be a good parent or a good wife or husband, then you need to stay focused on those goals. Don't let anything get between you and your objective. Don't let anything tug you away or get you off on a detour. Focus like a laser beam.

7. Be Bold, Be Daring, Be Courageous

Someone once said, "Being brave is easy. You just gotta want something so much your life ain't important." Courage and boldness come from caring about people more than you care about your own safety, security, and comfort. Courage comes from having a cause to live for—and to die for. If you care enough about bringing the races together, healing division, saving the lives of children, improving the lives of the poor, stopping crime and hunger and teenage pregnancy, and serving Jesus Christ, then you don't worry so much about what other people might say about you or do to you.

Someone once said that if you're trying to decide between two equal choices, always choose the bolder path. Don't be reckless, of course, but don't play it *too* safe, either. Go for it, man!

Back in '56, the great Johnny Unitas was quarterbacking the Baltimore Colts in the first overtime game in history. They had gone into that game favored by 4 points, which meant that if the Colts lost or even if they beat the New York Giants by less than 4 points, the bettors would lose. The two teams were tied at 17 when regulation play ended. In overtime, Unitas drove his team to within field goal range and could have easily won the game by calling in a kicker. But he refused to settle for an easy three points. Instead, he set up a much riskier and bolder lateral-pass-and-handoff play. It worked, and the Colts ended up winning by six points in overtime.

Unitas was later asked why he went for the bolder touchdown

play instead of the easy field goal. His reply: "Are you kidding? I had a thousand bucks on that game with a four-point spread! I'm not going to blow that off with a lousy field goal!" Which is probably one of the reasons it's now illegal for players to bet on the games! The point is, if you want to win big, if you want to be a champion, you've got to take some calculated risks.

8. Be Persistent

Don't give up. Don't let anything or anyone stop you. Do what is right and do the work God has given you to do. Very few touchdowns are made with a single 99-yard pass. Most touchdowns come at the end of a ten- or fifteen-down drive made up of five-yard plays, three-yard plays, and even some lost yards. If you don't hang in there, you'll never get to cross the goal line and do the Lambeau leap!

A lot of games are won by sheer persistence. Call it toughness—the ability to absorb hits, to accept punishment, to take your licks and keep moving forward. Call it resiliency—the ability to bounce back and keep playing after you've had your faceguard pounded into the turf a dozen times. Whatever you call it, if you don't have it, you'll only be a wannabe, an almost-was. But if you've got it, man, you'll be a hero!

Persistence is the power to put a dismal first half behind you and to come back in the second half for a big win. I've seen enough games won by fourth-quarter comebacks to know the power of persistence. I remember our entire 1991 season with the Eagles being a season of bad breaks, early losses, and setbacks—followed by stunning, unexpected comebacks. That was the year Randall Cunningham was sidelined for an entire season in the first quarter of the season opener with a bad knee. That was the year the Eagles went through four starting quarterbacks, the year the sports reporters all counted us out after the first few games. It was also the year our entire battered, bloodied team played with incredible heart and persistence, so that our defense finished number one in the NFL against the rush, against the pass, and overall. That was the year we came back from being 3–5 losers to 10–6 finishers.

We capped that season off with an incredible comeback game against the Washington Redskins. By the end of the third quarter, we were not only scoreless, we had not even moved the ball closer than 37 yards to the goal line. It looked hopeless, and a few fans had already started walking out of the stadium in disgust. A lot of teams would have given up at that point—but we wanted to win, so we *stayed* to win and we *played* to win. As a result, the final fifteen minutes of the game were legendary. Our quarterback, Jeff Kemp, connected with 11 of his final 16 passes for 98 yards, and Roger Ruzek amazed a breathless Philadelphia crowd with a game-winning 38-yard field goal in the final seconds, winning it 24 to 22. That's the power of persistence.

If you are persistent, if you are dogged and relentless in the pursuit of your dreams, if you are the kind of person who doesn't let people or circumstances stop you, then you'll be a champion. Ain't nobody gonna stop you.

A HERO TO MY KIDS

One of the top goals of my life is to be a hero to my kids, Jeremy and Jecolia. Someday, when they are asked, "Who are your heroes?" I hope both of them say, "My mom and my dad!" I think I will have failed as a father and as a human being if they say anything else. And I don't want to fail. I want them always to look at Sara and me as the two great role models for their lives.

To be a hero to my kids, I need to build a strong relationship with them. I want Jeremy and Jecolia to feel that Sara and I are their best friends. Obviously, they are going to form friendships outside of our family, and they should, that's healthy—but I want them to always be able to say, "My mom, my dad are my best friends. I can tell them anything, and I will always be accepted. I can go to them with any problem, and I'll always be encouraged and strengthened."

In order for them to feel that way, we have to tell them and show them we love them every day—and we do that. I kiss Jeremy every day, I hug him, I let him know it's a man thing to hug your son, to hug your dad. It doesn't make you weak. I'll probably keep hugging Jeremy after he gets married and has kids of his own, because I want him to know that he has a father with strong arms, a strong voice, a strong heart, a strong love—a father who will care for him, protect him, and do anything in the world for him.

The day Jeremy was born, I took him in my arms and I cried,

because he was my own son, and I never imagined how beautiful it would be to have my own child in my arms. I cried when Jecolia was born, because now I had not only a son, but a daughter. Both Jeremy and Jecolia were good babies, and as they have grown older, they have been a blessing.

Some friends of ours told me they spanked their kids' hands, starting at around six months, when the kids started getting into stuff that could be bad for them. I wasn't sure how I felt about spanking, but when Jeremy got to be about that age and he put his hands into something he shouldn't have, I spanked his hands. I found out that a child is able to understand the concept of "Don't do that," even at that young age. By eight months, he'd do whatever I told him to do. If I told him "no," he'd back off.

I know a lot of people reading this will think, "Hey, that's child abuse!" No, I didn't abuse my child, I didn't hurt him, I cared enough to teach him right and wrong—"Do" and "Don't"—at an age when he could understand a mild spanking but couldn't understand language. I've never liked spanking my kids, because I have a very soft heart where they're concerned. If I have to spank, I do it as a duty, reluctantly, not angrily. They'll cry for a little bit, then I sit down with them and have them tell me why I spanked them. I give them a hug and kiss, and I play with them. I let them know they're loved.

If I just get mad, haul off and whup my kids, then walk away— well that's abuse. If you spank a kid reluctantly, in sorrow rather than in anger, and you love them afterwards, that's discipline. There's a big difference. When you hit a son in anger, he feels rejected. When you discipline a daughter in love, she may not like it, but at least she is able to say to herself, "Hey, he spanked me for a reason. He didn't want to do it, but he did it because he loved me. He didn't turn his back on me, he gave me a kiss, he talked to me while I was crying, he played with me and spent time with me afterward, he showed me I'm accepted and loved."

Jecolia was born about two years after Jeremy, and though she didn't obey as quickly as Jeremy, she was always a sweet little girl. As she got older, she responded more and more. As my kids got older, one thing I told them over and over was, "If you're honest with me, if you always tell the truth, it'll keep you out of a lot of trouble." Our kids really took that to heart, and they're two very honest kids.

I'll tell you, Jeremy—our ten-year-old—is so honest, he actually got in the habit of telling me every time he had a temptation or a guilty thought. He would bring everything to us, and he'd think we were going to be mad at him because of this or that little thing, and we'd say, "No, Jeremy, we're not mad at you. We're proud of you that you tell us these things." Sometimes he'd call me at the facility or on my car phone and confess some little thing to me, and I'd say, "That's natural, Jeremy. Let's just pray about it." And we'd pray together over the phone and that would be the end of it—until the next time.

One day, I was driving home and I thought, *I've gotta stop this! That boy's calling two or three times a day, telling stuff on himself. He's really getting on my nerves."* But then I felt God speaking inside me, saying, "Why would you want to stop him? Aren't you trying to teach your son to be honest?" I said, "Yeah." God said, "Don't teach him to be dishonest. That's just you being selfish." So when I got home, and every time after that, I just let him tell me whatever was on his conscience, and I thanked God that Jeremy felt comfortable laying everything on the table with me.

Fatherhood has been the most gratifying, rewarding experience of my life. It has given me the opportunity to train up two wonderful kids, and to watch them grow and mature into the kind of people God wants them to be. It makes me proud enough to pop my shirt buttons to see Jeremy and Jecolia demonstrating compassion and generosity at such an early age. Both of them received money from doing some commercials, and we had put that money in the bank for their college education. After our church burned down, Jeremy came to me and said, "Daddy, would you take a thousand dollars out of my college fund? I want to give it so the church can be rebuilt."

Jecolia—our eight-year-old—is the same way. Once, during school (this was before Sara began home-schooling), the kids were sharing prayer requests, and one little girl stood up and asked for prayer. She needed orthodontic work done, but her teeth would have to wait because her parents needed the money for the new house they were planning to buy. The girl asked if the class would pray that her family would get some extra money to get her teeth

fixed. Jecolia came home and told Sara about the little girl and
said, "She needs $210, and I want to give it to her out of my own
money." She did that, and both the little girl and her mother shed
tears over it—and frankly, I got a little misty-eyed myself.

I'm excited to see that my kids have latched on to the principle
that God doesn't bless us just for us, He blesses us so that we can
bless others. I guess all parents say they've got the best kids in the
world. But Sara and I actually do.

I would like to think that the caring and the desire to bless
others that we are seeing in Jeremy and Jecolia is a reflection of
what they see in their mother and me. Everything I've been saying
is summed up in the Promise Keepers' song:

> Lord, I want to be just like you,
> Because he wants to be just like me.
> I want to be a holy example
> for his innocent eyes to see.[2]

If my kids see me as a hero, a positive role model for their own
lives, they will begin to imitate me. The more I imitate Jesus, the
more Christlike my own kids will be. And I believe that one of
the most important ways I can model and exemplify the character
of Jesus Christ to my kids is by really loving their mother. The
Bible says, "Husbands, love your wives, just as Christ also loved
the church and gave Himself for it."[3] The way Jesus sacrificed
Himself for the church is an example to me of the way I am to
sacrifice myself for Sara.

My kids know how much I love them by the way I love my wife.
If I demonstrate Christlike love to Sara, then Jeremy and Jecolia
will see the love of Christ in me. They will know that they live in
a loving home, and they will grow up feeling safe, secure, and
cared for. But if they grow up seeing me behave in a nasty, disrespectful way toward Sara, hurting her feelings, abusing her emotions, or worst of all, physically hurting her, they will wonder, "If
that's what Daddy does to Mom, how does he feel about me? Does
he love me? Does he care about me? Or am I next on his hit list?"

I love peace in my house, and so does Sara. If there's a problem,
we try to achieve peace as soon as possible. We try not to disagree
with one another around the kids, but if we ever do (for example,

if Sara and I have a disagreement going on in the front seat of the car while Jeremy and Jecolia are in the back), then we try to handle it with maturity, and we let the kids see the resolution of that conflict. I want them to know that their dad and mom are big enough to say, "I'm sorry," and to resolve conflict in a healthy, caring way.

I think it's also important, if I want to be a hero to my kids, to apologize to them when I'm wrong. One time, I disciplined Jecolia for something I thought she had done to another child who had come over to play. The other child had told me Jecolia slapped him, and when I asked her, she admitted it. I later found out that she hadn't actually slapped the boy across the face as I had thought—she had just given him a little tap on the ankle. She shouldn't have done it, but it was a way less serious offense than the boy first made it sound, and I certainly never would have disciplined her as I did if I had known the real facts.

When I found out what really happened, I apologized to Jecolia. "And just to prove I'm sorry," I said, "I'm gonna get you something special." A few weeks went by, and I forgot that I had made that promise to her.

One day, she came to me and said, "Daddy, remember you were going to give me something special?"

I said, "Yeah."

"Well," she said, "I know what I want."

What she wanted was a little gray cat she had seen in a pet store window. That little cat runs around our house today, and his name is Tiger. He's my repentance cat, my apology cat, my way of saying I'm sorry to Jecolia for disciplining her unfairly. I see that cat around the house, and I am reminded of the need always to search out the full truth of a matter before I discipline my children.

I know that a lot of guys think that to be the man of the family means acting like a dictator or a terrorist. They make their wives and kids afraid around them. I know guys who say, "When I get married, the family's gonna be run the way I want it. If I say cook, my wife cooks. If I say go to the store, she goes to the store. If I look sideways at my kids, they better run and hide." Man, that's not right. Sure, the husband is supposed to exercise leadership in the home, but it is to be a caring, understanding form of leadership—leadership that is actually servanthood. Jesus has said that the greatest among you shall be the servant of all.[4] So fathers, as leaders, are actually servants to their families, not dictators.

If there's a challenge to men, it's that we need to learn how to be servants to our families. We need to sit down, listen to our wives, listen to our kids, truly hear what they are saying to us, because they have a lot to tell us that we don't understand. We think we do, but we don't. Wide-open, honest lines of communication are crucial to a healthy marriage relationship and a healthy father-child relationship.

People call me a football hero, and I try hard to live up to that responsibility. But above all else, I want to be a hero where it counts the most: right here in my own house. When I die, I want Jeremy and Jecolia to look back on my life and say, "My dad was a great father, a great friend, and a real man of God. He was my hero." If someone wants to mention at my funeral that, hey, Reggie White played a decent game of football, too, well that's all right. But being enshrined in the Football Hall of Fame in Canton, Ohio, doesn't mean diddly compared to being enshrined in the hearts of my wife and my children. The wedding band on my finger and the ring of love that surrounds me in my family mean more to me than any number of Super Bowl rings you could offer me.

A HERO TO KIDS WITHOUT DADS

I love being around kids. One of the great joys of my career has been the times I've spent surrounded by kids at Jerome Brown's football camp in Brooksville, Florida (which his old Eagles teammates still run every summer in his memory), or at Keith Byars camp in Dayton, Ohio, and at my own camp which I've been running in Chattanooga, the place where I grew up, since 1991. I patterned my camp after Keith's—we get sponsorship from companies like Coca-Cola and Krystal Hamburgers, and we offer it free to neighborhood kids. Over the years, a lot of my friends have helped out by donating their time and talent to the kids—guys like Ronnie Lott, Keith Byars, Keith Jackson, Edgar Bennett, Jerome Brown, Jim McMahon, Leroy Butler, Clyde Simmons, Seth Joyner, Eric Allen, Sterling Sharp, Reggie and Raleigh McKenzie, and others. We also had a lot of help from local sponsors Sam Woolwine and Dottie Heard of the *Chattanooga Free Press* and coaches like Big Doug Carter, R. V. Brown, and LeRone Jennings.

It's a free camp, and before our first year, I figured we'd have so many kids we wouldn't know what to do with them all. Instead, we got 150 kids. I was discouraged, and was just about to call it quits, but then I heard the Lord saying to me, "Reggie, the kids are important, not the numbers." The Lord was right. I decided then and there to keep offering the camp every year, even if we only got ten kids. Sign-ups remained pretty steady at around 150 throughout most of the time the camp was in existence—until 1996. That's when we lowered the age from 13 and up to 6 and up—and suddenly we had 650 kids in the camp! We work the kids hard, teach them a lot about football and a little about life, and give them heroes to look up to.

One of the goals of the Reggie White and Friends Football Clinic is to give kids the same kinds of formative experiences I was blessed to receive when I was a kid at FCA camp. I especially want to reach out to the many fatherless boys in the Chattanooga area. Having spent many of my early years without a father in the house, I remember how much I wanted to be around my coaches, my pastor, my camp counselors, and the men in our church who volunteered their time to take us kids on outings and camping trips. I remember how much I just ate up their friendship, their affirmation, their pats on the back, their shouts of "Good job!" or "Way to go, Reggie!" All boys need that, and it breaks my heart to know how many boys grow up in this country never receiving that. Kids are growing up without heroes these days, and a kid without heroes has no reason to become anything other than an addict, a rapist, or a bad-dude gangsta in the 'hood.

If you want to have an impact on our society, on all our many social ills, then take time to be a mentor and a part-time dad to kids who don't have a dad. Statistics show that fatherless youngsters are much more likely to get caught up in gangs, drugs, and crime than kids who grow up with fathers. Why? Because fatherless kids tend to grow up lonely, hurting, and angry over being deprived of a father's love. They grow up lacking the moral guidance and positive role model (that is, a hero) that a good father provides. Today, the poverty rate among families headed by a single mom is 33.4 percent, versus only 5.7 percent for two-parent families. And 70 percent of long-term prison inmates (including 72 percent of teenage murderers and 60 percent of rapists) grew up in fatherless homes.

If you want to attack the problems of crime, drugs, gangs, and poverty right at their source, then help some fatherless kids find male guidance and male heroes. This is not an indictment of single mothers, because they are taking on an incredibly difficult job, a job that is tough enough for two people to handle—and they are doing it all themselves. Good, caring single moms are heroes too! Much of my early life I was raised by a single mom and she did a good job, the best job any single mom could do. But I believe that those of us who are men, and who have some time to give, should help out those struggling single moms by providing fatherless kids with a positive male influence. You want to make a real difference in this world? Then be a dad to a kid who has no dad.

Publisher's note: The first edition of this book appeared in August 1996. Less than six months later, Reggie White and the Green Bay Packers went to Super Bowl XXXI in New Orleans. We left the following section of the book exactly as Reggie originally told it, including his prediction that by the end of the '96 season, the Packers would go to the Super Bowl and "take the title back to Titletown." Well, the Packers did exactly as Reggie predicted. So, following this section, we have added an entirely *new* chapter, in which Reggie tells the story of the Packers' miraculous 1996 season, and of the thrilling capstone of his career, Super Bowl XXXI.

EYES ON THE PRIZE

One of the marks of a true hero is that he sets goals—and he either reaches those goals or he fails gloriously in the attempt. I have some tall goals that still haven't been reached, but I fully intend to achieve them before I hang up my pads and helmet for the last time. I've played pro ball for eleven years, and I've been on winning teams all those years—*winning* teams, but not *championship* teams. I've been to the playoffs seven seasons out of eleven—but I've never set foot on a Super Bowl field.

If you go to the Football Hall of Fame, you'll see a lot of guys who have finished their careers with greatness—great fame, great achievements, great stats—but without a championship ring. They have become legends in the game, yet never got close to a Super Bowl. I refuse to join their ranks. I refuse to end my football career without a championship ring.

The game of football has been good to me, and I think I have been good for the game—both on the field and in my off-the-field efforts to reform the game. Football is a part of me. I have given it everything I have, and I have never left anything on the field. There is only one place I've never been, one level I've never reached in this game. Once I have competed at the pinnacle of this game, I will be satisfied. My life in football will be history. I can hang it up and walk away, knowing I've done everything I came into the game to do.

As I write these words, the '96 season is about to begin—my twelfth year in pro football. I'll turn thirty-five years old as we approach the playoffs. I expect to have an exciting season. Thinking back on the miracles of the past couple years, who knows what lies ahead? Whatever comes my way in the trenches, I'll tackle it with all I've got. When I signed with the Packers, I figured I would play out my four-year contract and retire at the end of the '96 season. But here I am, going into that fourth season, feeling at or near the top of my game, and I'm thinking, *I see a few more good seasons still ahead of me. Why stop here?*

Man, the fans and the community have been so good to Sara and me. To this day, we still mist up when we think of all the money and love the Wisconsin community poured out upon our church in Knoxville. We've never been received the way we've been received by the people of this state. Wisconsin, we love you. I want to keep representing you as long as I have something to contribute to the Green Bay Packers.

It has been one of the greatest privileges of my life to add my name to the legendary tradition of this football organization. The Green Bay Packers invented the Super Bowl some thirty years ago, and won the first two Super Bowls ever played. The Super Bowl trophy is named after Green Bay's immortal Vince Lombardi. Back when Lombardi ran the team, they called Green Bay "Titletown, U.S.A.," and the Packers were viewed with the same kind of awe that the 49ers and the Cowboys have commanded in recent years.

Under the leadership of head coach Mike Holmgren and general manager Ron Wolf, and powered by the mighty right arm of Brett

Favre, the Packers have come within a few yards of restoring the full, awesome glory of the Packers tradition to Green Bay. On Saturday, January 6, 1996, a day after my eleventh wedding anniversary, we beat the 49ers in their own stadium. It was the biggest Packer victory in a quarter-century. From there, we went into Texas Stadium, a place where we had lost five straight times, including our last two divisional playoffs. Our 13–5 record was certainly a match for the Cowboys' 13–4. We had earned the right to be there, and we played hard, we played loose, we played well. The lead in that game see-sawed five times before the final gun. We fell short. We lost—*that* year. The Cowboys went on to the Super Bowl and won the right to be called America's Team—*that* year.

But *this* year? Hey, it's time we take the title back to Titletown!

The Packers were America's Team in the Lombardi days, and I truly believe the Green Bay Packers are about to become America's Team once more. We haven't earned it yet—not quite yet—but it's gonna happen soon. We have our eyes on the prize.

There isn't another team in the NFL that is better suited to wear the mantle of America's Team. After all, who owns the Green Bay Packers? Not some rich guy with an ego the size of Texas. Uh-uh, no way. *Americans* own the Packers. Real Americans. Ordinary, everyday, working class Americans. Salt-of-the-earth Americans. People-who-will-give-you-the-shirts-off-their-backs Americans. Some owners will put a gun to the heads of a community and say, "Give me this, give me that, or I'm moving this team to Kalamazoo." Not the Packers, because the Packers owners *are* the community.

And what kind of a community is Green Bay? Oh, man! It's the most special, most beautiful community of people on God's green earth! Everything I've seen, including the outpouring of love I've felt, tells me that God is on the verge of winning a spiritual championship in the state of Wisconsin, a victory that will spread across this nation. To me, the city of Green Bay, Wisconsin, *is* America— at least, everything that is best about America.

And who coaches the Packers? A real, humble, regular American-type guy. Coach Mike Holmgren—former high school history teacher and master offensive strategist—is one of the greatest men to ever coach the game. Yet he walks around like a guy who doesn't even know his own greatness. Before Coach Mike came to town, Green Bay produced only 2 winning seasons out of the previous 19. The year before Mike came, the Packers finished 4 and 12; his first year as coach they finished 9 and 7, and every season since has been a winning season. In my mind, Mike Holmgren is America's coach.

And who leads the Packers on the field? A humble, fun-loving country boy from Kiln, Mississippi. A guy who keeps playing and winning, even with a separated shoulder, even when he's spitting up blood—a real American hero, the genuine article. Brett Favre is the best America has to offer. In my mind, he's America's quarterback.

America's Team, the Green Bay Packers? You bet. I'm proud to be a Packer, and I will be a Packer until the day I no longer play the game. And then I'll be a Packers fan—big-time.

How many more years will I be in the trenches? As long as I'm having fun, man. As long as I'm having fun.

And I'm having *a lot* of fun right now!

Chapter 13

MISSION ACCOMPLISHED

O ur 1996 championship season didn't begin with the season opener. It didn't begin with the first preseason game, or the July training camp, or the April minicamps.

No, for the Green Bay Packers, our championship season began in the dark hours of the evening of January 14, 1996, after the weary and defeated Pack boarded a bus outside Texas Stadium. We had just lost the NFC title to the Dallas Cowboys, and we were angry, sad, and full of hurt. As the bus lurched onto the freeway and headed for Dallas-Fort Worth airport, Brett came over to me. Brett's an intense young man, and he can't stand to lose. He was crying as he gripped my shoulders and said, "Big Dog, I promise you, we're gonna win it all this year. We're goin' all the way to the Super Bowl, and we won't let anything stop us this time."

"You're right, man," I said. "I know we are. This season's over. Next season's gonna be our season."

And week by week, as the start of the new season neared, I became more and more convinced that Brett and I were right. This was gonna be our year. We acquired some excellent talent for the '96 season—not only playing talent, but leadership talent.

We picked up Eugene Robinson as our starting free safety—he'd played eleven seasons with the Seattle Seahawks, was a two-time Pro Bowler ('92 and '93), and was the top interceptor in the NFL.

Though he would go on to lead the Pack with six interceptions in the '96 season, Eugene was even more valuable to us in providing experienced leadership to our defensive backs. Our secondary is talented but young, and Eugene provided the seasoning that elevated the performances of cornerbacks Doug Evans (six interceptions in '96) and Craig Newsome (71 tackles and no pass interference penalties), rookie defensive back Tyrone Williams (remember his one-handed lunging interception in the NFC Championship game?), and veteran strong safety LeRoy Butler. Among them, Eugene, LeRoy, Doug, and Craig would rack up an awesome 22 interceptions for the season. When I saw the things Eugene was doing with our defensive backs, I knew we had a great shot at the Super Bowl.

We also picked up left tackle Santana Dotson from the Buccaneers to help us out in the middle. His specialty: stopping the run. Playing to the right of me in the trenches, he would end the season with 6½ sacks. Other acquisitions who would prove immensely valuable to us as the season wore on included wide receiver Don Beebe (from the Bills—he had been to four consecutive Super Bowls without a win), linebacker Ron Cox, and, of course, kick and punt returner Desmond Howard.

A Heisman Trophy winner, Desmond (a.k.a. "Dangerous D") had struggled as a wide receiver and returner for the Redskins and the Jaguars. It's a real testament to the judgment of Ron Wolf and Mike Holmgren that they saw Desmond's potential and signed him as a kick and punt returner for the Packers. His future with the Packers didn't look too bright at first. Sidelined with a hip pointer on his very first day of practice, it looked like he would be cut before getting a chance to prove himself. Desmond's got the most positive attitude and the biggest grin in the NFL, but even so, there were times when he was depressed about his career. He and I spent a lot of time during training camp talking and praying together. He made the cut, got healthy—and the rest is history.

And I'm talking *Super Bowl* history.

THE PRESIDENT DROPS BY

The NFL preview issue of *Sports Illustrated* hit the stands in August, and there we were on the cover—Brett, Robert Brooks, and me. *SI* picked the Packers to face the Kansas City Chiefs in Super Bowl XXXI. I thought, *Oh, man, that's all we need!* I'm not superstitious, like those people who think getting the cover of *SI* is a jinx or the kiss of death or something like that—but I knew it meant added pressure, distraction, and expectation that we didn't need as a team.

The really big pressure we faced, however, was the schedule. Because we had won the NFC Central title for the '95 season, we had drawn what most sports commentators agreed was the toughest schedule in the NFL. In addition to our divisional opponents, we were paired with the NFC West champion 49ers (11–5 in '95), the NFC East runner-up Eagles (10–6), the NFC East champion Cowboys (11–5, and we played in Dallas *again*), plus San Diego, Denver, and Kansas City from the AFC West—the toughest division in the NFL, with no teams below .500. All in all, we faced a slate with a combined '95 record of 146–110.

In the preseason exhibition games, we beat the Patriots (24–7), the Steelers (24–17), and the Ravens (17–15). I don't know if some of us were just feeling confident or starting to get a bit cocky, but a lot of guys on the team were talking a lot about the Super Bowl during August. Right after the Steelers game, however, Coach Holmgren sat us down and read us the riot act. "I don't want to hear anyone on this team mention the Super Bowl anymore," he said. "That kind of talk is over right now, and I mean it. We've got a tough schedule ahead of us, and the Super Bowl is a million miles away. Just keep your focus on what you've got to right here, right now." We were embarrassed two weeks later by the Colts (30–6) in our last exhibition game of the preseason—a loss that underscored Mike's words.

For our season opener, September 1, we went to Tampa Bay and scuttled the Buccaneers, 34 to 3. The local papers said that about a third of the fans in Tampa Stadium were Cheeseheads—and I believe it, because sometimes it sounded just like being at Lambeau Field. Brett was on fire, throwing 20 completions for 247 yards, spreading the ball around to eight receivers—including three touchdown passes to my man, Keith Jackson, whom I've suited up with for over a decade ever since our Buddy Ryan days in Philly. Keith was explosive that day.

That game was a milestone for Brett. With a 27-yard pass to Antonio Freeman on third-and-17 in the third quarter, Brett tied Joe Namath as the third-fastest player in history to reach 15,000 passing yards. Dan Marino achieved that mark in 56 games, Jim Everett did it in 64, while Brett and Broadway Joe made it in 66 games.

On Labor Day, the leader of the free world dropped by. President Clinton came to the field during practice, chatted and threw the football around with a bunch of the players, and got his picture snapped with us. There was an election campaign going on, so there were a lot of reporters and camera people around. As President Clinton and I were walking down to the field, we had about a minute or so to chat. We talked about the torching of my church in Knoxville (which is unsolved to this day), and the burning of so many other churches across the South in the past two years.

"Mr. President," I said, "a lot of churches are still burning to the ground, and we're no closer to solving the problem than before. I'm concerned that the whole problem is going to move to the back pages of the newspaper, and people will forget about it. I have some ideas that I think could help the situation with these churches, and I have some concerns about the way the investigations are being handled by the federal agencies."

"I'd like to hear your thoughts about it," he said. "I'll tell you what I'll do—I'll have someone from my staff call you real soon."

"Sir," I said, "I'd appreciate it if you could call me personally."

"Well, I'll try to do that as soon as I get back to Washington," he said.

But I never heard back from him.

LOPSIDED SCORES

We played our second game of the season a few days later, on September 9. It was a special game because it was a Monday night home opener—the first ABC Monday Night Football game at Lambeau in ten years, and only the fourth Monday night game in Lambeau history. The crowd was rocking, the tundra was jumping, and the noise really fired us up for battle. We hosted the Philadelphia Eagles, coached by our former defensive coordinator, Ray Rhodes—and to be honest with you, we weren't very hospitable.

We rolled over my former team, 39 to 13, powered by two Robert Brooks TD receptions (it was the eleventh 100-yard receiving game of Robert's career).

Defensively, we shut down their running game, holding quick Ricky Watters to just 38 yards on 10 attempts. They tried to run the ball away from me—but then they just kept bumping up against Gilbert or Santana or Sean. Turnovers were decisive. We forced one fumble and three interceptions. Early in the fourth quarter, Santana and I shared a sack in the end zone for a safety.

Brett started out as he often does, with a little too much adrenaline in his throwing arm. In the first series, he overthrew everybody but the Ayatollah. Then he settled in, finishing the first half with 14 of 27 for 222 yards and two TDs. It was classic Favre— those deep, cruise missile passes were launched with laser-guided accuracy whether he was standing in the pocket, rolling out, or dancing away from a platoon of rushers. He gave us all a scare, however, when he scrambled to the seam and was shoved out of bounds and into the brass band. He limped back onto the field and finished the game.

Our third regular season game, September 15, was at home against the San Diego Chargers. Their quarterback, Stan Humphries, plays a deep-set passing game, dropping seven or nine yards into the pocket. So the two "old men" on the front line— Reggie White and Sean Jones—had farther to go to get to him. But we got to him, all right. Sean and I each got a pair of sacks in that game. Gabe Wilkins and Shannon Clavelle teamed up on a fifth sack, and our secondary provided great coverage. We held the Chargers to 141 net yards, including only 33 yards rushing.

Robert Brooks had another great 100-yard day, and our offense gained 132 yards on the ground—the third straight game we had rushed for 100 yards or more, proof that Green Bay has a mechanized infantry as well as an air force. When 6-foot-1 250-pound fullback William Henderson caught his first-ever NFL touchdown pass, he ran for the stands to make his Lambeau leap—and you shoulda seen the fans run screaming from the wall when they saw him coming!

This game was a great test for LeRoy Butler's new contact lenses—they really worked! He got two interceptions, the first on a ball tipped by Craig Newsome, and the second one, for a touchdown, came when he swiped a pass intended for running back Terrell Fletcher. LeRoy tore past Stan Humphries and down the wide-open left sideline. This was LeRoy's first chance to vault into the stands since he invented the Lambeau leap back in December of '93. His lack of practice showed—he only made it halfway up the wall, and the fans had to reach down and pull him the rest of the way up. Robert Brooks gave him a 6 on a scale of 10.

About five minutes before the end of the game, Desmond Howard showed the kind of stuff that would later make him MVP of Super Bowl XXXI: He ran a punt return 65 yards for a touchdown. This was no accident, by the way. Mike Holmgren wanted to have every unit of the Packers working together to produce touchdowns—including special teams. He knew that Dangerous D had a superhuman quickness that could be put to good use if he had good blocking in front of him, so Mike challenged the blockers on the return teams to block hard and open holes for D. It was a strategy that worked right through the season, the post-season, and the Super Bowl.

We beat the Chargers, by the way, 42–10.

Game four, September 22, was a case of murder in Minnesota—and we were the victims. The Packers hadn't won in the Metrodome since December 21, 1991—and this game was no exception. We gave up 13 points in the fourth quarter and lost to the Vikings 30–21. Minnesota was hitting us with a mix of blitzes and four-man rushes, and Brett spent a lot of time on the ground. He was sacked seven times—the most times he was ever sacked in a single game.

We bounced back in game five, grabbing a lopsided victory in the Seattle Kingdome, 31–10. In the first quarter, Seahawks quarterback Rick Mirer rolled to the right and tried to fire a pass. I got my hands up, deflected the ball, then pulled it down and ran 46 yards with it.

We won game six in Chicago with a 31-point margin of victory—Packers 37, Bears 6, our biggest win ever over the Bears.

ONE BIG KICK

Game seven, October 14, was a Monday night thriller—a long-awaited rematch between the Packers and the 49ers. The last time we met, it was in January at 3Com Park for the divisional playoff—

and we had whupped 'em in their own house, knocking them out of Super Bowl contention. Now they were coming to our house, hungry for revenge, and the atmosphere on the field was as fierce and desperate as any playoff game. There was a lot of trash-talking and shoving, a lot of high emotion in that game. We wanted to win it for Coach Holmgren because it was the team he once assisted as offensive coordinator. But the 'Niners wanted the win too—and they played a punishing, physical game that night in front of a record-high crowd of 60,716 Cheeseheads.

'Niners starting quarterback Steve Young spent the entire game pacing the sidelines, because of a pulled groin. His backup, Elvis Grbac, was up to the task—in his four previous starts for San Francisco, he was undefeated. We kicked off to the 'Niners, and they got some good plays and a couple first downs—then LeRoy Butler busted their drive by stripping the ball from 'Niners running back Tommy Vardell.

On our very first offensive play, Robert Brooks was thrown to the ground while blocking out 49ers cornerback Tyronne Drakeford. Robert had his right leg out in front of him as he went down, and it popped the ligament in his knee. The trainers came out and wrapped an inflatable immobilizer around the knee. Then they carried him to the sidelines and sat him on the bench. I had a sinking feeling as they worked on Robert—it looked bad. Finally, they carted him off to the locker room. As he left, he told us, "Don't worry about me! You guys just go out there and dominate!" Before his injury, Robert was our second-leading receiver, with 23 catches for 344 yards and four touchdowns; after that play was over, so was Robert's season.

Our defense thundered in that game. We stuffed the running game and pressured their passing game, coming away with two interceptions—LeRoy's in the 'Niners opening possession and another one in the first quarter by Eugene Robinson on a long pass intended for J. J. Stokes. That set up a drive to a 25-yard Chris Jacke field goal.

The 'Niners defense was every bit as tough as we were. They took away our running game, allowing us eight rushes in the first half for a total of 12 yards. Without a ground game, Brett had to keep the ball airborne most of the time. Two big passes—a 50-yarder to Keith Jackson and a 54-yarder to Don Beebe (who stepped into Robert Brooks's slot) set up a pair of early field goals, giving us a 6 to 0 lead. Prior to that game, we knew that if we could get the ball into the red zone, we could get it into the end zone—of 23 possessions inside the 20-yard line in our previous seven games, we had scored 15 touchdowns. But that night, against the 49ers, it seemed like we could only get close enough to kick. Before the game was over, Chris Jacke would tie his own club record of five field goals in a single game.

The tide began to swing San Francisco's way midway through the second quarter. By halftime, we trailed 17–6. But we still had thirty minutes of football to play, and we still had one of the best second-half coaches in the history of the game. Mike Holmgren got us settled and focused, made his adjustments to the game plan, then sent us back out on the field.

Halfway through the third quarter, things began to flow our way once more with a 59-yard touchdown pass to Don Beebe. There was a lot of controversy about that play. Don made a diving catch almost 30 yards downfield, hauling it in and rolling on the ground. 'Niners cornerback Marquez Pope was close to Don, and a lot of people thought he touched Don while he was rolling, which would have meant a dead ball. But Don thought the ball was still live, so he got up and kept going. The official agreed with Don. And me? Hey, I've gotta side with the official!

For the 2-point conversion, Brett rolled right and fired a bullet into heavy traffic. Edgar Bennett came up with it on the 2, lunged for the goal line, and grabbed 2 points. Score: San Francisco 17, Green Bay 14. At that point, the crowd notched up the noise about another forty decibels or so. You couldn't have heard an atomic bomb go off in that place. It was tremendous. I sacked Grbac for a loss of 3 yards in that quarter, registering 160 sacks for my career.

In the fourth quarter, we were closing in on the 'Niners. With 3:35 left, Jacke kicked his third field goal, a 34-yarder, bringing us dead even with San Francisco, 17 to 17. We knew we could beat 'em. We felt it. The game had swung our way.

Then disaster struck. With just over two minutes left, Brett shot a slant pass to Derrick Mayes—but Marquez Pope got to the ball first, snatched it, and returned it to our own 12-yard line. Their first two downs yielded only 2 yards. On third down, after the two-minute warning, San Francisco head coach George Seifert called a play that would come back to haunt him. Why he didn't try at least one pass to Rice or Stokes in the end zone, I don't know. He could have at least tried to take a little more time off the clock. Instead, he had Grbac down the ball between the hashmarks for no gain to set up the field goal. Then he called Jeff Wilkins in to kick a 28-yarder from dead center, leaving 1:50 on the clock. The kick was good. San Francisco 20, Green Bay 17. We didn't have a lot of time, but when the pressure's on, you can get a lot done with 1:50.

After the kickoff, we got some help from 49ers dime back Steve Israel, who was first penalized 5 yards for illegal hands to the face—then increased the penalty to an additional 15 yards and ejection for unsportsmanlike conduct when he dissed the official. The next few plays were magical—Brett scrambling, one arm out-stretched, directing traffic, then dumping off perfect wrist-flick passes—11 and 9 yards to Beebe, an 8-yard sideline clockstopper to Desmond, followed by a scramble to the 13 for a first down and our last timeout. It all happened bang, bang, bang, within the final minute of regulation play. He tried two more passes—incomplete. After unleashing that second pass, Brett was hit hard by a 49er defender and driven into the ground. It took him a few moments to get to his feet and clear the cobwebs. He was hurting.

The clock was down to 17 seconds, third and 10, no timeouts left, and lots of pressure. Brett could win the game with a pass into the end zone—but if he threw it under and the receiver was stopped short of the goal line, there'd be no timeouts left and no time to bring in a kicker for the field goal. They lined up. Brett took the snap, dropped back under pressure, and threw a lofty one. It sailed high over the goal line, through the end zone, out of the end zone, and was caught—

By some guy in the marching band.

Jacke went in and kicked a nice, high field goal, with just the slightest hook to the right. It was Green Bay 20, San Francisco 20, with 8 seconds left in the fourth quarter.

The 'Niners won the overtime toss. We kicked off, and they went three and out. We took the punt on our own 43, and moved the ball to the San Francisco 35. From there, Chris Jacke booted his fifth field goal of the evening, a 53-yarder that was still rising when it split the uprights. We had won it by seconds and inches, 23–20.

Under incredible pressure from a pounding defense, Brett completed 28-of-61 for 395 yards—way below his usual percentage, but he threw so many balls in the air, he was able to make things happen. We won it even after Robert Brooks left on the very first offensive play. Guys stepped up—especially Don Beebe, who finished with 11 catches for 220 yards. It was a grinding, brutal, physical contest on both sides of the ball—and we battled our way back from a 17–6 halftime deficit to a nail-biting, sudden death win. Two dominant teams went after each other with everything they had, grinding each other down to a stalemate—then settled the matter with one big kick. Like Brett said afterwards, "Oh, man, what a game!"

DISSED IN DALLAS

We won our next two games—Tampa Bay and Detroit, both at Lambeau—but we lost Antonio Freeman with a broken forearm against the Bucs. We were 8–1 going into game ten in Kansas City, November 10. There were almost 80,000 red-clad Chiefs fans in Arrowhead Stadium that day. We had no illusions. It was gonna be a tough game. The Chiefs really pounded the ball on us, gaining 182 yards on the ground. It was the first time all season our defense had allowed the other side to run so much. These Kansas City guys don't play finesse football, but they are tight, they are tough, and they know their roles. Steve Bono is a smart quarterback—not agile and creative like Brett, but certainly cool and controlled under pressure.

The K.C. fans made so much noise the tackles couldn't hear Brett count down to the snap. Their heavy blitzing defense, anchored by Neil Smith and Derrick Thomas, pinned down our offense something awful, sacking Brett four times and forcing an interception and a fumble. They often hit us with a "fire zone" attack—a blitz with zone coverage instead of man-to-man. They mixed things up and kept our offense off-balance throughout the game. Already forced to do without Robert Brooks and Antonio Freeman, we had four more guys go out of that game because of injury: tight end Mark "Chewie" Chmura, wide receivers Terry Mickens and Anthony Morgan, and defensive lineman Sean Jones.

With a minute left in the game, Derrick Mayes gave us a chance to win, grabbing a one-handed touchdown pass out of thin air, bringing us to within 7. But K.C. recovered our onside kick and ran out the rest of the clock. The game lasted three-and-a-half long, terrible hours. Final score: Kansas City 27, Green Bay 20.

Game eleven was the most painful of all: Dallas, November 18. As long as I've been a Packer, as long as Coach Holmgren has coached the Packers, this team has never beaten the Dallas Cowboys. Going into this game, we were 0 and 6 in Texas Stadium. We left there 0 and 7. The Cowboys led 15 to 0 at the half, and were dragging us down to a shutout until Brett hit Mayes with a TD pass inside the final two-minute warning. It was an *ABC Monday Night Football* game, and you probably saw it—the game where Dallas beat us with nothing but field goals—seven, to be exact.

"Oh," you're probably thinking. "*That* game! The one where Reggie and Michael Irvin got into an argument at the end!"

I'm glad you brought that up. A lot of people thought Michael Irvin and I were arguing, but that wasn't so. I wasn't mad at Mike, and Mike wasn't mad at me. Fact is, a lot of things happened at the end of that game that the ABC Sports cameras didn't catch and that the guys in the broadcast booth misinterpreted. When that incident took place, the Packers were already beaten. Traditionally, when a team has been beaten like that, you don't keep them standing on the field while you kick the ball through goal posts. You take a knee, you run the clock down, you shake hands, and let everybody go home. But that's not Barry Switzer's style.

I have nothing but respect for the Dallas team. They didn't want to kick that field goal. In fact, Dallas quarterback Troy Aikman and a lot of other Cowboys were mad at Barry for sending Chris Boniol in to kick that last one.

Here's what you didn't see on TV: Troy had already taken a knee and was running down the clock. With less than half a minute to go, Troy went up to the center and was getting ready to take a knee again and end the game. Just then, the special teams guy trotted out to Troy and tapped him. Troy waved him off and yelled, "Get outta here! We're running out the clock!" The special teams guy insisted, "We're calling a time and kicking a field goal! That's what Barry wants!" Troy still wouldn't leave the field. "Get outta here! We're not kicking a field goal!" But Barry started yelling at Troy from the sidelines, so Troy left the field. He was boiling mad. Then Boniol came out and kicked the field goal.

The next thing you saw on TV was Michael Irvin and me, yelling at each other, surrounded by our teammates. The TV announcers said, "Whoa! Do we have a fight going on?" Hey, Mike and I weren't fighting. If you have a tape of that game, take another look. My friend Mike has his hand on my shoulder and he's saying to me, "This is for a record, man! A record for Chris! That's all this is about!" He's not arguing with me—he's trying to calm me down! He knew I wasn't mad at him—I was mad at Barry!

"Mike," I said, "I understand what's happening, but it doesn't have to be done! You don't do that, even for a record! You already won the game, Troy was running the clock down, but Barry wants to rub our noses in it by kicking that field goal!"

You have to understand everything that had gone on before. This wasn't the first time Barry had dissed us. In the past, when we lost to the Cowboys, the first thing Barry would do is go on TV and say, "We kicked their blanks." That's nothing but no-class disrespect. Same with that field goal—it wasn't about the record books, it was Barry Switzer's way of rubbing it in on national TV. Troy knew it, and that's why he wanted no part of it. I think Mike Irvin knew it, too, but he was hoping to calm me down.

As I went to the sidelines, the crowd booed me, and the TV announcers criticized me. But I'll tell you something: I've seen this kind of thing from the other side. I played for Philadelphia when Buddy Ryan did a similar thing to a team we had just beaten. I didn't agree with rubbing somebody's nose in it when I was the victor anymore than when I was the vanquished. If I was a coach and there were ten or twenty seconds left and my team had already won the game, I'd let the clock run down. To me, a real record is something that happens in the course of the game, not something you tack on at the end. What Barry did is something we took personally. When you defeat a foe on the field of battle, you don't spit on him—you salute him.

The irony of that night was that we were the only team to score a touchdown—and we *still* got beat! Final score: Dallas 21, Green Bay 6.

MY BIRTHDAY WISH

We had lost two straight, and there was no question that a big part of these back-to-back disasters was our injury-hobbled offense. We just couldn't get our receivers open in either the K.C. or Dallas game—and that had hurt us bad. As it turned out, the very day of the Dallas game, the Jacksonville Jaguars had placed a very talented receiver on waivers—Andre Rison. Before the game, Packers GM Ron Wolf met with Coach Holmgren and Sherman Lewis, our offensive coordinator, and they talked about claiming Andre. He was an eight-year NFL veteran and a four-time Pro-Bowler, and they believed he could make things happen in Green Bay. But there was one objection to consider: In his previous tours with Indianapolis, Atlanta, Cleveland, Baltimore, and Jacksonville, Andre had acquired a reputation for being "difficult."

The day after the loss in Dallas, Green Bay put in a waiver claim for Andre. As soon as he arrived in Green Bay, Mike Holmgren sat him down and said, "Andre, Green Bay is a fresh start. Anything that happened before is then, this is now. And right now, the Packers need you and you need the Green Bay Packers. Let's make this thing work."

It turned out that Coach Mike was exactly right—Andre Rison and the Packers were a perfect marriage. The one thing Andre felt he never received on all those other teams was respect, not only as a player but as a person. And one thing you can count on finding in the Packers organization is respect. From the time Andre joined the team, and right on through the Super Bowl, the Packers were undefeated. No question, Andre played a part in that—and he's never been "difficult" on this team.

Andre made his debut in the twelfth game of the season, November 24 in St. Louis, a 24–9 win. He wore Sterling Sharpe's old jersey number, 84, and he caught five passes for 44 yards. Not bad for his first day on the job. Andre viewed his fresh start in Green Bay as a kind of career rebirth. Despite his eight years in the NFL, he would later remark, "This is my first year in the league. I'm nothing but a rookie. This is my first start, my first team."

Next, we beat Chicago at Lambeau, 28–17—our sixth consecutive win against the Bears, and the first time the Packers had beaten the Bears six straight since 1930. The following week we beat the team with the best record in the NFL, the 12–1 Denver Broncos. Denver coach Mike Shanahan decided to bench his quarterback John Elway, who was still healing up from a hamstring injury. In sub-freezing weather, we beat backup QB Bill Musgrave 41–6.

On December 12—four days after beating Denver and a week before my thirty-fifth birthday—I signed a five-year contract, guaranteeing I would finish my career as a Green Bay Packer. I got my birthday wish—to play as a Packer, retire as a Packer, and go into the Hall of Fame as a Packer. The next day, I was named to a record-tying eleventh straight Pro Bowl.

I collected two more sacks when we beat the Lions in Detroit, 31 to 3.

Our final game of the season was against the Vikings at Lambeau three days before Christmas. We were waiting on that one. Minnesota had beaten us in their own house, the Metrodome, back in September. But now they were in our house, and we intended to rock their world. After the previous games, some of the Vikings claimed they had "dominated" us. In our minds, one loss did not constitute being "dominated." The season-ending rematch was a physical game on both sides of the ball—and there was a lot of yappin' and helmet-buttin' going on. But the main thing that happened that day was that the Packers won it, 38–10, and we stretched our home-game winning streak to 16—the longest in the forty-year history of Lambeau Field.

THE LAST LAUGH

We had a two-week layoff after we beat Minnesota. During that layoff, I had a lot of time to think and pray. The Lord started dealing with me. In my thoughts, I sensed God asking me a question. *Reggie, why do you think I have allowed you to come this far, to get this close to a championship?*

I thought about it, and finally had to confess, "I don't know. It's not because of my faith, because I have often doubted that I would end my career as a champion."

And in my spirit, I felt God saying to me, *You're exactly right, Reggie. It's not because of your faith, because your definition of faith is wrong.*

I was like, "Well, what do You mean, Lord?"

He said, *You think faith is believing that if you ask Me for something, I will give it to you, I will make it happen. You think faith is about getting what you want. Reggie, that's not faith. That's desire.*

I said, "So what are You saying to me, Lord?"

And God said, *Faith and obedience go hand in hand. Go to Hebrews chapter 11 and read what it says.* And I looked up Hebrews 11, that great hall of the heroes of the faith. I read the stories of all those men and women of faith in the Old Testament, and I saw what God was showing me. Not one of the people listed in Hebrews 11 asked God to give him or her something. Instead, they are said to have had faith because they believed God, followed God, and obeyed God. It wasn't their desire but their obedience that God counted as faith.

Then I sensed God saying, *Reggie, I have brought you this close to the championship not because you desired it or because you asked me for it, but because you obeyed me. When human wisdom told you to go to San Francisco, you heard Me telling you to go to Green Bay. You took a lot of flak for that decision, you were misunderstood and criticized. But you went, you trusted Me—and I counted that obedience toward your faith.*

I am convinced that most of us have a mistaken definition of faith. When God tells us to do something, and we move on His word, that's faith. When you do that, people are gonna think you're crazy, just as everybody thought Noah was crazy when he built the boat, and just as everyone thought I was crazy when I went to Green Bay. People laughed at me and scoffed at me. But I had the last laugh.

God led me to Green Bay, just as I said all along. And God allowed me to play on a championship team.

OUR CHAMPIONSHIP SEASON

During the '96 season, the Pack allowed the fewest points of any team in the NFL (220) and scored the most (456)—the first time one team had led both categories since the undefeated Dolphins in '72. And our team record of 13–3 was Green Bay's best since 1962.

Our defense gave up an NFL-low average of 259.8 yards a game, plus the league-lowest totals of touchdowns allowed (19), yards

allowed (4,156), and first downs allowed (248). We finished the
season with a total of 39 takeaways—23 more than in 1995. The
Packers defense went from 14th in the league in '95 to first in
the league in '96.

It was a great year for my personal stats as well. I led the team
with 8½ sacks for the year and extended my NFL career total to
165½ sacks in 184 games. I took my leadership role very seriously,
both on and off the field. There are a lot of young guys on the
team, and I wanted to imbue all of them with the benefit of the
seasoning and battle scars some of us old dudes had acquired in
the trenches. I called a lot of meetings—LeRoy Butler says I called
more meetings than Congress. I know the guys got a little sick of
it at times, but I wanted to make sure we kept our focus and our
confidence. I wanted to make sure everyone on the team realized
how close we were, and that we were playing well enough to win
it all.

Our performance during the '96 season secured home-field advantage for us in the playoffs. And that meant the 49ers had to
trudge through the frozen tundra one more time for the divisional
playoffs. We entered the playoffs supremely confident. I don't
mean we were arrogant or cocky. We simply knew that we were
playing well in every facet of our game. If we could maintain that
level of performance through two games in Green Bay and one
game in New Orleans, we could celebrate the rest of our lives.

In the days before the playoffs, I had a recurring dream. In that
dream, the Packers were playing the Panthers in Carolina. I
dreamed that I was rushing the Panther quarterback, Kerry Collins.
As I came at him, he reached back to throw, and just as he released
the ball, I jumped and tipped it—And then the dream was over. I
had that dream several times, and it always ended in the same
place. It was frustrating, never knowing if that tipped ball resulted
in a completion, an incompletion, an interception, or what. In my
dream, I always thought I was playing a real game—and then I'd
wake up and think, *Oh, man! It's just a dream!* I played both
playoff games—the San Francisco game and the Carolina game—
at least three or four times in my sleep before I ever stepped on
the field. It was torment.

Finally, on January 4, 1997, before a record crowd of 60,787
rain-soaked Cheeseheads, we took the field opposite the San Fran-

cisco 49ers. A freak January rainstorm had turned our tundra into a swamp. Our attitude was perfectly expressed by one of the banners hung by the fans: RESISTANCE IS FUTILE—WE HAVE ASSUMED CONTROL. The 49ers won the toss and accepted the opening kickoff—then promptly went three and out on their first possession. You had to admire the courage of Steve Young, taking the field with his sides taped up and shot full of Novocain to mask the pain of his busted ribs. He had been injured during a goal-line lunge in a wild-card playoff game the previous Sunday against the Eagles.

Punter Tommy Thompson tried to kick the ball to the right seam, away from Desmond Howard, whose league-leading three TDs on returns made him a punting squad's worst nightmare. As the ball sailed skyward, the wind caught it and carried it toward the center of the field, right into the hands of Dangerous D. Desmond ran it all the way to the 'Niners 7-yard line before he was tripped up by cornerback Frankie Smith. Two plays later, Andre Rison caught a 4-yard TD pass from Brett. Nine minutes into the first quarter, D received another punt—and ran it back for 71 yards and a touchdown, eluding seven tackles in the process.

There was plenty of 49er trash talk, both before and during the game—but we shut down the talk with action. We played a tight game on a sloppy field, turning the ball over only one time; the 'Niners, meanwhile, suffered five turnovers. Fritz had us playing base defense, which held the 'Niners to 196 total yards. Nothing fancy in the way of defensive schemes—we just pounded them into the mud.

We ran the ball at them 39 times for 139 yards, which made up for Brett's career-low 15 pass attempts for 79 yards. The quicksand he was playing on wouldn't let him make big plays in the air. So Brett patiently shifted to short passes and a running game—and our ball carriers came through. Edgar Bennett ran for two touchdowns, and nearly got a third when he fumbled the ball into the end zone in the third quarter (Antonio Freeman, back from his broken arm, recovered the loose ball for a touchdown).

By the time the mud had sloshed to a standstill, we had clinched the division title with a score of 35–14. I heard that a week later, when they resodded the playing field, they were still pulling 49ers out of the mud.

Most of us on the team were hoping for Dallas to emerge victorious against Carolina in the other division contest on the following day—we were eager to get our hands on the Cowboys in our own ballyard for the NFC championship. But Barry and the 'Boys folded in Carolina, so we hosted the Panthers on January 12.

The week before the championship, Coach Holmgren was getting very intense. His mood was starting to filter out to the rest of us. We knew how important it was to stay loose, so I went to Mike and said, "The guys think you're too tense. It's making all of us tense." At first, Mike was, like, in denial. "Who, me?" he said. "Me? Tense? Not me!" While he was saying this, he was so tense, the quills in his mustache were standing at attention. I said, "Mike, you're tense. You've gotta loosen up on the team." So the next day, he apologized to the team and completely turned things around for us. Instantly, the tension evaporated, and we knew we were going to have fun going after Carolina.

A couple of days before the game, Mike sat me down and said, "Are you ready?" I said, "I'm ready, Mike." He nodded. "Good," he replied, "because you've waited your whole life for this game. You've been talking about it for years. Now it's really gonna happen. So make sure you focus all your energy on it. Go out and do all the things you've been promising. This team looks to you for leadership and emotion. If they see it in you, they'll find it in themselves." I said, "I know. I'll be there. Count on it."

The day of the game, we thundered out of the tunnel growling "Dominate!" We were ready for anything—even temperatures just above zero with a minus-25 degree windchill. But in the first few snaps, our offense had some problems settling in. Five minutes into the game, Brett dropped back to throw a slant to Beebe and was picked off by Sam Mills, who nearly ran it into the end zone. Kerry Collins scored a short time later with a 3-yard TD pass to fullback Howard Griffith. Right after the interception, Carolina linebacker Lamar Lathon grinned at Brett and said, "You're good, Favre—but this is gonna be a long day for you." Brett just shrugged and walked off the field.

At the beginning of the second quarter, Brett answered Lathon with a 29-yard touchdown pass to Dorsey Levens, tying the game at 7. On his next drive, however, Brett fumbled while scrambling away from Lathon and Mike Fox. Lathon recovered the ball, and the Panthers got a field goal for a 10–7 lead. Still, Brett was fired up, Edgar and Dorsey were hot, the offensive line was solid—and the busier they were, the more time I had to rest. In the course of the game, Edgar Bennett carried 25 times for 99 yards, while Dorsey carried 10 for 88. In the skies above Lambeau, Brett nailed 19 of 29 for 292 yards. A 6-yarder to Free in the end zone put us on top at the half—and we held that edge through the rest of the game.

During a time out in the second quarter, the giant instant replay screen lit up with a video of me singing "Amazing grace, how sweet the sound, that saved a wretch like me . . ." And the whole stadium sang along. It was awesome. At the end of the song, the screen went dark except for the words, "We believe."

The play everyone will be talking about for years came early in the third quarter. It was pure Favre—creative, spectacular, and against all the rules of sensible quarterbacking. In a third-and-7 situation on the Carolina 32, Brett was flushed out of the pocket and found himself being sacked by Kevin Greene and Lamar Lathon. He was falling forward and decided to make the best of it, shoveling a two-handed pass 5 yards downfield, where Dorsey Levens stood in the open. The ball squirted into Dorsey's hands, and he whirled around and answered Brett's prayer, turning disaster into a first down. As Brett picked himself up off the ground and checked himself for missing parts, Greene walked past him and said, "Wow!" Brett had been hammered so hard that, until Greene said that, Brett didn't know if the pass was complete or not.

I have a lot of respect for the Carolina Panthers. Kerry Collins is on his way to becoming a great quarterback. I've known Dom Capers since I played at the University of Tennessee—he was a defensive back coach there. He's a fine coach, a fine Christian, and a man of integrity. Carolina is a young, strong team, and they don't have anything to hang their heads about—they made us work for that win. In the end, however, our defense shut down their running game, while our offense provided the perfect mix of passing (292 yards) and running (201 yards). Even when we were trailing through the first half, we never doubted we'd come back and get the job done. At the end of the game, Panthers linebacker Lamar Lathon paid us a great tribute. "The Packers are a team with great heart, a great quarterback, and a great coach. We should pattern ourselves after them."

Even before the game was over, while 60,219 fans were screaming in triumph, I wrapped my arms around Mike Holmgren and hugged that bear of a man, and I thanked him for leading us to this place in history. Then I took off my helmet, jumped up on the Packers bench, and raised my hands to the crowd, thanking them for their love and support. Brett ran over to me and we hugged each other, and he shouted in my ear, "Reggie, this is why you came to Green Bay! This is your moment! You deserve this!" I've got to tell you, when he said that, years of working and striving for that moment spilled out of my heart and down my face. I was totally overcome by everything that moment meant to me. And one by one, my teammates came to me and embraced me. We had carried each other to this place, and our hearts were bursting with joy and love for each other.

As the clock ran out, sealing our 30–13 victory, a victory platform was rolled out to the middle of the field. A bunch of us crowded onto that platform and waved to the stands. The legendary Terry Bradshaw introduced Virginia McCaskey, daughter of the late George Halas, a co-founder of the NFL and longtime coach of the Chicago Bears. She presented the George S. Halas trophy—a beautiful wood-and-silver symbol of the National Football Conference championship that we had just won on that very field. Packers president Bob Harlan accepted the trophy, dedicating it to the fans, and to Ron Wolf and Mike Holmgren, who had "restored the Green Bay Packers as America's team."

Then I spoke to the fans. "Four years ago," I said, "God brought me here for a purpose. God has His hands on this team, and I have to give Jesus the praise! All glory goes to God! Thank you, Lord!" The fans roared back their gratitude to God. Then I said, "Green Bay, I hope you're proud of us, because we're proud of you." And the crowd roared again.

Next, Brett came forward, and he was all choked up. "I remember telling the fans and the media before the season started," he said, "that we were going to go to the Super Bowl. And in two weeks, we'll be in New Orleans."

It was incredible. It was true. All of us on that podium were going to New Orleans for the biggest game of our lives. Me, Brett,

Sean, Santana, LeRoy, Edgar, Eugene, all of us. As the sun sank into an orange haze over the top of the stands, I hoisted the Halas trophy over my head and took a victory lap around the field, a broad smile on my face, tears of joy flooding my eyes. And I could see the individual faces of the fans—some of them shouting and waving, and some of the weeping for joy. Green Bay, thank you for that moment in my life, which I'll treasure as long as I live.

THE BIGGEST GAME OF MY LIFE

I went to New Orleans expecting to win—but I also expected a tough game. I had, and still have, enormous respect for the New England Patriots and their former coach, Bill Parcells. I was surprised, in a way, that my emotions weren't higher—it seemed that my most intense feelings, from anxiety to excitement to joy, had been spent in the playoff games against San Francisco and Carolina. Now that I was in New Orleans for Super Bowl week, I was confident and ready to take on the challenge. Sure, I was nervous, too, because I wanted to win so bad. In the back of my mind were crazy thoughts like, *Oh, man, if we lose? We'll be the first NFC team in thirteen years to lose the Super Bowl! Can't let that happen!*

My teammates and I were pretty well insulated from all the hype that surrounds the Super Bowl. When I wasn't at practice with the team, I was in my room. I only saw Sara the night she came into town. After that, I didn't see her or the kids throughout the week. I wanted to stay concentrated on the game. I didn't go out on Bourbon Street or do any of the other New Orleans stuff. I only left the hotel a couple times on my own to get something to eat—and then I was mobbed so bad, I couldn't really enjoy it. I don't blame the fans for crowding around, and I appreciate the fact that they want to be around me, but there were times I just needed to walk around and be alone.

The week before the Super Bowl was a week of preparation, just like any other week. Coach Holmgren didn't do anything special in practice—just tried to make it as normal a week as possible. We went through the same paces we always do, and he kept practices to reasonable hours so we had time to relax and enjoy ourselves.

One of the things that really motivated us during that time was all the hype about Bill Parcells. We kept hearing from reporters that we had the edge over the Pats on the field, but that Bill had the edge over Mike Holmgren in terms of Super Bowl experience and strategic ability. That made us mad, and we took it personally, because we knew that Mike is an excellent coach and game strategist. He took a backseat to no one, including Bill Parcells. That kind of talk just fired us up all the more.

The night before the game, Mike surprised us with a little extra incentive to win. At a team meeting, he was giving us his usual pep talk, which we had pretty much heard before in one form or another. Then he stepped over to a table that was draped with a blanket. "I want to show you guys something," he said. He grabbed the blanket, whisked it away, and revealed a mound of green—a hundred thousand dollars in cash.

Now, all of us on the team have big bank accounts, but none of us had ever seen that much money in cash before. "Gentlemen," said Mike, "I want you to remember that this is what we get if we win this game." Well, a lot of guys got pretty excited about it. I don't know if the sight of all that money powered our performance the next day—but I do know it didn't hurt.

After Mike's pep talk, our media people showed us a highlight video they had put together, set to the song "Chance of a Lifetime" by Take 6. It was a compilation of great plays we had made throughout the year. At the end of the song, an image of the Lombardi Trophy fades in. The entire team sat transfixed and silent, with our eyes focused on that trophy. It helped us to have something visual, something tangible to concentrate on, to remind us of why we were in New Orleans, and what we had come to accomplish.

Also that night, Fritz Shurmer met with the defensive squad. He was very open and emotional. In fact, he broke down as he told us about his brother, who had died in early '96. Before he passed away, he asked Fritz to do one thing for him—win a championship. It really touched and inspired us all that Fritz would share something so personal with us. All the guys on defense really love Fritz. He's an intense person, and he really relates to us, even though he's a generation (or two) ahead of us in years. He knows when to have fun with us, when to get serious with us, and when to really let us have it. He prepared us well.

The next day, January 26, 1997, we came out of the tunnel and onto the field of the Louisiana Superdome, ready for battle. The ceremonies of the coin toss and the national anthem were powerful, and helped us to get centered for the battle that was about to be joined.

We kicked off. After the Patriots first five-play possession and punt, Brett opened up the game with a quick strike—a 54-yard touchdown pass to Andre Rison. The play was not in Mike Holmgren's script—Brett read the blitz in the Patriot defense and audibled at the line. The play came off exactly as Brett planned. We got the conversion, then kicked off. The Patriots only got two plays for 1 yard before we intercepted and grabbed a field goal. At 6:18 into the game, we led 10-zip.

On his next possession, Patriots QB Drew Bledsoe started sucking us in with play-action fakes—faking the run, hiding the ball, then passing. Their offensive line was chipping me and doing a lot of cut blocks. Their pass protection was solid and Drew hid the ball well, so our defense just wasn't getting to him at all. We expected the Patriots to run early on, because that's what Bill Parcells's teams usually do. I played against Parcells's N.Y. Giants for eight years when I was with Philadelphia, and one thing Bill always did was establish the run early in the game. So we fully expected them to pound the ball on us in the first quarter, and they totally surprised us when they put the ball in the air. Thanks to Fritz, we finally adjusted to the Patriots' scheme and started blitzing more, bringing our safeties and corners in more to try and knock them off a rhythm.

Bledsoe fired one pass to my good friend and former Eagles teammate, Keith Byars. It was broken up in the end zone by Craig Newsome—but Craig (who had not been penalized once in the entire '96 season and postseason) was hit with a pass-interference penalty. The ball was spotted on the 1-yard line and easily turned into a touchdown. On our next possession, we went three and out, and New England was able to get a second touchdown on four plays totaling 57 yards. Twelve and a half minutes into the game, we were trailing, 14–10.

Fritz really got in our faces at that point. "Enough is enough!" he shouted. "Go get Bledsoe! Do whatever it takes! I'll blitz every play if I have to—just get in his face! Make him wonder where

you're coming from next!" We did what Fritz told us to do, and it
worked. Under intense pressure, Bledsoe missed six of his next
seven pass attempts. Finally, LeRoy sacked him on his blind side—
Bledsoe never saw him coming.

On our first possession of the second quarter, Brett hit Antonio
Freeman with an 81-yard TD pass—the longest play from scrimmage in Super Bowl history. Free beat strong safety Lawyer Milloy
in single coverage, and we took a 17–14 lead. We extended the
lead by a field goal on our next possession. Just before the end of
the half, Brett ran the ball into the left corner of the end zone,
diving at the last moment, nicking the plane of the goal line as he
sailed out of bounds. Only the scantiest amount of ball ever actually made it into the end zone—but it was enough. At the end of
the half, it was Green Bay 27, New England 14.

When we came out on the field for the second half, it was as if
a thick blue haze of war hung over our battlefield. Of course, it
was just smoke and fumes from the pyrotechnics and the Harley-
Davidson motorcycles from the halftime show—but the lingering
smoke made the air hot, oily, and hard to breathe.

Halfway through the third quarter, I noticed I was really getting
tired. I was laboring for breath and my legs were getting weak and
wobbly. I went to the sidelines and told Fritz and Larry Brooks,
our defensive line coach, "Man, I'm getting tired out there. I don't
feel like my legs are there." They told me, "Reggie, we've been
watching you and you're playing well. Just hang in there and keep
up the pressure." I played a couple more snaps, then went back to
the sidelines and told Fritz and Larry, "I'm really tired, I think I
better come out." They said, "You're moving well. Just keep going."

Finally, I took myself out of the game for a couple snaps. Santana
came out at the same time. I just had to catch my wind so I could
go down the stretch. I went back into the game on the same play
that Curtis Martin ran in an 18-yard touchdown straight up the
gut. New England was ecstatic. They had closed to within 6 points
of us, and we knew the threat was real.

I went to the sidelines and I grabbed Eugene Robinson. "Eugene," I said, "I'm tired, man. I don't feel my legs are there. Man,
you've got to pray for me or do something for me."

So right there on the sidelines, Eugene quoted Isaiah 40:31 to
me. "Big Dog," he said, "'those who wait on the Lord shall renew

their strength; they shall mount up with wings like eagles, they shall run and not be weary, they shall walk and not faint.' Just trust God, man. He'll be with you out there."

I hugged him and watched as the Patriots kicked the extra point, then set up for the kickoff. I was breathing easier, and I felt more strength and feeling in my legs.

As I watched from the sidelines, the Patriots kicker, Adam Vinatierie, sent the ball end-over-end, deep in our own territory. Desmond Howard, who had already returned four punts for 75 yards in the game, was waiting for it at the 1-yard line. He grabbed the ball and lit out like his feet were on fire. He sprinted like a jackrabbit through briar, up the middle into his wedge, then veering left behind his blocker, Don Beebe, and finally robot-walking into the end zone. It was one of the most incredible sights I have ever witnessed—a 99-yard kickoff return. Coming just seconds after the Patriots rallying touchdown, it completely broke New England's spirit. After Brett tacked on two more points with a pass to Mark "Chewie" Chmura, the score was Green Bay 35, New England 21.

After the kickoff, I lined up again. The ball was snapped and Max Lane, the Patriots third-year right tackle from Navy, dove to cut-block me. I ran right over the top of him and got to Bledsoe a split-instant after he threw the pass. Keith Byars caught the pass for a gain of a few yards. *Man,* I thought, *I'm feeling good! I'm moving like I haven't moved all game! Eugene was right! God has renewed me totally!*

We lined up again for a four-man rush. The ball was snapped. I took the inside move on Max, using the club move to lift him out of the way with my right arm, then I lunged for Bledsoe, wrapped my arms around his knees, and hauled him to the turf. That was my first sack of the game, for a loss of 8 yards.

We lined up again, this time for a three-man rush. It was third and 13. Max thought I was going to club him again, so he set himself to contain me on the inside—but instead, I beat him around the corner and flung him aside with the rip move. He was trying to hang on to me, his legs flailing in the air, as I rushed Bledsoe and tackled him for a second consecutive sack, this time for a 7-yard loss.

It was amazing, the transformation that took place after Eugene prayed for me and spoke God's Word to me. Eugene showed up for me big-time. He knew exactly what to say when I needed God's strength and renewal.

That finished out the third quarter—and the fourth quarter was no better for New England. Drew Bledsoe tried valiantly to rally his team in the final fifteen minutes of the game. In the process, he was intercepted twice, bringing his total for the game to 25 completions of 48 attempts for 253 yards, plus four interceptions. I got a third sack with 1:45 to go in the fourth quarter, using the club on an inside move again. I didn't know it at the time, but my three sacks in a single game set a new Super Bowl record.

The game officially ended—and the celebration began—at 8:48 P.M. In Super Bowl XXXI, before a crowd of 72,301 spectators and a television audience in the hundreds of millions, the Green Bay Packers earned the title of NFL Champions with a score of 35–21. The title had come home to Titletown, U.S.A. The Lombardi Trophy was returning to Lombardi Avenue.

The celebration was incredible—the roaring crowd, the hugs and smiles everywhere, the white confetti dancing in the air like snowflakes, the grin and wave of my wife and my kids in the stands, kneeling on the field of battle and praying with my brothers in Christ from *both* teams. Then we went up onto the platform for the presentation of the Vince Lombardi Trophy to Packers president Bob Harlan, general manager Ron Wolf, and coach Mike Holmgren. After thanking the people of Green Bay and the players of the new "America's team," they put that trophy in my hands, and it gleamed and sparkled as if it was lit from within.

I held the trophy high and told the world, "God brought me here! I want to say, thank You, Jesus! It's not all about us. It's not all about what we accomplished. It's about what God has done in these players, in this team. And Lord Jesus, I just want to say, thank You for this opportunity!"

Then I ran out onto the field and hoisted that trophy high over my head. The people in the stands sent up a shout of triumph and joy. You've seen those NFL commercials that say, "Feel the power!" Well, I felt it. Oh, man! My emotions were bursting—not just for us as a team, but for the fans who lifted us up, just as I was lifting up that trophy. Most of all, I felt the power of God, who had lifted up this team for His own glory. I was in awe of how God had put this entire journey together. It wasn't because of Reggie White. It wasn't because of anybody who lined up on the field. Too many things went too right for us during the year. Things had happened that could only be called supernatural. God had set this up, and I can't take any credit.

I once heard someone say that the reason God rested on Sunday was because He knew that was the day the Packers would be playing. I wouldn't go that far. I wouldn't say that God is a Packer fan. But I do believe God has a plan for the Green Bay Packers.

I have been privileged to play on a championship team. But I have to tell you that an even greater privilege is that of playing on a team where I am surrounded by so many faithful, committed brothers in the Lord. Every week, I suit up and line up with men who are committed to serving the Lord Jesus Christ with their entire lives.

When I decided to come to Green Bay, when I told the media I believed this team could win a championship, a lot of people thought I was foolish. I could show you dozens of newspaper columns that scoffed at me for my decision. No one's scoffing now. But at the same time, I haven't seen anyone step up and say, "I was one of those scoffers, and now I have to admit that Reggie was right. Maybe God really did speak to Reggie. Maybe he wasn't as crazy as we thought he was." The scoffers are real quiet right now.

I'm not saying that God is in the business of choosing winners and losers and who gets to go to the Super Bowl. He's got a lot more important things to be concerned about than football games. I'm not saying God loves the Packers more than any other teams or individuals. I'm just saying that God has his own purposes in eternity, and if He can use the hype and media circus of a Super Bowl game to elevate His message and further His purpose, then He will do that. Ultimately, it is not winning championships that matters—what matters is that lives are impacted and God is glorified.

I want people to know that God had his hand on this team, and God sent me to this team for a reason—not just to put a Super Bowl ring on my finger, but to give me a platform from which to tell the world about the love of Jesus. It's great to win a championship—but if all I gained was a ring for my finger, if I never impacted anyone's life in the process, then that ring wouldn't mean anything.

Before I came to Green Bay, I said this team could go to the Super Bowl. When the first edition of this book came out, I predicted we would get there. I knew we had the quarterback to lead us and the coach to inspire us and drive us on to victory. Everything I predicted came to pass. My quest for a championship is complete. But I still have a few more good years left.

Hey, I wouldn't mind winning another one!

NOTES

Chapter 1. Life in the Trenches

1. "Injury ends season for Reggie White," *Philadelphia Inquirer*, December 14, 1995, p. D3.
2. Quoted by Bob Sansevere, *St. Paul Pioneer Press*, January 24, 1996, p. 1D.

Chapter 3. Big Dog

1. Ray Didinger, "Welcome, kid: Cowboys' rookie tackle unshaken after experiencing Reggie White," *Philadelphia Daily News*, December 1, 1994, p. 86.

Chapter 4. Incredible Wealth

1. Proverbs 31:13, 15, 16, 17, 20, 26, 28, and 30.

Chapter 5. Buddyball

1. Frank Dolson, "You can't fool fans with fake NFL games," *Philadelphia Inquirer*, September 23, 1987, p. F1.

Chapter 6. An Eagle in the Storm

1. Stan Hochman, "Buddy should stay; Clash of styles is no reason to let him go," *Philadelphia Daily News*, January 7, 1991, p. Sports 77.
2. "The Buddy system: The Eagles never stopped believing," *Philadelphia Inquirer*, December 20, 1988, p. A12.
3. Isaiah 40:31.

Chapter 9. The Rambos of Lambeau

1. Bill Lyon, "When game was on the line, White couldn't deliver," *Philadelphia Inquirer*, September 13, 1993, p. C1.

Chapter 10. Miracles in the Trenches

1. Matthew 14:14.
2. Matthew 20:34.

Chapter 11. Fighting Fire

1. John 8:48.
2. Luke 4:18–19.
3. John 2:19.
4. John 2:21.
5. Deuteronomy 32:30.
6. Matthew 24:7; Mark 13:8; Luke 21:10, 25–26; Revelation 17:15.

Chapter 12. How to Be a Hero

1. Colossians 3:23.
2. "Knowing You," sung at Promise Keepers by the Maranatha Promise Band.
3. Ephesians 5:25.
4. Mark 10:44.

The Urban Hope Corporation, founded by Reggie White, is a national faith-based organization, whose mission is to empower and revitalize the people in urban and rural areas.

If you would like to make a tax-deductible contribution to the Urban Hope ministry, please send a check or money order to:

Urban Hope
P.O. Box 11475
Green Bay, WI 54313

Or, if you would like to learn more about Urban Hope, please write to the above address or call us at our toll-free number (888) 8-REGGIE.